Produce Your Play
Without a Producer

A Survival Guide
for Actors and Playwrights
Who Need a Production

Published by Smith and Kraus, Inc.
177 Lyme Road, Hanover, NH 03755
www.smithkraus.com

Manufactured in the United States of America

Cover and Text Design by Julia Hill Gignoux
Cover Illustration by Larry Howard

First Edition: February 2001
10 9 8 7 6 5 4 3 2 1

The Library of Congress Cataloging-In-Publication Data
Hillenbrand, Mark.
Produce your play : a survival guide for actors and playwrights who need a
production / Mark Hillenbrand.
p. cm. — (Career development series)
Includes bibliographical references.
ISBN 1-57525-255-4
1. Theater—Production and direction. I. Title. II. Series.

PN2053 .H53 2000
792'.0232—dc21   00-0484491

Produce Your Play Without a Producer

A Survival Guide for Actors and Playwrights Who Need a Production

Mark Hillenbrand, MBA, PhD

CAREER DEVELOPMENT SERIES

A Smith and Kraus Book

must clear before the production becomes viable. Of course some producers get lucky and stumble onto a wonderful, dirt-cheap space, but it always seems like those lucky strikes happen to the other guy, the guy with the grail in the nap sack.

The space chase doesn't have to be a random search, for the following *This book is dedicated to my parents.* producer find the correct space—without getting burned by dragons or theater managers.

Network with other producers. The best sources for information about theater spaces are people who have successfully produced theater. The new venture producer should begin her investigation via the telephone by calling theaters and speaking to either the producing director or managing director of local semiprofessional and community theaters. Most experienced producers are very willing to share information about space and producing with others, primarily because of an altruistic love of theater. The novice producer should learn to ask the right questions by first listening to the voices of experience, then assimilating what was heard, and, finally, formulating questions based on the consultation. Also, networking can lead to the discovery of various state theater associations. Appropriate state or regional theater associations should be contacted because their directory would be a gold mine of producers and venues, an almost endless source of free information about venues and knowledgeable people. Any experienced producer knows that the cliché should be varied to read, "half the fun is planning how to get there."

Consult resource books. Many major cities have resource books for actors that cover issues such as venues, rehearsal spaces, and a host of other needs. Contact Applause and The Drama Book Shop (New York), and Act One (Chicago) to inquire if a resource book exists for your city. Actors' resource books also provide contact information for tech-

Contents

Introduction vii

Chapter 1: Putting on the Producer's Hat 1

Chapter 2: The Ground Floor: Readings 9

Chapter 3: What's Your Budget? 20

Chapter 4: Passing the Hat: Fund-Raising 41

Chapter 5: The Hard Hat: Finding a Space 56

Chapter 6: Working With the Artistic Team 78

Chapter 7: Working With the Design and Technical Team . . . 96

Chapter 8: Legal Issues, Tax Law, and Insurance 110

Chapter 9: Box Office and House Management 127

Chapter 10: Getting the Word Out: Marketing
     the Production 143

Chapter 11: Creating a Buzz: Publicity 175

Chapter 12: Moving On 205

Bibliography: The Producer's Library 211

The Little Black Book: Useful Contacts for Producers 227

National Theater Organizations 312

Drama Bookstores 317

Rights and Royalties Agencies for Plays and Musicals 318

Regional Arts Organizations 325

State Arts Agencies 326

The Producer's Timetable: Suggested Parameters 334

ideal venue is a formidable one. If the wrong venue is chosen, a play may never find its audience, critics may never find the theater, and the producer may never find his income.

For example, *The Fantastics* is a charming musical that needs a relatively intimate venue to do justice to the script and music. Subsequently, the producers settled on a relatively small theater, one not comparable to a Broadway musical house, but one that offered the production a setting conducive to the four-character action in the musical. Likewise, the early plays of Sam Shepard and Lanford Wilson played best on small stages which facilitated a close proximity between actors and audience, as did the plays of Beckett, and the chamber theater productions of Ibsen and Strindberg. Contrast these productions with those of many modern musicals and farces, which need a larger venue to give some distance between the performers and the audience.

The character of a venue, however, is far more important than its capacity. "Character" can be defined by the type of space, the established audience draw, and its location in town.

Established Theater Spaces

An established theater space is a venue set up for live performances. Most of the spaces that are considered legitimate theaters fit this category. In an established theater space, a producer should find audience seating already in place, stage lighting, a sound system, a lobby area, and restroom facilities. The equipment and amenities make producing in an established space far less taxing than producing in a space that requires basic outfitting of theatrical equipment, a stage area, and seats. Indeed, producing in an established space has a number of definite advantages over a new venue, such as location recognition by audiences and critics, as well as a track record of (hopefully) suc-

Introduction

Producing, like acting, has a set of clearly defined functions, and many producer's talents can be acquired through both practice and study. Playwrights and actors can become producers, provided they have the drive, personality, and skills to create a project from the ground up. This book explores producer's functions as well as "insider's information" that aspiring producers need to know to avoid the quagmires of producing theater. Moreover, if this book's reader never embarks on a producing mission, he or she will still benefit from theatre production knowledge, which might make the playwright or actor a bit more savvy about the realities of the stage.

Indeed, all playwrights and actors should be streetwise regarding theater production because all production variables will affect the outcome of the script in performance. For example, if a playwright produces or is produced by another, then the theater chosen for production can have bearing on the success of the playwright. Theater buildings and even empty spaces have their own personalities, which will, in part, determine how the audience receives the play. Most large- and medium-sized cities have venues that attract a young, hip audience who may be receptive to an avant garde play. Likewise, it probably wouldn't be a good idea to produce *The Sound of Music* in New York's East Village. Although the choice of space is ultimately the producer's, such a choice has great bearing on the aesthetic quality of the play and its reception among critics. Other issues such as fund-raising, marketing, relationships with the local media and press, and the technical side of theater are subjects actors and playwrights should comprehend whether or not an actor or playwright ever produces original work. Naiveté is amusing for Ibsen's Peer Gynt, a character who blithely stumbles in and out of predicaments well beyond his comprehension, but actors and playwrights cannot afford to be like Peer, for naiveté can result in frustration and a lot of money down the drain.

The producing world, indeed, has its share of quick sand, icebergs, and mirages. A Pollyanna might assume that producing is easy and fun. It isn't. When I was in New York, I called a playwright who had just produced a play. I asked this playwright for an interview regarding the experience of writing and producing theater. The writer immediately responded with, "It's a pain in the ass. Talk to my psychiatrist." As it turns out, however, I was granted the interview and while the writer's experience was a big pain, it was also very rewarding. Producing is probably the most work an actor or playwright will ever do. Although this book attempts to provide useful and smart information to playwrights and actors, it cannot covey the real-life tribulations of producing. It also cannot convey the intangible and emotional rewards of seeing a script or character come to life on stage before an audience.

Produce Your Play Without a Producer: A Survival Guide for Actors and Playwrights Who Need a Production is unlike practically every other acting and playwriting book on the market, for this book begins where most playwriting and acting books end. This work is centered on the premise that playwrights and actors always have and must continue to take control of the means of production themselves. This book explores the issues of stage production and advises actors and playwrights on this topic. A play does not breathe in a manila envelope perched atop a stack of hundreds of other manila envelopes somewhere on a bowed shelf in a theater office. Playwrights and actors can and should learn how to produce their own work, *especially an artist who is early in his or her career.*

This book shows how to build a production structure from the inside out. In fact, many actors and playwrights are doing this. It is very common today for actors to showcase their talents, usually with a full production designed to introduce their work to producers and directors. Playwrights, too, produce their own work from the hundreds of playwright-sponsored productions at the New York International Fringe Festival, to new work produced in hometown America. Echoing the words of playwright Megan Terry, "Do it yourself, it's the American way."

Rental Issues

Term of lease. Rental agreements can be written by the day, the week, the weekend, the month, or any variation of term. Some theater owners will insist that the theater be rented the entire week prior to a given weekend, while others will begin a lease on a weekend date. If the producer is rehearsing the play at another location, these issues become critical. Every producer's goal is to pay for the theater space only when it is actually used, whether it is for performance or rehearsal.

Performance dates. Coupled closely with the term of the lease is the availability of specific dates for performance. Every producer should get a firm commitment from the theater owner regarding performance dates prior to signing a lease because not all dates may be available. For example, some theaters discourage performances on Sundays, and others may not allow both a Saturday matinee and evening performance. It is also possible that a theater may have a date or two scheduled for their own auditions, which could conflict with a desired performance date. Moreover, a theater owner will obviously be far more receptive to a production date proposal if the dates fall within a time frame that fits her schedule. Many theaters are dark over the summer months and do indeed rent space during this time. Another smart strategy is to look for T.B.A. (To Be Announced) slots in theater schedules. If the producer's proposal is strong enough, a theater owner may give consideration to a new production. After all, theaters usually fill slots with T.B.A. because they haven't settled on a specific production and, thus, may be especially receptive to new ideas.

Rehearsal space. A producer should never assume that a rental agreement automatically carries with it the right to rehearsal times on stage. Whenever the demand is great for theater space, most theaters will realize a higher profit

Chapter One

Putting on the Producer's Hat

A theater producer is essentially a monomaniac with a mission. Producers can be actors, directors, designers, or playwrights. A producer is the catalyst that makes the production a reality. Theater is, in fact, still produced by those people who have the ambition and vision to establish their own production mechanism to make their unique vision a stage reality. Most theaters, including regional not-for-profits, began this way. This book examines the theater producer as a role that playwrights and actors can assume, thereby creating opportunities for themselves as well as exposure for the script and the company of artists who embody the production process.

Many Playwrights Have Put on the Producer's Hat

The off-off Broadway movement of the 1960s characterized this take-charge spirit. The activity was centered in New York's East Village, and at its core was a group of young artists who produced their own work. Sam Shepard is a good example.

1

It makes no difference that his early plays were produced in nontraditional theater venues such as churches, or cafes, or the basement of a garment shop. What does matter is that he took control of the means of production himself. Richard Foreman is another contemporary, distinguished example of the playwright-producer who developed during the early years of the off-off Broadway movement. David Mamet's early work in Chicago echoes a similar premise. Anyone who finds a space, talks a friend into directing, gets some actors together, and encourages people to view the work is, in every sense of the word, a producer. Currently there are literally hundreds of playwrights producing their own work in New York. Certain organizations such as the International Fringe Festival, The Producer's Club, and Expanded Arts are very receptive to the playwright-producer. Outside New York prospects are also bright due to the proliferation of theater spaces. Since the American theater decentralized, more spaces and greater audiences have developed, which is encouraging to any playwright-producer. Cities such as Chicago, Minneapolis, and Seattle have vibrant, large, thriving theater communities with many talented non-Equity performers.

Moreover, looking back a bit further, one would discover that George Bernard Shaw produced some of his first plays. Likewise, the brilliant French playwright Molière was a producer. Shakespeare? Historians don't know if he produced theater, but they tell us that he held a share in the producing company as well as the acting company. In 1597 when The Theater was dismantled, ferried across the Thames to escape Puritanical laws, and reconstructed as The Globe, it is not too far fetched to imagine that Shakespeare pitched in, pulled a few nails, hauled some lumber, and cursed the splinters that ended up in his right hand. Today, our vision of these playwrights has been somewhat sanctified by academe, which paints a rather pristine and literary impression of these writers. The familiar portrait of Shakespeare in his

Renaissance gentleman's garb comes to mind. But many great playwrights got their hands dirty doing theater. Indeed, playwriting can be rather grubby. So can producing theater.

Many Actors Have Put on the Producer's Hat

Examples of actor-producers abound, dating back to antiquity and continuing on in today's theater world. One notable example of actors who produced theater (and themselves) revolves around the Steppenwolf Theater in Chicago. Steppenwolf was largely founded by a group of midwest theater students shortly after their graduation from college and arrival in Chicago. The group included a young Gary Sinise and, a bit later, John Malkovich. During the early days of Steppenwolf, the actors grappled with the same problems any producer must solve—finding space, raising money, attracting an audience, and paying the rent in their church basement theater. If, however, Sinise and Malkovich had not been a part of the *producing* team at Steppenwolf, it is safe to guess that their careers would have gone in another direction. The Group Theatre in the 1930's under Lee Strasberg, Harold Clurman, and Stella Adler also saw these actor-directors operating as producers, as they fought battles with not only the politics of the time, but also budgets, ticket prices, and performance space.

Perhaps one of the best contemporary examples of the actor producer is Kathy Najimy, the actress who has recently made a name for herself in the *Sister Act* movies and the sitcom *Veronica's Closet*, and a number of successful films. Kathy Najimy and her college roommate began producing their own two-woman play *The Mo and Kathy Show* shortly after their graduation from San Diego State University. The *Mo and Kathy Show* moved to New York where it played for a number of years in small spaces. Eventually, *The*

Mo and Kathy Show caught the attention of feminists and comedians and its creators were soon connected in New York and then in Los Angeles and they later won a spot on HBO, as well as an Obie Award. Examples also abound of comedians who *produced* their own one man or one woman show and later found wider acclaim in broader venues—Woody Allen, Robin Williams, and Lilly Tomlin to name a few. The founding members of the Second City comedy/improv troupe produced their own shows during the group's early years. The rest is history.

Moreover, some of the more interesting, albeit, avant garde theaters were begun by actors who produced their own work. The San Francisco Mime Troupe, The Living Theatre, The Bread and Puppet Theater were all founded by actors who developed their own production mechanism. Judith Malina, actress and cofounder of The Living Theatre, continues to face every issue covered in this book on nearly a daily basis. Indeed, many producing organizations were founded by actors with the producer's flair for risk-taking and foresight.

Indeed, some marvelous plays had rather humble origins. Many productions currently on Broadway, off-Broadway, or in leading regional theaters did not begin with first-rate, full-Equity productions. Some plays are able to transfer to higher plateaus because of quality and a venturesome producer's foresight. The musicals *Hedwig and the Angry Inch*, *Godspell*, and the plays *Driving Miss Daisy*, *Steel Magnolias*, and *Torch Song Trilogy* had rather modest initial productions sponsored by the playwrights. Although most self-produced work does not evolve beyond its initial production, the chance of a playwright achieving critical acclaim without the initial risk-taking venture is naught. True, success is often the result of a body of work that has developed over time, but that cannon must build upon an inaugural production.

Producing also builds connections for the playwright-producer or actor-producer to other theater artists. If one takes on the challenge of producing, then one will immediately be placed in a position that necessitates contact with other producers, actors, directors, designers, graphic artists, and media personnel. Producing will bring the extrovert out of an introverted person. Also, in a producing situation, sometimes relationships develop that will yield great benefits to the producers as well as the company of artists on the production team for years to come. Perhaps some of these connections will result in positive and unforeseen future potentialities. One never knows who will know who in a few years. An accurate description of the theater world might be "three degrees of separation," for it is a small world, and producing puts one somewhere on the continent, not in a life raft looking to find land.

Producing theater can also open doors to unexpected talents. Too often people are labeled an actor, a designer, or a playwright. But because producing theater requires a diverse repertoire of skills, calling on hidden talents can bring those abilities to the fore. Playwrights may discover a keen marketing sense that may prove to be necessary in marketing themselves, or an actor might unearth a prowess as a wordsmith. Indeed, producing encompasses so many diverse tasks that it challenges the producer along many lines, and meeting those challenges can broaden one's view of one's self.

The Producer Must Wear Many Hats

Ideally, the term "producer" is an all-encompassing word—broad in responsibilities, deep in convictions, and vast in abilities. A producer must wear the green visor of the banker and assume the role of accountant, bookkeeper, and money manager. Producers also need considerable skill in fund-raising, even if this means asking family and friends for support, or soliciting support from local businesses. The producer must prepare budgets, set up the box office operation, balance the books, and say no to the designer who wants five more lighting instruments. He or she must also be aware of tax regulations, perhaps file for nonprofit status, and pay the company. And that's just the beginning.

A producer must put on the hard hat of the structural engineer and find space for the production. This means scouting theater spaces in town, sizing up the qualities and character of each space, determining the preestablished audience draw, and striking an agreement with the theater owner. Producers can, and often do, create their own space from a church, or a storefront, or even a corner in a park. Creating a theater space from scratch means dealing with an array of challenges, from finding seats to fire code regulations, from handicapped access to parking availability, through restrooms to adequate lobby space. And more. Much more.

A good producer must wear the hat of the actor-managers who dominated theater a century ago when hiring a director and working with the company of artists. It involves knowing how to let go but yet maintaining control of the production budget. Indeed, every producer must embrace the uneasy truce between art and commerce, that high-wire professionals have been balancing on from the ancient Greeks to today's professionals on Broadway. The balance can be a precarious one, and it can even mean dismissing an actor who misses too many rehearsals, or pulling the plug on one's own production. Producing is a business, but the business is an art that entails a wide array of temperaments and talents that must blend to do justice to the play as well as the paying audience. It is the producer's job to make sure that the mix of elements works together to produce an artistic alchemy greater than the sum of the individual parts— a performance that will attract people by virtue of its ability to communicate something uniquely dramatic. If the producer slides too far toward commerce, or too close to artistry, the delicate balance can be lost and the resulting stress may show through to the performance itself.

The producer must also feel comfortable wearing P. T. Barnum's bowler. Barnum was a theater producer who worked around the turn of the century, selling his attractions of theatrical spectacle and wonder— everything from Jenny Lynd, the world-renowned soprano, to Jumbo the Elephant, the world-renowned (you guessed it) circus elephant. Barnum recognized that selling the production was paramount. Modestly did not play well in his arena, nor does it play well in ours today. Although no one can condone Barnum's unabashed fabrications, today's producer can, however, emulate his enthusiasm and be the force behind the generation of attention. At a minimum, if a playwright or actor wears the producer's hat, then he or she must write compelling press releases, design attractive and eye-catching posters and flyers, target-market the play toward specific groups, and establish a good relationship with the local media. Although all this takes time, energy, and money, the producer should not be discouraged since such activities are ultimately behind every successful play. Someone is always wearing Barnum's hat.

Summing Up: Producer's Points

- Many actors and playwrights developed during the early years of the off-off Broadway movement by producing their own work. Anyone who finds a space, talks a friend into directing, gets some actors together, and encourages people to view the work is, in every sense of the word, a producer.

- Historically, many playwrights and actors developed their craft in a company of artists where producing theater was a part of their trade.

- Many artists self-produce because it is the only means of achieving goals.

- From small beginnings, productions and artist can and do grow to a high degree of professionalism and acclaim.

- Producing builds connection among theater artists.

- Producers must be fund-raisers, budget managers, gamblers, employers, psychologists, salespeople, and cheerleaders. And that is just the beginning.

Moving On

Readings are a good way to test the waters. Actors and playwrights can learn a great deal about producing by starting with the relatively simple task of staging a reading. The next chapter dives into readings, their requirements, limitations, and rewards.

Chapter Two

The Ground Floor: Readings

Production Values

The word "production" conjures up many images, and without a grounding principle, those images can take over and obfuscate the art of theater. For example, *Cats!* has been critically derided for its entire theatrical life. The production values are not suspect—they're actually extraordinarily good, with outstanding costuming, lighting, and dancing. But *Cats!* reinvigorated the kind of production values that blind the average theatergoer into seeing only those superficial values without glimpsing into Shakespeare's mirror of human nature. Theater patrons have now come to *expect* those blinding production values without expecting to see something of their own nature. Subsequently, many Broadway producers perceive that patrons *only* want big, spectacle-saturated shows, and they provide precisely those, complete with helicopters, sinking ships, or rain on the Lincoln Center stage. This supposition extends outward to the regional and community theaters, with productions of *Oklahoma* complete with live cows, or productions of *The Music Man* with seventy-six actual trombones. Theater historians tell us that spectacle has always existed, from the ancient Greeks, to medieval theater, to the melodramas that gained popularity in the nineteenth century. Spectacle and drama once enjoyed a much more congenial coexistence, but recently, I believe, the balance has been steadily tipping toward spectacle in many venues.

Any first-time producer must be vigilant not to get caught in this spectacle trap, especially a producer who is new to the game and producing an original play. Many of the great producers in the twentieth century who discovered and produced new playwrights maintained the very core nature of theater. For example, Margo Jones, the director and producer of Dallas' Theatre '47, produced and directed the early plays of Tennessee Williams and William Inge on a bare stage set in-the-round. George Devine of London's Royal Court directed and produced an entire generation of playwrights known as "the angry young men" including Arden, Osborne, and Bond on a very simple production aesthetic. Devine dubbed his productions "essentialism," because he only wanted what was absolutely necessary to the play's essence on stage. A producer operating in today's world should take a page of advice from Jones and Devine and manage the production values to bring forth the humanity inherent in any good play and not allow spectacle to take over and dazzle the patron. Theater can be a place where imagination thrives so long as it is allowed to live and not be squelched by spectacle. Besides, it's economical to keep things simple, as Jones and Devine well knew.

What Kind of Production Is Best for the Script?

There are hundreds of shades of gray among theater productions. A production is not defined by a specific amount of money, but rather a very fundamental exchange between actors and audience. Indeed, these two elements define production. Productions can be as simple as a reading in a classroom, or a staged reading in a theater, or as complicated as a fully mounted show on Broadway. An actor or playwright wearing the producer's hat must decide what production type best suits the script and the company of artists that will support the venture. If the script is new and raw, it is best to aim for some type of reading, since the cost and expectations are much more manageable than a full production.

Closed Cold Readings

The most basic form of reading is the cold reading. Although cold readings can have a small audience, let us consider that a cold reading is defined as one without an audience and is designed to allow the playwright to hear his or her words filtered through an actor's interpretations. A cold reading is dubbed cold because of the lack of rehearsal time, usually next to nothing, that proceeds the reading. The basic procedure is to seat the actors in a defined performance space and to seat the writer in the spectator position while the play is being read. The producer of a cold reading must keep a few key points in mind.

Try to do the cold reading in a theater. The space for the reading matters in so far as it should be quiet and free from people passing. A living room is acceptable, but the host should try to maintain closure among the actors and playwright. If the phone rings or the dog romps around the room, then concentration can be broken. Such disruptions, common in a living room, can break any rhythm or any semblance of dramatic action that can come out of the reading.

Producers must always be thinking one step ahead. The more salient reason for holding the reading in a theater space is that it initializes contact with a theater owner or manager. It can be the beginning of a relationship that may become far more important in the future. It takes very little to ask for permission to do a cold reading in a theater. If the theater space is empty, and if the group doing the reading seems trustworthy, then most theater managers will give such a request consideration. The simple relationship that can begin with the theater owner might prove to be essential if the play is eventually produced. Maybe the owner has a necessary prop, or will loan out a costume, or can provide marketing advice. If the basis of the relationship is formed early on, then later it can bring value to the production. Most people get involved with theater because they love it and they feel driven, and most people in theater are generous with their time and advice, so it behooves the producer to build networks as soon as possible. This holds true for New York, as well as a local community theater. Moreover, as a producer, one must get over any trepidation of asking people for advice, time, and physical properties. No one produces in a vacuum, and the more allies the producer has in the present, the better the chance of a quality production in the future.

Secure the space for the appropriate amount of time. This seems simple, but it is often overlooked. Frequently, a reading will get underway only to be broken up by another group that has the space reserved for another purpose. Everyone then has to gather his or her things, scout out a new location, and resume the reading. This type of disruption happens frequently on college campuses, but it can be avoided with a little planning by the producer. If such a simple detail is attended to early on, the reading ambience can take on a semblance of some consequence, that something can happen that may someday lead to fulfillment.

Organize the scripts. Again, this is a simple detail and it should be attended to a day or two before the reading. It is annoying for everyone involved not to be on the same page at the same time. If the actors do not read from identical scripts, then at some point, the reading will abruptly halt while everyone compares and deciphers who has the correct version of the play. It is really the playwright's responsibility to organize and distribute the scripts a day or so before the reading.

Organize the reading space. Make sure that the group can get into the space by making arrangements to have the room unlocked at the appropriate time. Secure enough chairs for everyone and arrange them in a setting that is conducive for the reading.

Remind all people involved a day ahead of time. Nothing dampens the reading atmosphere like a missing actor or two. In a reading situation, no one is getting paid and everyone is doing the playwright a favor. A friendly reminder is almost always appreciated and can help in avoiding some last-second scrambling for actors.

Establish trust among the group. During a cold reading, not much is at stake production-wise, save for the relationships that are formed among the actors and playwright, and possibly a director. As producer of the reading, treat people as if they are honoring you with their time and talent. Trust among artists and a positive atmosphere will renew itself in the future because such qualities attract good people.

Open Staged Readings

The next logical step is the staged reading. The staged reading is a type of production because an essential element is present along with the actors—the audience; thus it is dubbed open. The American staged reading format often follows the lead of the O'Neill Center's National Playwright's Conference. The format was developed by Lloyd Richards and is defined as a rehearsal process, a script-in-hand performance before an audience, a brief period wherein the playwright reworks the script, and another script-in-hand performance for an audience. Professional actors, directors, and dramaturgs work with the playwright during the developmental process. Gray modular set pieces represent furniture or other necessary set elements. The staged reading production, however, introduces a feature that the fully mounted production does not easily accommodate, namely last-minute revisions by the playwright. In fact, the staged reading production encourages a writer to listen to his or her script and make revisions, often on the spot, perhaps during rehearsal, or immediately prior to the reading. The staged reading is a *developmental* production geared to the script and playwright. It is a unique beast among theatrical productions, and ironically, anyone who has been to a few staged readings enviably sees one which far outshines a later, fully mounted production of the same script.

The producer of the staged reading must be cognizant of all elements necessary for the production of a cold reading along with several additional components.

Because an audience is present, the producer must prepare the audience space, as well as the stage area. Basic considerations involve chairs, clearly marked exits, and a location that audience members can find without much difficulty.

The producer should hire or secure a facilitator. The facilitator welcomes the audience, creates a relaxed, supportive atmosphere, and conveys the developmental nature of the production to all present. The facilitator also leads the after-play discussion. It is vital that the facilitator has some experience with new play development so as to guide the audience discussion toward honest reactions rather than prescriptive comments regarding script changes. The staged reading production should not become ground for an ambush on playwriting.

The staged reading production also requires a minimal amount of exposure through publicity and marketing channels. It requires nothing elaborate, but a few well-placed flyers and simple posters announcing the date, time, place, and event title can help to round out the audience.

The producer should invite local theater professionals and established theater artists. The invitation should be in the form of a personal letter announcing the event, followed by a request for attendance. A few days before the event, the producer might want to follow up with a phone call, but this depends on how well the producer knows the invitee. Contacting local theater directors, designers, stage mangers, teachers, as well as local actors is important. Once again, the producer's aim is the establishment of relationships with people who can benefit future productions.

Invite local critics. This point goes against a lot of common wisdom. However the aim of such an invitation is not the generation of a printed review; rather it is establishing a relationship with the local media. Perhaps the reviewer might be interested in the event itself, covering the fact that a group of people is concerned with new play development. This strategy can work if the reading is taking place in a small to mid-sized city. In New York, Chicago, and Los Angeles, however, critics will very rarely attend a reading, and the reality is that a producer must often enlist the aid of a well-connected press agent if there is to be any hope of a critical review for a fully mounted production.

Prepare a simple program. Simple is defined by a single sheet of paper duplicated on a photocopier. The audience usually wants to know a little about the play and playwright(s), as well as the actors and the director. The rule of thumb here is no more than one page and nothing of pretension. The program should also remind the audience of the after-play discussion.

Do not charge for admission. After all, the audience is doing the writer a favor, and admission charges imply that the production is finished and polished.

Try to provide coffee and cookies. This can be construed as an inconsequential detail, but simple amenities create an atmosphere that is a bit more social and relaxed. Keep the amenities off stage.

As a matter of courtesy, the producer should request that the actors not leave until the reading is over.

The producer must also make arrangements for the technical requirements. Usually a staged reading has some semblance of a set, but this can be accomplished with a few well-placed folding chairs. If sound is necessary, keep it simple by using a quality home stereo. If lights are necessary, or if lights are readily available, keep the lighting plot basic. Only three cues are really advisable: lights up, lights down, house light to half. Sometimes, there is a temptation to turn a staged reading into a technical exercise, with multiple light cues, costumes, sets, and even special effects. As a producer, it is best to avoid any temptation to lean in this direction and to discourage others who may have a fascination with dimmers, gels, jig saws, and digital audio equipment. But be sure to invite those folks to the party after the reading (if there is one) because you may need to enlist their help for a future project that can provide technical people with opportunities to develop their craft and expertise. It works both ways.

Secure rehearsal space for the necessary time. Staged readings come in all shapes and sizes; some carry the weight of a couple weeks of rehearsal, some just an afternoon. Moveover, the performance workshop is usually characterized by an intense weekend of rehearsal followed by a reading. The producer must make arrangements for rehearsal space and work with the space manager to insure an unfettered rehearsal period.

The Actors' Showcase

If this book had been written twenty years ago, perhaps the actors' showcase production would have been discussed in this chapter. But today, actors' showcases are, in every sense of the word, full productions—with sets, costumes, lights, and glossy publicity pieces. To the theater patron, an actors' showcase can look exactly like a production, save for the presentation of a series of scenes, rather than a complete play. The aim of the actors' showcase is, of course, showing the talents and personalities of the actors to perspective agents and producers. Because showcases have evolved to full productions, they shall be considered throughout the remainder of this book.

Success

As a producer, one should be concerned with the relationships among theater professionals, technical people, actors, and even local critics that can form during the developmental process of the staged reading. The nucleus of a company can begin to take shape under the banner of "readings." Relationships are vital in the theater world, more so than in many other arts forms because of the collaborative nature of the art. Perhaps the play being read will lead to nothing, but perhaps a relationship will form between the producer and an actor or director that will lead to fulfillment of artistic promise. The producer should not define success solely on the possibility that the script can move to another level of production; in fact, most readings do not "move." If the playwright is the producer, success should be defined dramaturgically, as well as in terms of how favorably the "production" was received by participants and audience. Moreover, readings are a good place to start a producing venture.

Readings, however, can be misleading for the producer and artists, especially readings that occur on a localized stage, one unlike the O'Neill stage. The deception can occur because of the amiable nature of the audience and participants. The reception of such readings should not be construed as indicative of that of a paying, nonpartisan audience. A producer should temper the reception of the reading with the realization that well-intentioned approbatory responses can and do occur more often than before a paying audience.

Summing Up: Producer's Points

- A new venture producer should not be blinded by the spectacle-driven production values of established theaters. Doing so will probably compromise the reading effort by placing the focus on the glitz, not the dramatic action or actors.

- The closed reading is designed to allow the playwright to focus on the script, not its reception before a paying audience.

- Producers should always try to stage a reading in a theater because this establishes connections with professionals who may be of future benefit.

- Establishing trust among the core group is essential if involved production ventures are undertaken in the future.

- Producers should court an audience for open readings since that group may provide support for future efforts. Producers should always think ahead to the next project.

Moving On

Playwrights and actors who take the next step toward a full production will come face to face with the daunting issue of money. Budgeting is all about planning—how to spend money, not actually passing cash between hands. Indeed, budgeting is a planning skill that should be honed early in the producing process as to avoid costly mistakes that often result from unforeseen and last-minute expenses. Producers should take a page of advice from the Aesop fairy tale of the ant and the grasshopper. The ant planned ahead, and the grasshopper didn't. Guess who got through the winter?

Chapter Three

What's Your Budget?

Many American companies fail because of poor management, and the same can be said for artistic organizations. Management can be defined as planning and organization. Budgeting is an important part of management because it represents the most basic of all planning activities. Planning budgets are described as pro forma because they do not represent actual numbers, but rather projections of what may happen. This chapter discusses pro forma budgets, the items within the budgets, and the variables that can affect cost projections. A comparison between a pro forma budget (what the producer believed would occur) and an actual financial statement (what actually occurred) will follow. Other key chapter concerns pertain to budget realization, financial risk, and timing—that is when the producer can begin to spend money and when income begins to be earned.

What Is a Budget?

Picture Athena's scale of justice. It is a simple scale, usually depicted with two plates hanging on chains from a fulcrum. A budget is much the same, with one plate holding the expense, and the other holding the income. Too much on either side will tip the scales, in one direction deficit, in another, surplus. A budget is a *prediction* of how the scales will tip, or in the rare case, how the budget will balance. We budget every day, even if we don't realize it. If we ask, "will I have enough money to buy a new television next month?", we engage in a budgeting process that balances the cost of the television against available cash. Budgeting for a theater production, too, involves a balance between what we think the production will cost against what cash we will have both before and after the realized production. Some people fear the term "budget" because it conjures up images of C.P.A.s and piles of ledgers and a stack of broken pencils. Real problems, though, result from not doing a budget and not planning ahead for financial outcomes. Without budgets, producers can, and often do, lose control over expenses, and the result can be a frowning Athena with a broken scale and no future production plans.

Types of Budgets

Theaters and producers must write a number of different budgets. The basic budget types are as follows:

The Capital Budget
Capital budgets usually reflect major outlays of cash for start-up assets that hold value over time. The acquisition of a building, major renovations, landscaping, attorney's fees for incorporation are all items reflected in a capital budget. A producer who buys a building with the intention of producing plays will draw up a capital budget. This book does not focus on the process of starting a producing theater entity and, as such, capital budgets fall outside the scope of this discussion.

Annual Operating Budgets

An annual operating budget reflects activity over the fiscal year, and it is the responsibility of any theater producing a number of productions during the year to draw up an annual operating budget. Items such as the mortgage payment, the annual salaries for the artistic director, managing director, and technical director are included in the annual operating budget. Seasonal marketing expense, as well as office supplies used throughout the year, are also reflected in the annual operating budget. Likewise, this book does not focus on the process of managing a yearly producing theater and, as such, annual budgets fall outside the parameters of new venture, single-show productions.

The Production Budget

Most theaters that now write capital budgets and annual operating budgets began with a single production budget. The production budget as implied, reflects all activity pertaining to a single production. It is obvious that before a production budget can be tackled, the producer must make a firm decision regarding choice of script. Production budgets have two components: expenses and income.

Expenses

In several ways, expenses are more manageable than sources of income because the producer has more control over spending money than he does with income generated with ticket sales. If one asks, "How much does it cost to produce a play?" the answer is as varied as the answer to "how much does a car cost?" Productions come in all shapes and sizes, some with music and some with fully unionized players; some are housed in fabulous Broadway theaters while others are staged in a local church with an all volunteer cast and crew. The expenses, of course, depend on the scope of the production project. All productions, regardless of where the production is housed, however, usually share some common expense areas such as space costs, artistic and technical personnel salaries, set and costume costs, script duplication charges, box office expenses, insurance, and marketing and public relations costs. What follows is a breakdown of costs and what variables come into the mix when estimating dollar amounts for expenses. Subsequent chapters explore these topics in detail.

Space

Space is often the single largest cost item in any production budget. Plays are produced in all sorts of spaces; some are produced in theaters, some in churches, some in the corner of a park, and some in the middle of Times Square. The price of the space naturally depends on where the space is located and who owns it. Some producers are fortunate enough to use a theater for no cost, while others dole out thousands of dollars for the use of a prime spot on New York's Theater Row. The space selection, of course, depends on what the play requires and available funds. Other rental issues include the duration of the lease and technical equipment associated with the space.

Factors in Estimating the Cost of Space:

Location. To echo the real estate agent, "location, location, location" largely determines the value of a property. People may feel comfortable with an established locale and may not want to venture out to see a play in a questionable part of town. The same logic applies to critics. It so follows that the prime locations cost more.

Reputation. Spaces have reputations, not unlike plays, that build over time. A space with an established reputation will require a greater outlay of cash because the value of a sought-after space is found through its ability to attract more patrons (than a space with little or no reputation). Moreover, some spaces have an historical track record, or a character unto themselves that can add or detract to the cost factor.

Familiarity with owner. Of course, cost of space is still determined by who controls it. If the producer of a play has an established relationship with the space owner/manager, then perhaps a better price can be negotiated. Likewise, if the owner of the space has a personal interest in the project or believes in the play, perhaps an advantageous deal can be struck.

Terms of the agreement. Cash is not the only currency. Rental agreements can be offset by trading labor for cash, or a percentage of future box office revenue, which, in fact, transfers some of the risk to the theater owner. Production length and rehearsal time are also important factors.

Equipment. The amount, quality, and availability of the technical equipment adds to or detracts from the rental price.

Size. Usually, larger spaces have more overhead and utilities, not to mention greater mortgage payments for the theater owner, and this cost is, in turn, absorbed by the tenant.

Personnel

The producer must decide who will be paid. In certain production settings, the size of the house and union agreements make payment a foregone conclusion. Even on a small production scale, however, it is advisable to budget some money for key technical people as well as the director and actors. The amount is sometimes not as significant as is the gesture.

Factors in Estimating the Cost of Personnel:

If the actors are covered by Equity agreements, then some form of payment is usually required. Equity arrangements can range from transportation costs to fully paid rehearsals. The cost factors depend on the city, the size of the theater, the production budget, and projected income. Equity agreements are covered in Chapter 6; however, a rule of thumb is a producer can manage a limited run in a ninety-nine seat theater with Equity actors without a substantial payment. Equity agreements usually only come into play in major cities where most Equity actors work. Even if an actor is non-Equity, the producer should make every effort to pay the actors something—even if it is simply $5 per rehearsal to cover travel to and from the theater. The same logic applies to the director.

The stage manager is a key figure in any production. The stage manager is the glue that keeps the production together during both rehearsals and performances. As such, a good stage manager is gold to a producer. Good stage managers are hard to find, and scarcity leads to value. In other words, as a producer, be prepared to cough up some money for a good stage manager—you'll need her. How much money depends on the city and the availability of stage managers.

Designers are also valuable members of the team. In large cities, it is very possible to secure a designer just out of college for little or no money because that designer is especially interested in building a portfolio. The production requirements will dictate how much money should be allocated to design. Some plays need very little set but elaborate lighting. Others may need special costuming but few light cues.

Technical people, like stage managers, can be hard to find. The producer must consider the technical requirements of the play: do sets need extensive building time, do costumes require construction, do lights need to be hung, does the sound system need to be tuned up, do seats need to be placed in the audience area? If the answer is yes to a number of these questions, then technical help must be secured and it usually comes with a price tag.

One word about estimating personnel cost: It is possible to secure wonderful people for very little money. The producer who is successful with volunteer personnel must create a currency of value associated with the production experience. As such, most volunteers will be younger people who value the experience of theater—most community theaters survive on this standard, and most college students pay for the experience of working with professionals because of the value of the learning opportunity. Money is not the only currency in theater. This sentiment will be echoed throughout this book.

Sets and Costumes

Sets can range from a realistic interior, complete with practical lights, to a bare stage or a platform in a park. It is often a temptation for the playwright-producer to build a set that shows off his or her play without giving full regard to the financial considerations. It is also sometimes difficult to say no to a designer working on one's own play because objectivity can be influenced by the passion for the production rather than financial prudence. Actors, too, can fall prey to production overkill if they sense that an elaborate set will showcase their talents. Costumes, too, range from fully designed, elaborate creations to pulled stock, to clothes out of the actor's own closet, or "creations" from the popular Italian designer Salvation Armi. Costume budgets reflect the degree to which costumes are designed and built from scratch or simply pulled from existing stock. It is important to note that talented costume and set designers can be both economical and creative, and perhaps that is the very challenge of design within a tight production budget.

Major Factors in Estimating the Cost of Set and Costumes:

Can the play be performed on a bare stage? Some outstanding directors, such as Margo Jones, felt that any script could be performed on a bare stage. Indeed, the bare stage has been a defining convention in many periods of theater history. If today's novice producer can justify a bare stage, then obviously budgetary costs for the set would be minimized.

What set pieces, if any, need to be built? What can be borrowed? If the play requires a few key pieces of old furniture, can these items be borrowed or built inexpensively? What is the cost of material and labor? Most common set pieces are available from other theaters or perhaps the producer's own living room. Specialty pieces may need to be built, but even this is contingent on the production aesthetic; that is, if the director approaches the play through a realistic or an expressionistic eye.

Must the play have specific costumes? If the play requires period costumes, what is the cost of building such costumes? Can they be rented? Better yet, can they be borrowed? If the play is a modern piece, can the actors provide their own costumes and will the costume designer be willing to accommodate such an arrangement?

Scripts/Royalties

If the producer is putting up an original script, and the playwright either acts as producer or is involved in the company, then royalties should not be a major concern. If actors, however, showcase themselves with an established script or musical, then royalties will figure into the budget equation.

Musicals are far more expensive to license than straight plays. Of course, royalties are based upon the production circumstances, that is the size of the house, ticket prices, and location.

Factors in Estimating the Cost of Scripts/Royalties:

1. The play and playwright.
2. The location.
3. The size of the house.
4. The length of the run.
5. Ticket prices.
6. The number of scripts needed.

Note that Samuel French, Inc. and other licensing organizations will almost always require such information before quoting a royalty fee. A complete listing of licensing organizations can be found in the appendix.

Marketing and Public Relations

"Build it and they will come" is a catch phrase from the film *Field of Dreams*. Unfortunately, the saying does not apply as well to live theater as it does to a baseball park. Producers must aggressively promote their product, and aggressive marketing and public relations require money. A good public relations campaign requires the development of press kits, press releases, production photography, and public service announcements, all of which require some front money. Marketing, of course, requires a minimal commitment to the development and distribution of posters and flyers. A good marketing campaign can also entail the development of postcards, newspaper ads, radio spots, and the like.

Factors in Estimating the Cost of Marketing and P.R.:

The City. The larger the city, the greater the marketing and P.R. costs. Greater populations carry greater competition for marketing and P.R. because more people are attempting to gain attention through the same traditional outlets. For example, newspapers in New York or Chicago do not *automatically* run press releases for theater productions, while papers in smaller cities often do. The general price of doing business is also costly in large cities since the greater number of for-profit organizations contributes to overall marketing costs for all organizations.

Presentation. A slick presentation costs more than a simple one. "Slick" is defined not pejoratively but rather by professional presentation in all marketing and P.R. materials. Professional photography and design, as well as four-color process printing add to presentation luster but also to the marketing and P.R. cost. Slick materials can, and often do, contribute to income because they get noticed with greater frequency than homemade materials run off on a black and white photocopier. Recall the poster and newspaper ads that have grabbed your attention. Chances are they were professionally designed and produced with very high standards.

Reach. The greater the marketing and P.R. reach, the greater the cost. If, for example, the producer creates a postcard to advertise the production, then the greater the number of people on the mailing list, the greater the cost. The price scale of the advertising reflects the reach of the media outlet. Newspapers with large circulations, or radio stations with high wattage and good ratings, will be expensive advertising avenues.

The means. Television, billboards, radio, and newspapers all carry a hefty price tag. Television traditionally reigns as the most costly means of marketing, followed by billboards, radio, and newspapers. Of course, the display size and advertising frequency play into the cost equation. Posters, flyers, and postcards are less costly, yet generally they are less effective in market reach.

Box Office

Any box office operation requires some organization and set-up. When writing a budget, a producer will decide on the type of tickets and reservation system as well as how the box office will be staffed. Box office operations can range from an answering machine to a fully staffed enterprise with networked computers, credit card capability, and a full-time manager.

Factors in Estimating the Cost of Box Office Operations

Staffing. Most budding theatrical endeavors do not posses a dedicated box office manager because most budding theaters do not have box office space under their purview. A box office manager usually comes with a price tag, of course, adding to the cost. If the producer cannot afford a manager, then an answering machine can take reservations and dispense information. Most off-off Broadway theaters operate with this arrangement. Someone, be it the producer or a volunteer, will staff the box office during performances.

Printing tickets. The choice of tickets also impacts the budget. If reserve seating tickets are specially printed, then this will drive the cost up. If the producer decides to go with general admission seating, then generic ticket stock can be purchased from either a ticket distributor or even a local party supply store. Sometimes, the evening's program serves as the admission ticket. Another option is contracting with a ticketing service to handle all phases of box office arrangements.

Income

Estimating income is far less certain than estimating expenses. If the theatrical enterprise has not secured non-profit status, then ticket revenue will produce the bulk of overall revenue, although it can be supplemented with private fund-raising efforts. Securing nonprofit status is a complicated procedure. It usually requires the counsel of a lawyer, always requires the establishment of a board of directors, and almost always occurs after the theater company has at least a couple of productions under its belt. This book assumes the producer has not yet secured nonprofit status.

The key factors in estimating ticket income are ticket prices, number of seats, number of performances, and projected attendance. Once set, the first three variables are controlled with absolute certainty, but the projected attendance is always based on hypothetical assumptions. The best indicator of future attendance is past attendance, and if the producer is beginning a new venture, then historical data cannot enhance his or her attendance projections. Some new production ventures sell out, while others play to a handful of audience members night after night. There is no formula of success in theater, and often, producers attempting to replicate a success meet with attendance disappointments. Indeed, predicting attendance is a high-stakes game because the money at risk is largely the producer's personal assets (or those of investors in a Broadway setting), and expenses must be balanced and controlled against projected income or substantial losses can follow.

Many theater producers calculate attendance based on the rule of 60; that is they assume 60 percent of the seats will be sold. In a pioneering producing environment, however, this projection is too optimistic. Producers should be conservative when making attendance projections. Forty percent attendance is a very conservative projection, yet it is not too reserved. Moreover, it is better to error on the side of conservation, rather than profusion. In other words, plan for the worst and hope for the best.

If the producer decides to run a play for a total of eight performances in a ninety-nine seat theater with a uniform ticket price of $10, the income projections would be:

Gross potential: 8 performances X 99 seats X $10 = $7,920
Projected attendance 40%
Budgeted ticket income: .40 X $7,920= $3,168

Major Factors in Estimating Ticket Revenue:

The number of performances. The greater the number of performances, the greater the possibility of selling seats, but the greater the expense of theater rental and production running costs.

The number of seats. The greater the number of seats, the greater the potential ticket revenue, but usually the greater the theater rental expense. Also, Actor's Equity agreements can have bearing on the number of seats allowed in an Equity production. (Equity Agreements will be discussed in Chapter 6.)

The ticket price. The greater the ticket price, the greater the potential revenue, but fewer price-sensitive patrons will attend. At the heart of the issue of ticket price is elasticity. Elasticity, in short, is consumer price sensitivity for a certain product. A theater producer could set ticket prices at $1000 per ticket, but no one would purchase the tickets. Likewise, a producer could set ticket prices at $1 and sell out the house but not make enough money to meet expenses. Finding the price where income is maximized is the goal of pricing strategies. Most new venture producers will set ticket prices slightly lower than ticket prices at comparable, yet established, theaters.

Other Sources of Income Include:

Income from fund-raisers. While a small *for-profit* venture will not receive a penny from foundations, corporations, or government granting agencies, the producer can conduct simple fund-raising events that are aimed primarily at friends and family. More will follow on this topic in the next chapter.

Start-up money. This is money from the producer's own pocket.

Concessions. If the producer decides to sell refreshments at the theater, a small amount of income can be realized.

Sponsorships. Producers of for-profit ventures can, and often do, sell program advertising, or display space on posters, flyers, and postcards. This, too, contributes to income.

Good Budgeting

Good budgeting is good planning that results from careful estimations of costs and revenue. The figures in budgets do not correspond to actual final dollar amounts, and, as such, the figures can be tinkered with until a desirable plan is achieved. If the budget plan is to correspond to the final dollar figures, then a number of steps must be accomplished before budgets can evolve into a working strategy. Estimates must be garnered, timing must be considered, goals and objectives must be set, and problems must be identified early on so they can be addressed in the planning phases of production.

How should the producer budget for printing costs? A producer should pick up the phone and call a few local printers. Figures should be secured for posters, programs, and the like for both color and simple black and white photocopies. What does it cost to rent a theater? Producers should visit

theaters and inquire. What will it cost to rent a specific costume? A couple of phone calls will answer the question.
Lights? Ask a technical person. Every single budget item
should be estimated based on actual information. Estimates
are knowledge, and the greater degree of knowledge the producer has, the greater the accuracy of the budget. Moreover,
much information is free for the asking; it simply requires
a little legwork. Kick the tires on everything.

Goals

Good budgeting also sets artistic and managerial goals
through the establishment of financial parameters. For
example, if a producer budgets $5,000 in ticket revenue, the
goal will be selling 500 seats at $10 per seat. If the producer
budgets money for 200 posters, the goal will entail the subsequent distribution of the posters in prime locations. If the
producer sets the costume budget at $500, then the cos-
tume designer's goal is to design the best costumes possible within those financial boundaries. Every budget item,
even concession income, should have an identifiable or,
preferably, a measurable goal attached to it that corresponds to some production element. Setting achievable
goals impacts every phase of budgeting.

Timing

Budgeting also urges the producer to consider timing. The
rule every producer should follow is — don't spend a dime
until absolutely necessary. There is an order to cash allocation that minimizes financial risk. For example, budgeting is an exercise in itself that costs nothing, and it should
be engaged early in the production planning. Nothing is
risked in the process. Rushing out and putting down a deposit
on a theater space before securing a director is foolish. Some
producers have lost a good deal of money because they spent

too early, or waited too long to secure necessary properties or people and, as such, have made the producing function a gut-wrenching experience. The order of producing events is reflected in the overall organization of this book as well as the producer's timetable in the appendix.

Be a Fishmonger

Good budgeting also identifies problems before they occur. Generosity in paying people is a virtue, but without the means to do so, the production endeavor can quickly become an exercise in good intentions gone bad, resulting in a poor reputation for the producer and few people willing to work with the producer in the future. A producer should not promise a great deal of money based on rosy income projections. If budgetary problems arise early, the producer should become like the fishmonger—that is, every percentage should be haggled over, every item examined, every goal rethought. If the play's producer happens to be the playwright, then budgetary problems can affect the script. In an ideal world this would never happen, but in the practical world, less costly plays get produced faster than demanding scripts. The small-cast, unit-set play that is dramatically sound, is a dream of many smaller producers. In short, rectifying some budgeting problems might mean another draft of the play, one that cuts a location, one that cuts a character, one that demands fewer props. This is not an easy reality to grasp, but all producers should recognize that art and commerce sometimes make for uneasy bedfellows.

Likewise, the budgeting process should also be flexible enough to accommodate changes. A budget should never be followed as if it were a map leading to a buried treasure. Budgets can, and usually do, change with time. Producers will discover some things cost more than planned, but perhaps a price break may be realized on other items. The budget should be adjusted accordingly. Budget flexibility should even extend to dropping the production altogether. If, after a budget analysis, there is no possibility of breaking even, then perhaps the production should be shelved before inevitable losses occur. It depends on the size of the producer's wallet or purse.

Financial Statements

A financial statement looks much like a budget except for the word "actual" that can accompany the title. The financial statement is compiled *after* the activity occurs and shows profit or loss. Financial statements are important for record-keeping purposes, since income must be reported to the IRS. Usually in a new producing venture, the organization is set up as a sole proprietorship. Indeed, two-thirds of all American businesses are organized as sole proprietorships. Such a classification considers production income as personal income for the producer and is taxed as such. Moreover, any losses come out of the producer's pocket.

Analysis of an Actual Budget and Financial Statement

The following budget and financial statement reflects the activity of an off-off Broadway production. The play was produced in the summer of 1998 in New York's TriBeCa in a 99-seat theater with non-Equity actors. The information was provided on the condition of anonymity for the producer and production.

Budget for TriBeCa Production
EXPENSES

Actors 4 @ $300	$1,200
Designers 2 @ $500	$1,000
Director	$300
Stage Manager	$500
Set	$500

Costumes	$1,000
Sound	$200
Marketing	$200
Press Agent	$2,000
Post Cards	$750
Postage	$500
Advertising	$400
Photography	$450
Space Rental*	$2,400
TOTAL EXPENSES	**$11,400**

INCOME

Box Office (12 performances)**	$7,100
Fund Raiser	$2,000
Front Money***	$2,300
TOTAL INCOME	**$11,400**

* Included rehearsal space.

** Tickets were $12.

*** Note that the producer was prepared to lose $2,300 of his money.

Financial Statement for TriBeCa Production

Actors 4 @ $300	$1,200
Designers 2 @ $500	$1,000
Director	$300
Stage Manager	$500
Set	$1,100
Costumes	$1,200
Sound	$50
Marketing	$460
Press Agent	$2000
Post Cards	$750
Postage	$300
Advertising	$400
Photography	$470
Space Rental	$2,400
TOTAL EXPENSES	**$12,130**

INCOME

Box Office (12 performances)	$3,400
Fund Raiser	$1,900
Front Money	$1,900
TOTAL INCOME	$7,200
Loss	($4,930)
Loss including Front Money	**(6,830)**

Analysis of TriBeCa Production Budgets

The producer expected to lose $2,300 of his own money. This is probably not an advisable producing practice, but it happens with frequency. In this case, the producer was the playwright and seeing his play on a New York stage was worth the out-of-pocket money.

The producer paid his actors and artistic staff. Although the producer was very pleased with the artistic quality of the product, he spent too much money on salaries. In larger cities a producer can secure artists for little money, and in fact, many New York actors are not paid for off-off Broadway work.

Most of the production budget expense items came in close to the actual figures. Although sets, costumes, and marketing ran over, postage and sound were less than expected. In areas where estimates could be obtained, the producer did a good job of planning for expenses.

The producer hired a press agent for $2,000 who did not perform as expected. The play was not reviewed by any of the major New York newspapers. This was $2,000 down the drain. Producers should never hire someone to do a job they could do themselves. Perhaps in this case the producer could have done a better job than the professional press agent. Press agents are a separate topic and will be covered in Chapter 11.

The income projections were way off target because of too much optimism. Income figures were based on 50 percent attendance and fell far short of expectations. Also, a shorter run could have saved money.

The producer ended up losing $6,830. Some of this loss could have been offset by not paying the actors, cutting set and costume budgets, not hiring a press agent, and not using a professional photographer. Of course, cutting expenses can also mean cutting the quality of the production and marketing, which would probably hurt attendance. This balance of expense against product is indeed one of the producer's main functions. In hindsight, it is easy to be critical, and novice producers do not possess the benefit of experience to back up their budget plans.

The deficit figures are rather sobering but, unfortunately, typical of many off-off Broadway productions. Some producers have ended up with far worse debit than in the above example, while others have made money. Of course the sample foregoing budget and financial statement characterize a New York production, and the cost of doing theater in Manhattan is considerably more than in a small town. However, it would be misleading to present the reader with a nice, balanced budget and imply that is the way it naturally works. There is a big difference between a wished-for outcome and taking all the necessary steps to make the desired outcome possible.

Summing Up: Producer's Points

- Budgeting should be engaged in early on because it is a planning activity that controls spending.

- Expenses should be estimated with research that backs up the figures; guesstimates should always be avoided.

- Budgeting research is another opportunity to meet people who may be able to further the production effort.

- Producers should not plan to spend money unless absolutely necessary. If a budget item can be borrowed, then it should be.

- Cash is not the only currency. Goodwill, friends, and opportunities can buy the producer space, costumes, and performers.

- Conservative income predictions are justified and generally prove to be more accurate than optimistic projections.

- Budget figures should be translated into specific goals whenever possible.

Moving On

After writing the budget, the producer will have a good idea of producing costs. To meet the costs and balance the budget, all producers engage in fund-raising activities. Fund-raising need not conjure images of rattling tin cups on Times Square or fat cats pressing for millions from investors. For the new venture producer, the truth is somewhere between these extremes. Although no one enjoys asking for money, it is nevertheless an activity that enables the production to go from the planning stage to the actual stage.

Chapter Four

Passing the Hat: Fund-Raising

Perhaps a discussion of theater fund-raising begets images from Mel Brook's film *The Producers*. In the movie, Zero Mostel and Gene Wilder portray two down-on-their-luck Broadway producers who raise money courting little old ladies to back their "hit" musical. The comedy revolves around the scheme of raising far more money than is necessary to produce the musical and then pocketing the money by insuring that the musical flops opening night. Plans go astray when the musical turns out to be a big hit and the backers discover that they were swindled. The final image shows Mostel and Wilder raising money in the big house for a new production, thus conning the cons. Many of the old-time theater producers did, indeed, hatch a scheme to raise money (P. T. Barnum was a master), but today's producer is operating in a much more savvy and sophisticated fund-raising environment than in yesteryear.

Why Do Producers Fund-Raise?

All producers concern themselves with fund-raising. At any production level, whether it be Broadway, off-Broadway, regional theater, university theater, or community theater, producers spend a good deal of time trying to secure necessary funds. While the targets for fund-raising change from level to level and while some producers sell shares of the production to backers, while others court grants from government agencies, the basic impetus of securing funding remains for all producers. Historically, producers have needed patronage to survive, and today most producers continue to need contributors or backers to fund productions, since few have the pocket cash to mount the shows.

Today's new venture producer finds himself at a disadvantage from established producers for a number of reasons. Chief among them is the lack of nonprofit status. Nonprofit status must be secured through the federal government and it often takes months, the help of an attorney, the establishment of a board of directors, and written bylaws. Once the status is confirmed, however, the organization becomes tax-exempt and can solicit funds from granting agencies. Most nonprofit theaters receive a substantial percentage of their operating income through grants and gifts from organizations and individuals. It is enlightening to examine the Theatre Communications Group annual *Theatre Profiles* book because a breakdown of earned versus contributed income often accompanies the profiles of theaters. Many profiles describe theaters in which more than half of the operating budget is contributed income. In other words, most established theaters do not survive on ticket revenue alone. Moreover, for profit Broadway theaters need investors to meet their multimillion dollar budgets, as well as substantial ticket sales to meet the monthly running cost of the show. The moral of the story is that very few producers can afford to go it alone.

Producers of smaller, new venture productions have many of these same economic realities and pressures impacting production viability. The producer who has not secured nonprofit status has even greater difficulty raising money since he or she cannot approach traditional granting agencies and cannot offer an individual contributor a tax deduction. Likewise, the smaller producer cannot offer a potential investor the prospect of substantial returns, let alone the glamour of a Broadway production. All hope of securing funds, however, is not lost for the small producer. He or she can employ some innovative fund-raising strategies that have proven effective in raising capital. Although the small producer is locked out of the granting games, the good news is that two-thirds of all contributed money comes from individuals, and not all individuals see a tax deduction as a necessary precursor for support of an artistic venture — especially the friends or family of the producer's artistic circle.

The main reason for fund-raising is to gather enough money to supplement production costs and diversify the risk away from one individual. But beyond the obvious benefits of fund raising lie a number of tangential benefits. Most fund-raising activities are social in nature, and, as such, a producer begins to build artistic associations and an audience base while engaging in the fund-raising activity. For example, if a producer organizes a fund-raising party, then he or she will need a core of people to help plan the party, as well as a larger group to actually attend the party. Such associations formed at the fund-raiser will form the backbone of the production company and the *initial audience* for the production. Good producers are always planning at least one step ahead of the current activity.

Fund-raising also adds identity and legitimacy to the project. In other words, it is a great source of free and early publicity. Fund-raising strategies announce to one's immediate world (of family and friends) that a new effort is underway and that the producer is serious enough about the show to organize and present a fund-raising activity. To paraphrase Marshall McLuhan, the party is the message. At an early fund-raising stage, the money raised is important, but success can also be defined by expanding the core group of people, both artists and supporters.

Early Considerations

Fund-raising activities can, however, present problems. Any producer wants to be associated with talented people and generous supporters. The cost of expanding the core group of supporters can never come at the price of promising more than the producer can (eventually) deliver. In other words, associations with the core group should not be the result of promising actors roles or designers opportunities. At the early fund-raising stage, the producer is walking a fine line between generating and encouraging interest in the production, while not overly committing to any specific option, be it securing a certain theater space or casting the production. The best approach to such a situation is honesty. If the production is not yet cast, then actors should be told that auditions will be held with a director in the following months. If a director has not been selected, then the producer should tell interested people that enough money must first be secured before the production gets the green light. People accept honesty; playing a card two ways, however, can lead to poor producing and promises that cannot be kept.

Very few people are born natural fund-raisers. As a matter of fact, most people dread asking others for money—people with beautiful elocution can suddenly turn into stammering, nervous wrecks. Such fear is natural, but the good producer quickly learns that overcoming that fear is central to putting on a play. Many theatrical organizations got off the ground because of early help from close associations. Here, the multivenue performing arts complex in New York got $8,000 in seed money from family and friends of the initial organizers. From its modest start, Here has grown to become one of the most significant venues in New York for new plays and performance art pieces. If the organization's founding members lacked the courage to ask their closest friends and family for support, Here probably would have

been just a dream on paper. Fund-raising, like most producer's functions, has a set of challenges that can be mas-
tered with planning and practice.

Choosing the Right Strategy

Choosing the right fund-raising strategy depends on a
number of factors. Fund-raising itself can be a well-funded
fully staffed operation, and, in fact, many theaters have full
time development staffs. Fund-raising activities can range
from time consuming, complicated, expensive strategies
involving wining-and-dining the well-to-do folks over a considerable amount of time, to simple efforts aimed at a few
close associates and friends. The right strategy makes all
the difference. A strategy not well suited to a particular theatrical endeavor can lose money and cause stress among the
producer's core group. Thus, before selecting a fund-raising
strategy, a producer should consider the following points.

1. Target the strategy toward specific people. Who is the
target of the solicitation? If the producer asks close friends
for money, perhaps a phone call is appropriate. If a rich uncle
dotes on his favorite niece, perhaps a handwritten letter is
the best means of solicitation. If a producer is in his twen-
ties, thirties, or forties, and wants to reach friends of a similar age and ilk, maybe a cash-bar party is the best avenue.
If the producer targets the general public, then a rummage
sale can indeed raise a good deal of money over a weekend.
If a producer wishes to gain support from local businesses,
then canvassing businesses person-to-person will likely get
better results than a phone call or letter. The aim of planning fund-raising is the consideration what each person, or
groups of like-minded people, wants and expects. The good
fund-raiser then organizes a strategy that fulfills individual expectations and ideally enables the contributor to feel
good about the act of giving.

2. What is the cost-gross ratio? Every fund-raising strategy has costs associated with the activity, whether it be a monetary, labor, or time cost. Some strategies are relatively simple and involve little money and time, such as a phone call to a family friend, while other strategies are expensive, such as organizing a fund-raiser dinner for possible donors, or a large-scale mailing targeted toward thousands of prospects. The cost-gross ratio is not an exact one, and, like a budget, requires some prognostication on the part of the producer. For example, if the cost of setting up a cash bar is $75, and if the producer believes she can raise $450 with a cash party, then the cost-gross ratio is 75 : 450 or 1 : 6. Conversely, if a producer organizes a dinner for twenty people at a cost of $20 per person and raises $2,000, then the cost-gross ratio is 400 : 2,000 or 1 : 5. Utilizing the strategy with the highest potential ratio does not always generate the most money, as in the above example. The cost-gross ratio is a budgetary planning tool that encourages the producer to consider the likelihood of a good return on time and investment. When evaluating the potential cost of an investment strategy, the producer should budget more than he expects the cost to be, to cover inevitable overruns. When guessing the gross figure, the producer should estimate conservatively. Thoroughly planning fund-raising helps to avoid the second biggest mistake fund-raisers make: spending too much on the event itself thereby undercutting themselves on the profit.

3. Consider the production team. If the producer has managed to gather a core group of people around himself, then the enthusiasms and talents of that group must be considered in fund-raising planning sessions. If the core group wants to produce a benefit performance, then the producer should give serious consideration to such a proposal. Likewise, if the core group wants to throw a fund-raiser party and offers to help, then let them do so. Fund-raising is difficult alone, but with a support group, it not only becomes easier, but the number of prospective donors greatly increases. The greater the number of family and friends *beyond* the producer, the better the chances of meeting or exceeding fund-raising goals. A word of caution: the more people involved in the fund-raising effort, the greater the chance of losing control over the production. Once money changes hands, people inevitably expect something in return. If a friend's mother contributes to the production, it is a safe bet that the mother expects to see her daughter on stage. A producer should never give up essential control of the production because of early panic over fund-raising.

4. Who believes in the production? The truly astute producer will have previously laid the groundwork for solicitation by inviting donor prospects to the open-staged reading, thereby establishing a relationship with people who demonstrate support for the arts. The initial contact would not involve an ask for money, but rather an ask for implied support as demonstrated by their presence at the reading. If implied support is cultivated, then monetary support can follow. Indeed, while professional fund-raisers speak of cultivating prospects over a period of years, the small venture producer can apply the same strategy, just on a smaller scale. Prospect cultivation also enables more personal contact with impending donors, and personal contact is far more difficult for a prospective donor to refuse than a letter or a phone call.

Fund-raising is much easier if the target people believe in the artistic effort prior to solicitation of funds. "Friends and family " sounds like a slogan for a long distance phone service, and although it might be just that, it should also be the slogan of every small-scale producer. Not only will friends and family strongly consider supporting the production, but they will also form the core of the initial audience. In a related fashion, fund-raising experts live by the credo that if a person has previously supported a cause, they are likely to support like-minded causes. It is much easier to cultivate someone who has supported theater in the past than a cold prospect who does not share a history of arts support. It is easy to locate such people in a given community. While established theaters may be reluctant to share donor records with a new-venture producer, practically all theaters print the names of donors in programs. An astute producer will take note of the individuals and businesses supporting theater and target these potential donors with an appropriate strategy.

5. What is the time cost? Besides the financial cost of organizing certain fund-raising events, there is also a time cost associated with every effort. Indeed, some dinners and receptions take a considerable amount of preparation time because people expect to be fussed over. In small-scale fund-raising efforts, preparation time can be taxing. Even simple cash-bar parties take planning; from location discussions to invitations to supplies. If one associates time with money, it becomes obvious that events generating the most amount of money in the least amount of time should be considered.

With Any Strategy

Set fund-raising goals. Budgetary considerations should dictate fund-raising goals. The budget, of course, provides the producer with an idea of how much money will be necessary to produce the play. Fund-raising goals derived from the budget gives the producer and the core group a tangible dollar amount as incentive. Fund-raising goals are nearly always reached incrementally, a few dollars at a time, and efforts of moving toward the goal create momentum and encourage endeavors necessary to reach the final goal.

Keep records. The single greatest fund-raising mistake a producer can make is not to personally thank all contributors. If gifts are not acknowledged, donors can feel as if their contribution was not valued, and such feelings lead to lack of future support with both donations and attendance at performances. Good record keeping enables the producer to keep track of who gives and to personally thank donors. Perhaps the best investment a producer can make early on is a packet of thank-you notes, an investment that will *maintain* the good will established between producers and supporters.

Donation records should be referred to in the event that the production is canceled. If, for any reason, the production never materializes, then the donations should be returned. It is unethical for a producer to pocket donations that do not fulfill the cause—it also leads to a bad reputation and people will usually not donate to future causes if the immediate production fails.

Never be desperate. People do not give to starving artists, rather they give to support culture in their communities. People do not give because a producer has a budget deficit, rather they give because they believe that the people behind the project can create something of value. Choosing a positive perspective through a positive approach can make the difference. In other words, everyone wants to bet on a winner. A major task of the producer fund-raiser is to make people feel good about giving. Buzz words such as, "new venture," "new play," "creating theater," make people feel as if their money is going to something productive — and hopefully it will.

Be specific. To many people, "would you help support making costumes," sounds better than "would you help support our play." People who give money to a cause usually want to know where their money is going. Established theaters do precisely this with many of their funding efforts—

some theaters encourage patrons to donate toward a specific character's costume, while others make specific theater seats available for donor recognition. On a smaller scale, holding a fund-raising auction to support the rental of space is entirely appropriate, and it makes for smart producing strategy.

Ask for specific amounts. The producer who hopes to get a $20 donation at a fund-raising party should ask for at least $25 dollars. Additionally, producers should always be up front with potential donors and not make any attempt to disguise fund-raising efforts as something other than a fund-raiser. People do not like to be shanghaied. If a party is a fund-raiser, then potential donors should be told ahead of time that the party is a theater fund-raiser. Also, if a producer is half way to her fund-raising goal, then that information should be communicated to people. Producers should be up front, as well as specific.

Acknowledge contributors. Donors should always be acknowledged unless anonymity is requested. Likewise, any volunteers who help organize fund-raisers should be publicly thanked.

Fund-Raising Events for Theater

While fund-raising offers the producer numerous opportunities for creativity, a number of established events have proven to be rewarding for theater producers. The events are not mutually exclusive, and often more than one event is needed to reach the fund-raising goal. The events are:

- The cash-bar party
- Raffles
- Sell the junk
- The benefit performance
- Wish lists
- The reception

The Cash-Bar Party

The event. The cash-bar party is an unpretentious event that raises funds by charging people a party admission price and/or a charge for each drink. The cash-bar party is usually held in someone's home or a local bar. Participants must be of legal age if alcohol is served.

Cost factors. Low. The producer must consider the cost of the libations as well as the percentage of the profits given over to the bar proprietor. Generally, the cash-bar party has a modest cost factor.

Profit factors. Good. A substantial profit can be realized from this fund-raising strategy. The key in tallying a good profit is correlated with the number of people attending the party, and getting together enough people who know how to throw a darn good party. (Actors are good at this sort of thing.)

Degree of difficulty. Low. The only real difficulty is attracting enough people to make the party worthwhile. The more people associated with the production, the better the chance of success.

Prep time required. Moderate. Once the invitations are out and volunteers have followed up with a phone call, then prep time is similar to that of any party.

The Raffle

The event. Hold a raffle. Most everyone at some point in his or her life has purchased a raffle ticket. Raffles are simple: a prize (or prizes) is offered as bait, people buy tickets that represent a chance to win, and the winning ticket(s) is drawn from the pool of entries.

Cost factors. Varies. The astute producer will try to get prizes donated from local restaurants, established theaters, bookstores, and other businesses. The great danger in conducting a raffle is spending too much out of pocket money for the incentive prize. Offering potential ticket buyers a large number of small prizes works as effectively as offering one larger prize, especially if the raffle money is going to a cause people will back.

Profit factors. Moderate. The producer and her team must consider how much money to charge for the tickets, what goal to set, and what incentive to offer. All of these factors work together to either create a profit or financial frustration. The more people working to sell tickets, the greater the profit.

Degree of difficulty. Moderate. Acquiring the prize and soliciting enough volunteers to sell tickets are the difficulties with this strategy.

Prep time required: High. Securing the prizes and purchasing raffle tickets (double-printed tickets with corresponding numbers on each stub) and selling the tickets can be rather time consuming.

Sell the Junk (a.k.a. The Rummage Sale)

The event. Rummage sales are common to just about every neighborhood. People display their wares and others buy the goods. Local newspapers carry ads for rummage sales. These ads run every day.

Cost factors. None, except for the cost of parting with that cherished wagon-wheel coffee table.

Profit factors. Good, but highly dependent on others' involvement.

Degree of difficulty. Low.

Prep Time required. A day or two.

These last three fund-raising strategies are best employed close to the actual production run.

The Wish List

The event. The Wish List. A list of items needed for the production is complied and circulated to the friends and family of everyone involved.

Cost factors. None.

Profit factors. Profits are usually in-kind, meaning that goods and services are received, not cash.

Degree of difficulty. Very low.

Prep time required. A brain storming session with the production team.

The Benefit Performance

The event. Sometimes producers will slate a certain performance as a benefit for some specific cause. Historically, benefits were held to support the retirement of an actor, or restoration of a building, or even a charity not directly linked to the production. Benefit performances generally have higher ticket prices than the nonbenefits since the cause justifies the higher ticket prices. Usually benefit tickets are sold by special invitation.

Cost factors. Moderate. The extra performance and the invitations can incrementally increase production costs by approximately a factor of one. Also, there can be some cannibalization of the regular paying audience that should be taken into account.

Profit factors. Good.

Degree of difficulty. If the production is already set to open, then there is no extra difficulty in one more performance date.

Prep time required. Little extra time is needed if the production is set to open.

The Reception Fund-Raiser

The event. This event works somewhat like a benefit performance in that people are invited to attend a fund-raising reception after a specific performance. Sometimes wine and hors d'oeuvres are served along with additional entertainment. Food is always important in the fund-raising game. Food has a social quality to it; in other words if people are enjoying themselves, they are more likely to give than if their stomachs are growling and calling them home to their refrigerators. This principle holds true with most fund-raising strategies.

Cost factors. Low. Wine, cheese, and a few invitations.

Profit factors. Moderate. It depends on who shows up and how much wine they consume.

Degree of difficulty. None.

Prep time required. A few hours.

No one is born a fund-raiser. As a matter of fact, many prominent fund-raisers will readily admit that they first dreaded asking people for money. It gets easier with practice because experience teaches the fund-raiser about people—how they give, why they give, and why they don't give. Experience also teaches that every gift is significant because it establishes a relationship that can develop into greater acts of philanthropy over time. Experience also teaches the fund-raiser that people, especially today, expect to be approached by numerous organizations and are generally not put off by the request itself.

Summing Up: Producer's Points

- All producers raise funds, and it often consumes a great deal of their time and energy.

- No one likes to raise funds, but most producers do it.

- When soliciting funds, producers should never promise more than they can deliver.

- A new venture producer should target family and friends first, and later expand the scope of fund-raising to include others.

- Producers should consider both the monetary cost and the time cost balanced against the potential return before employing specific fund-raising strategies.

- The more people committed to raising funds, often the better the chances for success. Thus, motivating the entire production team is part of the fund-raiser's job.

- Producers should set clear fund-raising goals that are tied to budgetary needs. Goals provide the team with objectives and progress toward them can be a motivating factor in raising money.

- Producers should be specific, both in asking for amounts and in telling donors where their money is going.

- Producers should always thank contributors regardless of the amount. Congeniality helps to create a lasting audience base.

Moving On

Perhaps the single largest expense is the cost of space. Moreover, renting or borrowing a theater extends well beyond dollar figures since the choice of space carries aesthetic, marketing, publicity, and audience ramifications. Finding a space is a considerable challenge for the new venture producer, but once met, the production finds a home and begins to find its identity.

Chapter Five

The Hard Hat: Finding a Space

Every producer must eventually face the formidable task of securing a performance space. Theater, unlike many of its cousin arts, cannot be replicated and distributed through a wide network, such as video, music, or literature. Subsequently, the performance space that accommodates the play greatly affects the artistic and financial outcome of the production. Unquestionably, the play's artistic reception is partially colored by the esthetics of the performance and audience spaces. For example, the producers of *Rent* "refurbished" Broadway's Nederlander theater in a style complementary of the musical's New York East Village setting, replete with cracking plaster and blue lights on the audience's side of the proscenium. The choice of space also impacts the financial statement's bottom line, since theaters often have established audience draws, as well as a fixed seating capacity. Indeed, space decisions are as complicated, risky, and time consuming as casting or marketing decisions.

What Space Will Serve the Script?

A fundamental consideration in the choice of space is the script itself. What space will serve the play? Some plays can be adequately performed in the corner of a park, while others need elaborate technical equipment offered only by established theaters. The astute producer knows how to read a script for clues that will help in gauging what type of space will best show off the work. If the play is set in the ship's boiler room, perhaps staging the play in a nontraditional space such as the basement of a building would serve the script well. Some of the more significant off-off Broadway spaces were, in fact, nontraditional theaters; plays produced in the 1960s often found homes in churches, garages, and cafes. Moreover, if a play is set in a park, it is feasible that an outdoor setting could bring out the script's given circumstances better than an indoor theater. If the script is an historical piece, perhaps a theater with historical character should be sought out. Some dramas are delicate, intimate pieces that best play in small spaces that give the audience a close proximity to the actors, while other plays demand some separation between actors and audience. It is ultimately a question of fit among the play, the space, and the producer's budget. If a director is on board the production team, or if the playwright is available, consult with one or both of them. They can provide insights into the space question and perhaps conjure up visions of untraditional spaces appropriate for the script.

The Space Chase

A producer searching for space can probably empathize with King Arthur's quest for the holy grail—a lot of hopes, a lot of leads, a lot of dead ends, and just another fire breathing dragon blocking the road at the end of the day. Indeed, the space chase might be the single greatest hurdle a producer must clear before the production becomes viable. Of course some producers get lucky and stumble onto a wonderful, dirt-cheap space, but it always seems like those lucky strikes happen to the other guy, the guy with the grail in the nap sack.

The space chase doesn't have to be a random search, for the following general guidelines can help the producer find the correct space—without getting burned by dragons or theater managers.

Network with other producers. The best sources for information about theater spaces are people who have successfully produced theater. The new venture producer should begin her investigation via the telephone by calling theaters and speaking to either the producing director or managing director of local semiprofessional and community theaters. Most experienced producers are very willing to share information about space and producing with others, primarily because of an altruistic love of theater. The novice producer should learn to ask the right questions by first listening to the voices of experience, then assimilating what was heard, and, finally, formulating questions based on the consultation. Also, networking can lead to the discovery of various state theater associations. Appropriate state or regional theater associations should be contacted because their directory would be a gold mine of producers and venues, an almost endless source of free information about venues and knowledgeable people. Any experienced producer knows that the cliché should be varied to read, "half the fun is *planning* how to get there."

Consult resource books. Many major cities have resource books for actors that cover issues such as venues, rehearsal spaces, and a host of other needs. Contact Applause and The Drama Book Shop (New York), and Act One (Chicago) to inquire if a resource book exists for your city. Actors' resource books also provide contact information for technical expertise, agents and producers, marketing and advertising consultants. Numerous contacts are also provided in the back of this book.

Check newspaper listings. One excellent source of current and viable theater venues is the arts calendar in the local newspaper. The producer can easily scan the arts calendar for available spaces, research the newspaper's back issues for past theater venues, or even phone the arts calendar editor for information. Also, many mid-sized cities now have weekly arts-oriented tabloids that appeal to a hip, trendy readership. These tabloids should also be consulted for feasible spaces since mainstream, traditional papers might not cover innovative, off-the-wall productions. Again, a phone call to the tabloid calendar editor cannot hurt, and they should know of the theaters, and makeshift spaces, about town.

Contact technical equipment rental businesses. Most decent-sized cities have businesses that rent and set up sound and lighting for theatrical productions. The people who do such work will know where plays have been produced in the past. They will have a very good idea of the character of venues, as well as information on nontraditional theater spaces. Any astute producer will want to make friends with these folks early in the venture, not only for the information they can provide, but also for the services offered.

Space Characteristics

Theater spaces are somewhat like people; some are charming, some attract other people, some inspire creativity, and some hang out on the dangerous side of town. Indeed, theaters come in all shapes, sizes, and histories, and some have established a certain type of patron draw through years of productions. The producer's task of matching the play to the ideal venue is a formidable one. If the wrong venue is chosen, a play may never find its audience, critics may never find the theater, and the producer may never find his income.

For example, *The Fantastics* is a charming musical that needs a relatively intimate venue to do justice to the script and music. Subsequently, the producers settled on a relatively small theater, one not comparable to a Broadway musical house, but one that offered the production a setting conducive to the four-character action in the musical. Likewise, the early plays of Sam Shepard and Lanford Wilson played best on small stages which facilitated a close proximity between actors and audience, as did the plays of Beckett, and the chamber theater productions of Ibsen and Strindberg. Contrast these productions with those of many modern musicals and farces, which need a larger venue to give some distance between the performers and the audience.

The character of a venue, however, is far more important than its capacity. "Character" can be defined by the type of space, the established audience draw, and its location in town.

Established Theater Spaces

An established theater space is a venue set up for live performances. Most of the spaces that are considered legitimate theaters fit this category. In an established theater space, a producer should find audience seating already in place, stage lighting, a sound system, a lobby area, and restroom facilities. The equipment and amenities make producing in an established space far less taxing than producing in a space that requires basic outfitting of theatrical equipment, a stage area, and seats. Indeed, producing in an established space has a number of definite advantages over a new venue, such as location recognition by audiences and critics, as well as a track record of (hopefully) successful past productions that help to define the space along with any new production.

Established theater spaces are generally divided into four major categories. A *proscenium theater* is defined by a framing device that separates the playing area from the audience—the curtain rises and the performance begins. Most Broadway theaters are proscenium style houses, and the traditional high school theater space is typically a proscenium space. A *thrust stage* is characterized by an acting area that is thrust out into the audience area, thus breaking the traditional picture frame of the proscenium stage. A *theater-in-the-round* setting presents stage action that is surrounded on all sides by the audience. The alley stage presents the action in a central area that is flanked on two sides by audience space. *Black box* theaters are defined by flexibility in that seats can be reconfigured in almost any variation in relationship to a playing area. Although no one type of space is better than another, the producer should recognize that many audience members have come to expect some degree of "fourth wall" scenic realism with the proscenium setting, while not anticipating much scenery with thrust, in-the-round, and black box stages.

The Audience Draw

Certain theater spaces, like coffee houses, or churches, have an established audience that is predisposed to attending performances. A producer should be aware of the implied audience draw and use that to his benefit by matching the play with a theater and audience receptive to the style of drama. For example, a Todo Con Nada audience on New York's Lower East side is used to hip, off-the-wall, Richard Foremanesque, break-the-mold plays, while The Upper West Side Repertory Theatre produces mostly traditional, main-stream, academically accepted dramas. Renting either one of these theaters, then, is *both* a business and an artistic choice that has bearing on the play's reception among its established audience and critics.

The Location in Town

Coupled closely with the preestablished audience draw is the identity established by the theater's location within a city. While a trendy spot might be just the ticket for a new coffee house, it may or may not serve a theater well for a number of reasons. First, critics are often habitual creatures that will not go far out of their way to find a new theater to review a new play. Also, new locations in town can prove to be unattractive to agents and other producers because of their lack of an established legitimacy. Any producer should think twice before settling on an untried, untested locale.

How to Pitch the Production to the Theater Owner/Manager

Most new venture producers will try to secure an established theater for their production. Most established theaters do, from time to time, rent out the facility to an outside production company. They do this primarily for the income resulting from rental agreements. Besides, no manager wants her theater to sit dark for long, costly stretches of time, during which bills for rent and utilities pile up. Approaching a theater manager requires a good deal of preparation and planning. A theater manager will expect to see a production plan in writing. A production plan includes:

- A complete budget, with income and expense calculations, a statement addressing the issue of how money will be raised, including the personal commitment of resources on the producer's part. If a producer is willing to risk personal capital on the production, then the proposal can take on some added momentum because of the producer's beliefs and backing.

- A complete script of the play, as well as a statement from the director.

- A complete marketing plan, including budgets and plans for public relations and publicity.

- A statement regarding how profits are to be shared between the producer and the theater manager.

- A production calendar or timetable that gives the theater owner a good idea of the time commitment expected.

The production plan by no means addresses all of the issues regarding the theater rental. Rather, it is meant to be a proposal that gets the attention of the theater owner so that the finer points of space can be negotiated later. Moreover, a producer approaching a theater owner will have a much greater chance of success if the producer has some kind of a relationship with the theater manager. (Thus, setting the stage for a production proposal through an earlier staged reading is a wise strategy.)

Rental Issues and Space Issues

If a producer can attract a theater owner's interest, then a number of rental and space issues enter into contract negotiations. Any producer should have a firm grasp on such issues before finalizing any contracts with a theater owner, for without a firm understanding of the basic issues between the parties, unfounded assumptions can lead to tremendous disputes close to production time.

Rental Issues

Term of lease. Rental agreements can be written by the day, the week, the weekend, the month, or any variation of term. Some theater owners will insist that the theater be rented the entire week prior to a given weekend, while others will begin a lease on a weekend date. If the producer is rehearsing the play at another location, these issues become critical. Every producer's goal is to pay for the theater space only when it is actually used, whether it is for performance or rehearsal.

Performance dates. Coupled closely with the term of the lease is the availability of specific dates for performance. Every producer should get a firm commitment from the theater owner regarding performance dates prior to signing a lease because not all dates may be available. For example, some theaters discourage performances on Sundays, and others may not allow both a Saturday matinee and evening performance. It is also possible that a theater may have a date or two scheduled for their own auditions, which could conflict with a desired performance date. Moreover, a theater owner will obviously be far more receptive to a production date proposal if the dates fall within a time frame that fits her schedule. Many theaters are dark over the summer months and do indeed rent space during this time. Another smart strategy is to look for T.B.A. (To Be Announced) slots in theater schedules. If the producer's proposal is strong enough, a theater owner may give consideration to a new production. After all, theaters usually fill slots with T.B.A. because they haven't settled on a specific production and, thus, may be especially receptive to new ideas.

Rehearsal space. A producer should never assume that a rental agreement automatically carries with it the right to rehearsal times on stage. Whenever the demand is great for theater space, most theaters will realize a higher profit margin if they rent the space primarily as performance space and encourage companies to rehearse elsewhere. This is often the case in New York and Chicago, where performance space is at a premium, but, interestingly, rehearsal space is rather plentiful and affordable in both cities. If rehearsal time is part of the rental agreement, a producer would be wise to negotiate specific hours in the day that the space would be availed to rehearsals.

Coproduction agreements and profit sharing. If a producer has a relationship established with the theater proprietor, then perhaps a coproduction agreement can be struck between the parties. A coproduction agreement essentially diversifies the risk of producing to the theater owner, thus resulting in lower cash outlay on the producer's part. It is almost always to the advantage of the producer to strike a coproduction agreement. The most common form of coproducing involves a split of box office revenue between the theater proprietor and the producer. The theater owner is gambling that the production will turn in a good box office performance, thus producing a fair chunk of revenue. Of course, if the play does not meet box office projections, then the theater owner absorbs some of the lost revenue. Why would a theater owner consider such an arrangement? Because the theater owner has some reason to believe in the producer or the production prior to the actual performances. In other words, if a relationship has been established, then a coproduction agreement can be broached. In the theatrical world, something called an "incremental commitment ladder" exists. The metaphor of a ladder of commitment is appropriate, since one gains position with an established theater one step at a time, whether the person is an actor, designer, playwright, or producer. If a high position of regard is held, then greater commitments on the part of the theater owner can be expected because some degree of trust has been established. Traditionally, the first rung on the commitment ladder is characterized by volunteerism.

Sweat equity agreements. Sweat equity agreements are another form of subsidized producing. The term "sweat equity" connotes that one's labor is exchanged for equity or a share of production time at a theater. Such agreements fall back to the barter system of exchange whereby one party trades labor for a good or service. In other words, sweat equity means working off part of the production cost by working for the theater owner. Work assignments may include duties such as box office management, bar tending, house management, custodial services, or even technical work. Sweat equity agreements are popular because the producer need not front a lot of cash, and the theater owner need not pay someone to perform needed duties. If a sweat equity agreement is struck, both parties must agree on very specific duties and an exact time duration of the labor agreement. Most sweat equity agreements are based on a specific hourly rate that translates to a lump dollar figure that offsets rental costs. Any producer is wise to get such agreements in writing before the term begins.

Scene and costume shop availability. The presence of a scene shop and costume shop does not automatically imply that they are included in rental agreements. Most often, people other than the theater proprietor manage such spaces. Indeed, even within a small theater, territories develop and control of space can become a high point for friction. A producer will save many problems if the rental agreement stipulates exactly what access is given to the shop areas, as well as what equipment can be used by the outside production company. Moreover, it is a grievous error to assume that shop staffs will pitch in and help with a production when, in fact, shop staffs hold no alliance to an outside company. Most likely, shop spaces will be off-limits to the outside producer.

Theater personnel. In certain rental situations, the producer is expected to pay for the established theater's key personnel. For example, the outside producer may have to hire the theater's technical director or box office manager as part of the rental agreement. This is not necessarily a liability, and it is not necessarily beneficial to the producer. The point is that if such an arrangement is expected, it is by far best to discover it *before* signing a rental agreement. Moreover, if the outside producer does pay for the services of theater staff, then duties should be clearly stated in any agreement.

Liability insurance. Any legitimate theater will carry a liability insurance policy. The policy protects the theater within set limits of an at-fault settlement or verdict in the event of a lawsuit. Lights can fall, patrons can slip in the aisles, seats can break, and fires do happen. In the event of such calamities, the outside producer must either be covered under the established theater's insurance or take out a liability policy to protect his own interests. If the theater proprietor's insurance covers the outside producer, then this must be secured in writing from both the theater and the insurer. Better safe than sorry. Liability insurance is covered in greater detail in Chapter 8.

Payment of rent. Any rental agreement should state the total amount of the rent, as well as when payment is due. It is usually to the new venture producer's advantage not to advance the entire rental amount up front, but rather to split payment so that at least part of the rent is due after the box office has produced some revenue.

Deposits. Most theaters require a deposit to secure the space for the agreed-upon time. If the theater requires a deposit, the producer should get in writing the policy for refunds and return of deposits. The policy should state when the deposit will be returned, what conditions are attached to the agreement, if the deposit can be refunded in the event of a production cancellation, and what percentage of the deposit is refunded if cancellation notice is provided within a set time limit. The shady theater proprietor can attempt to deduct charges for theater cleaning, utilities, or fire marshal services without prior notification of intent for such actions. Fortunately, most theater owners do not conduct business in this fashion. The producer can protect herself from such ruses by anticipating actions, and securing agreements in advance.

Office charges. Rental agreements can include office charges for services such as phone, fax, and computer usage.

Stop clauses. Stop clauses should not figure into a rental agreement for a modest production. Stop clauses are rental stipulation mandating that the production will close if box office revenue falls below a certain dollar figure. Producers should have stop clauses removed from any lease prior to final agreement.

Credit card handling. If the theater provides credit card handling, then the producer should determine the charges for such services prior to accepting credit cards.

Hours. Rental agreements should spell out the hours the space can be accessed by the producer and his team. This point is critical immediately before the production opens. More than one producer has been disappointed and embarrassed to discover that the space is not open at midnight for twelfth hour light focusing or floor painting. Often technical work is done at the last minute, and having the space available makes the hurried touch-ups possible. Unfortunately, paint still dries at its own pace.

The right to advertise. If the theater has outdoor signs or marquees, then the producer should be allowed to use the displays for her production. If this is not negotiated prior to the lease, then the theater may assume that their productions have exclusivity in outdoor displays.

Before finalizing a rental agreement, the producer should walk through the theater and inquire about a number of important issues. The right agreement struck for the wrong space is like getting a great deal on a Brooks Brothers suit that doesn't fit. The following issues should be closely scrutinized.

Space Issues

Capacity. Seats should be counted to determine exact capacity. The number of seats is an important figure for various reasons. Generally, the greater the number of seats, the greater the rental cost. The seat count also determines how many tickets are to be printed and available for each performance. A producer should also be aware of union codes, since Actors' Equity has rules in place based upon the number of seats in the theater available for ticketed patrons. The producer should also determine if seats are fixed or movable. Fixed seats are bolted into the floor, but flexible seats can be reconfigured in formations best suited to each particular play. Also, the producer should sit in a few of the seats; since not all theater seats are created equally comfortable, it is a good idea to know what the patron will be getting into.

Seating areas for the disabled. Does the theater provide wheelchair access into the building, and do wheelchair seating areas exist? Wheelchair seats require about one and a half times the space of a standard seat. The general rule of thumb is to provide three wheelchair seats for every ninety-seven regular seats. If the wheelchair seat is unsold, then a portable chair can be sold in its place. Producers should note, however, that local laws can often be more stringent than the American With Disabilities Act of 1990 and require additional accommodations for disabled patrons.

Fire Codes. All theaters have to comply with a local fire code. Codes are specific to each city; thus there are dozens of variations from location to location. However, certain universal features of fire codes are usually written into every city's regulations. They are:

Fire extinguishers should be located 75 feet apart from one another for every 2,500 square feet of space. Extinguishers should be tagged with the inspector's initials and be fully charged before every performance. Fire extinguishers should be mounted between 2 feet and 4.5 feet off the floor.

Proper storage of all flammable liquids and combustibles is mandatory. Combustibles should be stored in ventilated, metal cabinets positioned away from any electrical devices. Also, trash should never accumulate beyond the capacity of containers and should be disposed of daily.

No smoking signs must be in place since smoking is prohibited in almost every theater. Smoking on stage is permissible if it is necessary to the script and local authorities approve the request.

Exit signs must be displayed and illuminated during all performances. Also, exits must be left unlocked and unblocked during all performances.

The *Fire log book* must be kept in every theater to record on-site inspections by the theater stage manager or other fire inspector prior to every performance. Guidelines for fire log recordings are issued by local fire departments.

Fire proofing affidavits must be secured for scenery and draperies for every new production. Flame-proofing chemicals are available through theatrical supply catalogs and may be sprayed on scenery and draperies to fulfill regulations if materials are not flame retardant.

Open flames and pyrotechnics require special permits available through the local fire department. Usually, there is a fee for such permits, and they must be kept on file and available for inspection during the production run.

Sprinkler heads may be required in dressing rooms. Local

regulations vary, however, based on the code that governed the original theater construction.

Producers must be aware of fire regulations because serious violations can result in cancellation of performances. This does happen. During the 1998 New York International Fringe Festival a venue was closed down for two days because of fire code regulations. Other producers have lost a good deal of money because productions were shut down on opening night because of fire hazards. The best insurance against such actions is to comply with all regulations and to have a staff member who is a certified fire marshal. Fire marshals are usually not members of the fire department; rather they are individuals who pass a fire department examination, pay a fee, and obtain a fire marshal license. Thus, many established theaters have a fire marshal on staff, not to skirt regulations, but rather to verify and insure that regulations are met before opening night. Anyone who is serious about producing theater would do well to become a fire marshal.

Additional Space Issues

Access. During a walk-through, a producer should take note of the dimensions of doors. This is vitally important if scenery is built off-site and brought to the theater. Set designers need to know door measurements to scale scenic pieces accordingly. Also, notations should be made regarding ground floor access, elevator access, and dimensions of stairwells.

Electrics. The number of working outlets should be noted, along with their location and voltage. Special outlets called "disconnect boxes" should be in place for powering the light board and sound board. Back-up emergency lighting should be installed in case of power failure. Producers should also inquire about extra charges for utilities.

Fly system and overhead rigging. If a fly system is in place, inquiries should be made regarding its working condition and the load it will support. If overhead pipe rigging is installed, the same inquiries are relevant. Also, the coverage area of pipe rigging should be noted, along with the amount of space between the rigging and the ceiling, and the space between pipes.

Stage, wing and back stage space. Some plays require very little wing space, but others require space for storage of large props and special scenery. All space should be noted, and a diagram of the theater should be provided to the producer and design team.

Dressing rooms. Size and availability should be noted. Dressing rooms should be equipped with mirrors, electrical outlets, good lighting, and adequate hanging space for street clothes and costumes.

Audience lobby area/restrooms. Adequate audience lobby space is a plus for the producer because it enables her to sell concessions. Permission to sell concessions and the profit derived from such sales should be negotiated in advance of the final rental agreement. Also, public restrooms should be easily accessible. Most modern theaters have two toilets (gender specific) for every 100 seats.

Air conditioning/heating system. The theater should be adequately heated or cooled. Producers should check the air conditioning system and its venting. Some systems cannot be run during a performance because of compressor noise, while others operate quietly. Also, inquiries should be made regarding heating and cooling bills.

Lighting and sound equipment. A theater that regularly rents its space should be able to provide an inventory of all available equipment. Inventory lists should be broken down as to specific instrument type, number available, and the type of controlling board. Light boards are now computerized, and sound equipment is often digitalized; thus the correct operation is best in the hands of an experienced technician. Also, inquiries should be made regarding additional charges levied for the use of lighting instruments. Theater lights are expensive and burn out rather quickly, so such charges are sometimes merited.

Why a Theater Might Say No

Theater proprietors may refuse a well-prepared rental request. The reasons for refusal are varied, but often fall within a few general categories.

Damaging the theater's reputation may be a concern. If an established theater allows an outside company to produce, then the general public makes an association between the outside producer and the established theater by virtue of name recognition of the space, even though the established theater may have no stake in the production. It takes a theater years to build up name recognition, and such favorable regard is one of theater's primary assets. If this asset is compromised by an outside producer's mediocre play, then the established theater suffers some loss of prestige in the public's eye.

The timing may be wrong. Established theaters often have tight production schedules, and if a production proposal does not fit their framework, it will nearly always be rejected.

The outside producer may be seen as competition. If the production proposal is construed to be in any way competitive with the established theater's season, then it will be rejected. Theaters operate on a very small profit margin, and no theater owner will compromise the margin and put his theater at risk.

The play may not be good. Most theater owners will insist on reading the proposed play. If the play does not meet a subjective standard, they will likely dismiss it and the production proposal.

The theater manager may not have confidence in the people making the proposal. The real bottom line of any proposal is the people behind the project. If trust has not been established, then most theater managers will hesitate to give a project the green light.

In most sizable cities, however, there are spaces equipped to present plays and musicals that rent out to *anyone* with the money. Proposals are not needed at such venues; rather a set of dates and an open checkbook will secure the space. Such theaters, though, do lack the artistic prestige of an established theater and this can hinder marketing efforts.

The Empty Space: The Complexities of Renting a Storefront or Church

Every day, plays are produced in spaces that were originally designed and built for nontheatrical purposes. Storefronts are rented and converted into performance spaces, and churches house productions ranging from the classics to the avant garde. Indeed, in most mid-sized and large American cities, one can find creative conversions of space ranging from prisons, to fire houses, to schools. Brave people convert spaces into theaters every year, and some survive to become established venues. The new venture producer, however, should give thoughtful consideration to space conversion before attempting renovations for a number of reasons.

Renting Space and Equipment

Zoning. When choosing a space to rent consider that

cities have zoning laws that restrict business operations to definite districts. In other words, a producer cannot legally run a theater out of his basement unless his house is zoned for business.

Storefronts. A new venture producer will not want to sign a long-term storefront lease because of the uncertainty of theatrical producing. Most landlords are reluctant to lease a space for a few weeks because it might be more trouble to them than the money is worth. A new venture producer, however, must negotiate a lease that is long enough to produce the play and renovate the space, and short enough to get out if the production venture does not lead to future productions. It is a tricky balance.

Good space. Open spaces, free of columns, and with adequate height, are difficult to find. Consider also that finding a good open space—free from outside noise—is difficult.

Churches. Churches have their own schedules. Although they are popular places for theatrical performances, one must work around the church's schedule, which means certain nights are off limits, and equipment must be stowed away after some performances.

Equipment. All necessary equipment must be rented if the producer does not have access to it. Renting equipment is expensive and its installation is no walk in the park. However, many cities do have companies that rent and install theatrical equipment.

Renovating

Renovating. All the previously discussed concerns are magnified if space is to be converted. It is not a matter of examining equipment inventories, rather it is renting the instruments and equipping the space. It is not a matter of counting seats, rather it is finding chairs, transporting them to the space, and installing them in a proper configuration. It is not a matter of measuring stage and wing space, rather it is building a stage from scratch. And so on. Added to these concerns is that a newly converted space will carry no audience recognition.

Legally, if even one performance is held in a space, then that space must meet building, electrical, plumbing, and fire codes. An established theater should be up to code in these areas, but a raw space may need a lot of retooling to meet such codes. Renovations are very expensive and usually not feasible for a new venture producer.

Renovating a space is a huge job. Producing is also a huge job. The two combined could result in so much stress that the first production turns out to be the last.

Although the above can be discouraging, the producer should be aware that people do convert spaces into theaters with surprising frequency. If any producer is intent on converting a space, he or she would do well to read *Will It Make a Theatre?* by Eldon Elder. This book is a complete guide to finding, renovating, and financing the nontraditional performance space.

Summing Up: Producer's Points

- The performance space greatly affects the artistic and financial outcome of the production.

- Nontraditional spaces can house plays that have specific, but curious settings.

- Spaces, like people, have personalities that both attract some patrons and discourage others.

- Renting an established theater alleviates a myriad of problems associated with renovating a nontraditional space.

- Producers should never make assumptions that "what you see is what you get." Allowances for shop usage, insurance, and access hours must be negotiated prior to the final lease agreement.

- Producers should be aware of fire codes, as breaking a fire code could close the production and cause a considerable revenue loss.

- When approaching an established theater with a rental proposal, a new venture producer must have a well-thought-out, written plan which includes budgets and production concepts. Detailed proposals increase the chance of striking a favorable rental agreement.

Moving On

Although securing a space is a complex issue, it pales in comparison with the complexities of hiring artists, with their differing temperaments and expectations. Since no one produces in a void, the production team's complexion will make or break the play and its reception. The next chapter discusses hiring the director, playwright, and actors.

Chapter Six

Working With the Artistic Team

Producing theater can be seen as a process of carefully delegating production responsibilities to artistic and managerial personnel. Delegation is necessary because no producer can do everything alone. It would be nearly impossible for one to produce, write, direct, and act in a traditional stage production. Even the young Orson Welles surrounded himself with very talented actors and designers and managers. Theater is a collaborative art form, and it seems that producing also has a collaborative aspect to its character. The process of working with other artists, not lording over them, is one characteristic of the successful modern, new venture producer. Of course, there are anecdotes about dictator-producers such as Jed Harris and his colleagues from a bygone era, but those folks worked in another age and were not dependent on the good will and volunteer efforts on which many of today's producers draw.

Recognizing the collaborative aspect of producing can be especially difficult if the producer's own money is backing the effort. Delegating production control means giving a director and designers money and allowing them to make spending decisions within artistic and budget parameters. More-over, delegation can result in rewards via the efforts and talents of others' contributions through the collaborative process. For a playwright-producer, collaboration means allowing the director to make staging decisions and encour-aging the actors to develop a character beyond what is in the script. For an actor-producer, collaboration means becoming part of an ensemble and taking direction from another, and letting go of egocentric focus. Fundamental to a producer's success is the degree to which the producer sur-rounds herself with talented people who believe in the proj-ect. In other words, hire good people and let them do their job. How to attract and keep such people is the focus of this chapter.

Moreover, the artistic team can make many contribu-tions beyond artistry. Actors can help find space, designers may know of a good stage manager, the stage manager may have contacts with a local printer, and so on. The initial core audience will also be drawn from this inner circle of artists and technicians. Thus, in a new venture production, attract-ing and hiring people is not solely based on artistic merit, for it is also based upon what people can contribute to all aspects of producing— including fund-raising, finding space, marketing, and contacts with others who can bolster the production effort. Producing can be regarded as a series of complicated tradeoffs, and one aspect of the production alone should not guide all decision making.

Conflicts of Interest

In an ideal world producers produce, actors act, playwrights write, directors direct, and designers design. In a pragmatic world, though, actors produce, playwrights produce, and designers and directors also produce. Situations wherein artists produce can lead to conflicts of interest between artistry and the business of theater. The most precarious situation is one in which the director serves as producer. A director's charge is the artistic balance on stage, and a producer's charge is managerial and the two responsibilities can, and usually do, come into conflict with one another. For example, a director might desire a scenic design that is not within the producer's budget. If the same individual is wearing two hats, which one is tipped toward the other? The best approach is to have to two heads for two hats.

There are not as many conflicts of interest for the producer-playwright or the producer-actor. Playwrights can impart artistic control of the production to the director while still watching the budget; and actors can assimilate into an ensemble under a director's artistic oversight while keeping control of the production's managerial aspects. Although neither situation is ideal, producers should be quick to recognize that the pragmatic world is full of give-and-take, and striking the proper balance through a vision that encompasses all aspects of the production— managerial and artistic—is the producer's primary objective.

A Question of Vision: Whose Play Is It Anyway?

Most new venture productions grow out of someone's vision and passion. Should that person also produce the play, many questions can arise as to control of the vision during its development in production. For example, the majority of playwrights hold a vision of what their play should look like on stage; what type of actor best suits each role, and what production concept best fulfills this vision. Actor-producers, too, hold similar beliefs regarding casting, design, and production concepts. The rub can occur when a director is brought onboard to stage the play. What happens when the director's vision of the play develops in a fashion not parallel with the producer's? although theater is a collaborative art form, academia and the nonprofit theater community generally hold that the vision and concept are primarily the director's. In other words, the director wears Harry Truman's "The Buck Stops Here" hat in most production settings. However, that situation is one in which production funds are derived from a nonprofit corporate entity, such as a university or an organized, ongoing theater, not an individual. In a new venture production setting, and curiously with the high end of production, such as Broadway, funds are generally not derived from a nonprofit entity, rather funds are risked by an individual or a group of people who initially control all production. Thus, in new venture productions, "The Buck Stops With the Producer."

Should a producer discover that his vision is being radically compromised, it is entirely appropriate for that producer to step in and right the course of the production. This may sound rather heavy-handed, and indeed it can be. But producing theater is not simply raising money and turning over the production reins to a director. If it were, this book would be entirely focused on budgeting and fund-raising, but producing is much more—specifically guarding a vision that fostered the energy and will to venture into producing. And in a for-profit setting, he or she who controls the money also controls the production. This is not to suggest that directors cannot bring terrific insights to the production. Rather it is to suggest that before hiring artistic personnel they follow the same road as that traveled by the producer in matters of production vision and concept. As such, production concepts should be explored in-depth before offering artistic positions to any team member.

On Hiring and Working With a Director

Hiring a director is one of the most important decisions a producer will make. The director, of course, analyzes the play, formulates a production concept or approach, casts the play, and works with the actors and designers to create a unified production. Thus, a producer should devote considerable time to finding the right director for the chosen script. This is no easy task. However, most directors will not be put-off by a producer's inquiries, and indeed some will be flattered by a show of interest from a serious producer, regardless of the producer's stature. Finding a good director can be facilitated with a few guidelines.

Ask artistic directors or established directors for recommendations. Approaching an established theater's artistic director for a recommendation is perfectly proper. They might be able to provide a couple of names that can be approached. Most artistic directors know of directing interns or assistant directors who are looking for a chance to direct.

Visit directors' labs. If directors' labs or directors' workshops are offered nearby, a producer should visit the public performances. Such visits are a good way to network with directors and to see their work.

Producers should attend as much theater as possible to see directors' work first hand. There is no substitute for viewing live theater. While the director's exact contribution to the production is impossible to separate from the ensemble, it is possible to gauge if scenes built rhythm and tempo, if casting was appropriate within the frame of the play, if movement was purposeful, if the play's action was communicated to the audience, if relationships among the characters were defined, and if the play's given circumstances were unified through design and technical elements.

A producer should never hire a director based only on a resume. Paper can be misleading. Even a substantial record of directing achievements can never convey what actually transpired on stage. Hiring a director based on resume alone is like buying a painting based on a catalog description. A substantial record does indicate, however, that the director has had success working with producers, especially if the director has been rehired by a producer or artistic director. A resume is a good first indicator, but it is not definite criterion.

Resume references should be checked. If the director has a track record, it would be wise for the producer to call the last couple of artistic directors, producers, or playwrights the director worked with to ascertain how the director relates to actors, designers, playwrights, and producers.

A producer should work with a director who is on level with the production. If the producer is new to backing theater, it is wise for him to seek out a director of comparable stature. If there is a gross imbalance in experiences, then production control can be lost in acquiescence to experience. The problem is that most directors are solidly focused on production elements, not on the overall picture that encompasses producing, such as the bottom line. Moreover, relationships between producer and directors can develop in a parallel fashion if both careers are roughly comparable from the onset.

A producer should not explain away the play before a director has read it. A major mistake that a young producer can make is offering his views on plot, character, and concept *before* the director has had a chance to read it. The best strategy is to give the play to a director, give her plenty of time to read it, and then ask the director for her views and concepts. This strategy should reveal if the director has taken the time to read the script thoughtfully and if something in the script truly appeals to the director's sensibilities. Simply ascertaining if a director has read the play carefully can result in an objective standard which measures some degree of sincerity and interest.

Producers hire directors for artistic prowess as well as connections to other theater people. If the producer is not well connected within a given city, then it is wise to hire a director with connections. A good director can be invaluable in attracting good actors, designers, and technicians to the production.

If the producer finds a director and wants to hire her, then a number of issues should be spelled out in a letter of agreement. Issues such as the producer's involvement in casting (especially if the producer is an actor who expects to be in the production), the director's fee, employment dates, the production budget, the director's responsibility in marketing and public relations, and termination of assignment are a few of the issues that need to be stated in plainly written terms. Letters of agreement are covered in greater detail in Chapter 8.

On Hiring and Working With Actors

In almost every production setting, the director is responsible for conducting auditions, casting the play, and rehearsing the actors, but this does not imply that the producer has no role in the process of selecting actors. Most producers have some say on casting decisions, even if the input is as formative as calling the actor's references and sharing the results with the director or negotiating compensation. There are also a number of duties that must be coordinated by a combination of the stage manager and producer during the auditions and rehearsals.

Space must be secured for auditions and callbacks. Producers should make an attempt to secure a theater for auditions because such a move establishes contact with a theater manager, once again a connection that may prove to be beneficial when the play nears production. If a theater cannot be reserved, then a large, quiet room with an adjoining waiting area will serve the purpose. Since the director and stage manager conduct auditions, the producer should check with them regarding specific needs.

Audition notices should be written and circulated. An audition notice carries key information as to the play, the breakdown of roles, monologue/audition piece guidelines, the date, time, and place of auditions, callback information, and a contact number for additional information. Audition notices can be a simple flyer duplicated on a photocopier, or a listing in an arts/theater publication such as *Backstage* or a given city's arts tabloid. Many publications will run audition notices as publicity pieces; thus there should be no fee for such a promotion. Moreover, it is not unethical for a producer or director to personally contact actors and invite them to audition for a specific role. This process assumes that the play is being produced at a theater that does not have a contract with Actors' Equity (a nonequity house). If the production is governed by Equity, then EPA's (Equity Principal Auditions) must be held. For practically all new venture producers operating on a small budget, though, this is not a concern.

The producer or stage manager must secure scripts for the auditions if the director expects actors to read the play's roles.

Contact sheets must be prepared and duplicated. A contact sheet is the form actors fill out prior to auditioning. It includes the actor's name, address, social security number, and phone number. There is usually a section on the sheet for the director's observations of the actor's audition.

The producer or director should maintain a file of all actors who participated in auditions. Throughout the course of rehearsals, some actors may drop out of the production. Having a file of actors on hand will make the recasting process smoother if it is necessary to do so.

References should be checked. Pertinent questions asked of the reference may include the actor's work habits, congeniality, punctuality, and ability.

On a small scale, new venture production, casting a role is the result of not only ability, but also the actor's attitude toward teamwork in all production phases. If actors are willing to help in marketing, fund-raising, and even technical areas (if that is desired), then this participatory bearing should be made known to the director. Most new venture producers do not have the money to hire help in all phases of producing; thus an ensemble of people willing to pick up the slack can be invaluable and financially smart.

After the director has made her casting decision, the producer must prepare letters of agreement. A letter of agreement spells out the conditions surrounding the production and the obligation of both parties. Letters of agreement include the following items:

- Rehearsal start date
- The actor's name as it should appear in the program
- An approximate rehearsal schedule and rehearsal obligations
- The number of complimentary tickets the actor is entitled to receive and the number of tickets that can be purchased at a discount
- A statement addressing the actor's publicity obligations, including permissions for the dissemination of publicity photos
- Per diem allowance, if any
- Compensation and when it is to be paid
- Stop Date
- Termination of assigned role by either the actor or the producer/director
- Signature of both the actor and the producer

Letters of agreement are not meant to be instruments of coercion; rather they exist to anticipate problems or situations that may arise and provide an agreed-upon solution. If the producer pays the actors a token fee, then the producer should realize that the actors are, in fact, doing the producer the greater favor. Money talks, and if not much money is paid out, then "thank you" should be a well-worn phrase in the producer's vocabulary. Letters of agreement are detailed in Chapter 8.

On Working With Playwrights

If the producer is not the playwright, then obligations and agreements must be negotiated with either the playwright or the licensing agency. Issues include:

Payment of royalties. Arrangements must be made to secure the rights to produce any play not in public domain. Most published playwrights transfer simple rights (as opposed to grand rights, such as a Broadway or major regional theater production) to the licensing agent. Samuel French and Dramatist's Play Service are the two largest agencies and must be approached with a letter stating the number of performances and dates, ticket prices, venue, and number of seats. The licensing agency will usually respond with a standard price quote per the number of performances. Payment must be made prior to performances. If the playwright is not represented by a licensing agency, then rights must be negotiated directly with the playwright, generally about 6 percent of gross receipts. Most young playwrights desirous of a production will waive royalties or negotiate a nominal fee, however.

Sometimes a producer will ask a playwright to sign a contract giving a percentage of royalties to the producer if the production transfers to a professional venue. For example, in New York sometimes a simple off-off Broadway play will make its way to off Broadway (a full Equity, professional production) or even to Broadway. Transference contract riders are ethically questionable if the producer does not have the financial means to transfer the production himself. It is a questionable practice because transference contracts can make an off Broadway producer wary of taking on a play with strings attached, and often transfer royalties come out of the playwright's hide and pocket. Small venture producers outside of New York usually do not ask the playwright to sign transference or subsidiary rights contracts, and in small, new venture production settings this is a good, ethical practice to follow.

Script changes. Any changes in the script must be approved by the playwright. Although the Dramatist's Guild holds no power to negotiate collectively for playwrights, as does a union, the playwright is nevertheless protected under copyright law. While a strict interpretation of the law makes a playwright's words sacrosanct, most playwrights working closely with the production are open to suggestions and will develop the script in consultation with his or her artistic colleagues during the rehearsal process.

Revision limits. Negotiations with a playwright who is part of the production company should include a statement regarding a termination date for script revisions since some playwrights will rewrite up to five minutes before the opening night curtain. If the producer and artistic staff are willing to accept late revisions, then this statement is not necessary, but if the actors need some script solidity, a termination date is a good practice.

Staging/production management. A clear understanding that the director has artistic control of the staging and the producer has control over the production's management.

Rehearsals. A clear understanding regarding the playwright's role in rehearsals. It is not always advisable that the playwright be at every single rehearsal because the cast can feel constrained by a writer's presence.

Marketing. A statement regarding the playwright's role in marketing and public relations.

Actors' Equity Agreements and Codes

At times, even a new venture "one shot" producer must deal with Actors' Equity Association. Those times are defined by one key producer's decision: hiring an actor or stage manager who is a member of Actors' Equity Association. Just one Equity actor in the cast can change the parameters of the entire production; specifically the production budget, seating capacity, length of run, and other operating procedures such as rehearsal duration. Obviously, a new venture producer can side-step all Equity rules if he chooses not to hire Equity actors, but in some instances the best actor may indeed belong to Equity. Actors' Equity membership varies city by city, but, as one might expect, the greatest pockets of Equity actors are in New York, Los Angeles, Chicago, San Francisco, Seattle, and the Miami area. It is still very possible to cast a play in these cities without using Equity members, but if an Equity actor or stage manager is vital to the production, the wise producer will do some homework before making the final decision. What happens if the producer or director casts that Equity member? The answer is: it depends.

It is always possible to apply for an Equity waiver. In some instances Actors' Equity will waive rules, thereby relaxing the employment stipulations that govern Equity members. However, it is a common misconception among young producers that Equity waivers are easy to come by. In fact, Equity grants very few waivers. Waivers effectively diminish the power of the union through the granting of exceptions to the rule, and it follows that unions maintain their strength only through enforcing agreements between their members and the theater community. Usually Equity grants waivers only for charitable productions such as a church-sponsored production (not simply a production housed in a church), or productions sponsored by educational institutions. Most likely, the new venture producer will not be granted a waiver. Then what?

Contact the regional Equity office that geographically corresponds to the production. They are:

The National Office of Actors' Equity
165 West 46th Street
New York, NY 10036
212-869-8530

The Chicago Office of Actors' Equity
203 North Wabash Ave.
Chicago, IL 60601
312-641-0393

The Los Angeles Office of Actors' Equity
5757 Wilshire Boulevard
Los Angles, CA 90036
323-634-1777

The San Francisco Office of Actors' Equity
235 Pine Street
San Francisco, CA 94104
415-391-3838

The Orlando Office of Actors' Equity
10319 Orangewood Blvd.
Orlando, FL 32821
407-345-8600

The three most common Equity codes germane to the small venture producer are the Basic Showcase Code, the Los Angeles 99-Seat Theater Plan, and the Chicago Showcase Code.

The Basic Showcase Code

The actual code is nineteen pages in length, but what follows are some of the key points. A producer can obtain a copy of the code by writing to the New York AEA office. The key points are:

- Productions must be mounted in New York City.
- A maximum of 12 performances can be performed within a four-week window.
- Capacity can't exceed 99 seats.
- Ticket prices cannot exceed $12.
- Complimentary tickets must be made available to bona fide Equity producers and agents.
- Actors must be reimbursed for production-related expenses (such as basic travel to and from the theater).
- The total production budget must be under $15,000.
- The rehearsal period cannot exceed four weeks.
- Equity actors have the right to leave the production at any time.
- Non-Equity actors cannot be compensated more than any Equity actor.
- Producers must apply for Showcase Code status.

The Basic Showcase Code developed out of a mandate from Equity members who saw a need to produce their own plays and scenes to showcase their talents to others in the profession as well as the theater-going public. Prior to this code, Equity actors were actually constrained by their own union when it came to self-producing theater. Subsequently, the code provided an outlet for small-scale or off-off Broadway productions with Equity actors.

The Los Angeles 99-Seat Theater Plan

This plan is similar to the New York Code, but there are subtle (and not so subtle) differences.

- Productions must be mounted in Los Angles County.
- A maximum of 80 performances can be performed.
- Capacity can't exceed 99 seats.
- Four complimentary tickets must be made available to Equity Actors each four-week period.
- Actors must be reimbursed according to a schedule based on weekly gross box office income.
- Producers must provide AEA with a production budget.
- The rehearsal period cannot exceed eight weeks.
- Equity actors have the right to leave the production at any time.
- Producers must apply for 99-seat theater plan status.

The Chicago Showcase Code

The Chicago code is the most stringent set of regulations as compared with Los Angeles and New York.

- The Chicago code is only available for use by Equity actors, Equity stage managers, or Equity members serving as the producer of record.
- Productions must be mounted in Chicago.
- A maximum of 16 performances can be performed.
- Capacity can't exceed 100 seats.
- Ticket prices are "voluntary contributions" and may not exceed $10.

- Complimentary tickets must be made available to qualified talent employers for all performances.
- No Equity actor may contribute to the production expenses (except for an actor who serves as producer).
- Actors must be reimbursed for performance expenses.
- All net income from the production must be equally divided among Equity members.
- Producers must provide AEA with a production budget.
- Equity actors have the right to leave the production at any time.
- Producers must apply for the Chicago code status.

Note that the Chicago Showcase Code is granted only to members of Equity and stipulates that income is to be equally divided among Equity members. The new venture producer operating in Chicago should contact the Chicago Equity office before casting an Equity actor or stage manager. However, the Chicago theater community has a very large population of non-Equity actors and that talent pool should be given great consideration.

Producers Should Be Aware of Additional Equity Contracts

Production contract. The Production Contract covers the big shows—Broadway and national tours.

LORT contract. League of Resident Theaters (LORT) is the contract used by regional theaters. LORT theaters must demonstrate a sizable annual operating budget to receive a LORT designation.

Small professional theater contract. Small Professional

Theater contract is used in theaters outside of New York, Chicago, and Los Angeles.

Stock contracts (various). A stock theater hires a company of actors for a specific time and then disbands them after the season has been completed. Usually the plays are presented in a repertory format, that is, a slate of plays offered to the audience on varied nights. The various stock contracts apply to such circumstances.

Theater for young audiences. This contract covers plays performed by professionals for children and high school students.

Cabaret. The cabaret contract is for cabaret-style productions.

Guest artist. Theaters that occasionally employ professional actors use this contract.

Special appearance agreement. The Special Appearance Agreement covers Equity performers hired in theaters outside New York, Chicago, Los Angeles, and San Francisco

Off-Broadway contract. This covers off-Broadway productions. Seating capacity and theater location determine the off-Broadway classification.

Chicago area theater contract. Established theaters within the Chicago area use this contract.

Hollywood area contract. This contract is used by established theaters of less than 500 seats within the Los Angeles area.

Umbrella contract. This contract is used in Dallas, Austin and Houston, Texas; Portland, Oregon; Seattle, Washington; and Phoenix and Tucson, Arizona.

Members project code. This code is similar to a Show-case Code, but it applies to cities other than New York, Chicago, and Los Angeles. AEA members must sponsor the production.

Backers audition code. This code was written for the purpose of providing potential investors with a preview of an Equity actor performance.

Staged readings. Some staged readings require an Equity agreement. Check with the Equity office.

Bay area project policy. This is San Francisco's version of the Showcase Code.

Summing Up: Producer's Points

- Delegation of artistic control is paradoxically a loss of direct influence but an advancement in leadership.

- Artists are hired for many reasons, some of which are artistic, some of which are purely pragmatic.

- Producers should be aware of the complexities of Actors' Equity rules before hiring an Equity actor.

- Most producers hire people they have worked with in the past; artistic talent gets one noticed, but not necessarily cast.

Moving On

The next chapter discusses the formation of the technical team and how to increase cohesion among the entire production team.

Chapter Seven

Working With the Design and Technical Team

In a new venture production, simplicity is the watchword in design and technical elements. Simplicity, however, does not imply that design and technical elements are easy and without challenge. Often the designer's greatest challenge is the full expression of her artistic concepts within the parameters of a tight budget. The cliché "less is more" has found its way into the theater because there is truth to it—less design and technical elements means the designers must imaginatively convey a suggestion of location and character that allows the audience to realize even greater possibilities in their own minds. The imagination is where the magic of theater, if you will, can live. In a purely pragmatic sense, the small venture producer cannot afford to dazzle the patron with spectacle created with tens of thousands of dollars behind every sequin and laser light.

Moreover, simplicity in design can imply stage design prowess. Producers should familiarize themselves with designs by Jo Mielziner, Robert D. Mitchell, and Loren Sherman, all of whom have designed clean, beautiful, brilliant, and lucid sets. Examples of clean productions are bountiful, from Peter Brook's production of *A Midsummer Night's Dream* to George Devine's productions at the Royal Court, to many of Richard Foreman's works at the Ontologic Hysteric Theatre in New York. These production designs were remarkable, not because they were cheap, but rather because the designs complimented the play by creating clean space that kept the focus on the actor-audience relationship, not the set itself. Subsequently, the producer looking to hire designers and technical staff would do well to find people who have worked within a clean production aesthetic, not a setting in which scenic production values are the main attraction.

The following position descriptions are meant to be producer's hiring guidelines. They are in no way meant to be discussions of set designing, costume construction, or stage management. These topics are books unto themselves. Of course, if the producer hires and pays very little or nothing, then the tables turn and selectivity is the province of the designer or stage manager. If, in fact, the producer's budget is modest, then attracting designers just out of college is a wise move because these folks want to build credentials and may be willing to work for little money. The producer should recognize that people have differing motivations, and money is not the only currency in theater.

On Hiring the Set Designer

Although producing theater is a business, the producer does make *artistic* decisions when hiring the set designer and artistic staff. If the producer makes sound choices in hiring artists, then the producer's own artistic sensibilities are filtered through the production by the artists creating the stage designs. In early stages of negotiating with the set designer, it is vitally important that the producer and director share the script, budgetary information, and preliminary concepts with the designer. Other hiring considerations include:

- The producer or director should ask to see the designer's portfolio. A designer who is even remotely serious about his craft will have a portfolio that showcases his designs. The producer should look at the portfolio and check for organization, the number of designs and where the designs were realized, and make a few inquires about design choices.

- The producer or director should ask the designer if he has constructed set models. Trained designers are instructed in the craft of model making because the representation of the set enables the director to visualize the design in three dimensions.

- The designer should be asked if he has experience with scenic painting or set dressing.

- The producer should inquire if the designer has ever built any of his designs. In a small scale production, a staff to build the design might be a luxury. A terrific design is worthless if it is not fully realized on stage.

- If the designer has read the script, the producer or director should ask the designer to share a few early ideas. Such a discussion will also provide clues as to whether the designer's reading was careful.

- If the designer has a few preliminary ideas, then the producer or director should ask for an approximate cost of building the design. It might be necessary to rebudget after this discussion.

- The producer should ask the designer about availability and salary expectations.

- The producer or director should check the designer's references.

On Hiring the Costume Designer

Costume design is critical if the set design is minimal because the costumes must carry the weight of not only character definition, but also the given circumstances or world of the play. Costumes also make statements about character relationships, mood, economics, and the style of the play itself. Moreover, a costume design need not imply that costumes must be built from scratch, with sketches, patterns, and stitches. A good costume design can be realized by thrift and careful shopping at secondhand stores, or the creative use of an actor's own closet. The producer and director should work in consultation when hiring the costume designer and fully consider the following points:

- The producer or director should ask to see the designer's portfolio. A costume designer should have a portfolio of sketches and collages, fabrics, and photographs from realized production designs. The producer should look at the portfolio and check for organization, the number of designs and where the designs were realized, and make a few inquiries about design choices.

- The producer or director should ask the costume designer if she has created renderings of costumes and characters. Trained costume designers are instructed in the art of figure drawing because the representation of the character and costumes allows the director to visualize the design with color and texture.

- The designer should be asked if she has experience with makeup design.

- The producer should inquire if the designer has ever built any of her costume designs. Again, in a small scale production, a costume shop staff would be a luxury.

- If the designer has read the script, ask her to share a few early ideas. Such a discussion will also provide clues as to whether the designer's reading was careful.

- If the designer has a few preliminary ideas, then the producer or director should ask for an approximate cost of building or buying the costumes. It might be necessary to rebudget after this discussion.

- Ask the designer for a rough timetable of design and completion. At this stage of discussion, the timetable would only be a rough approximation.

- The producer should ask the costume designer about availability and salary expectations.

- Check the designer's references.

On Hiring the Stage Manager

A good stage manager is gold to a producer. But, like gold, good stage managers are hard to find. In fact, the stage manager position may be the most difficult of all production positions to fill, and a good deal of prospecting on the streets may be needed to find the right person. The stage manager is critical to the production effort because the stage manager is the glue that holds the production together even when it may appear to be falling apart. Stage managers oversee the daily running of rehearsals and performances. They also end up being psychologists, nurses, arbitrators, disciplinarians, acting coaches, house managers, and assistant directors. The job is enormous, and good stage managers are well paid, even in small scale production settings. When hiring a stage manager, the following points should be considered:

- Ask to see the stage manager's books from past productions. Good stage managers keep records of past productions that should include cue sheets, daily logs, rehearsal notes, and a transcription of the director's blocking. The producer should check for book organization, since organization is a primary duty of stage management.

- The producer or director should inquire if the stage manager has ever run a production meeting. Good stage managers demonstrate leadership through conducting meetings and managing rehearsals.

- Inquiries should be made regarding familiarity with the operation of technical equipment, such as the sound board and light board.

- The producer should ask the stage manager about availability and salary expectations.

- References should be checked.

On Hiring the Technical Director

Some productions include a technical director on staff. As the position title implies, the technical director coordinates all technical elements, oversees the implementation of the designer's plans, and usually runs the technical rehearsals and supervises set load-in and strike. Moreover, the technical director often designs and builds props; designs, hangs, and focuses lights; and designs the sound. In a small production setting, often the set designer shoulders a lot of the technical tasks, and, sometimes, the positions of set designer and technical director are combined into one uber-position that both designs the production and builds the sets. In such a circumstance, the combined position is the production's keystone, since so much responsibility is delegated to one individual. If the producer can afford to hire a technical director, then the producer should consider the following points:

- The producer should look for experience in working from a designer's plans to build the set. Moreover, in an established theater, the technical director often runs the scene shop and oversees the carpenters and stage crews.

- The producer should look for a wide array of experience in technical areas. A good technical director has a working knowledge of all phases of lighting, properties, sound, and sets.

- If the producer has decided on a theater space to house the production, then it is an advantage if the technical director has extensive knowledge of the space. A technical director who knows the quirks, the ins and outs of a theater, can save the production staff a lot of time and money by avoiding particular problems or by providing solutions based on past experiences in the space.

- The producer should inquire as to the technical director's connection to designers and technicians. A well-connected technical director will know where to borrow items and who to turn to for advice.

- The producer should check all references before hiring the technical director.

- The producer should ask the technical director about availability and salary expectations.

Additional Design and Technical Positions

The number of design and technical positions depends on the producer's budget, the availability and salary requirements of qualified people, and the demands of the script. Some new venture productions get by with just a couple of key people, but others need far more than a stage manager and a set designer. The new venture producer is not alone in balancing budgets with personnel; even established theaters give careful consideration to the script's technical demands before selecting people to support the production. The following positions, or a combination of positions, may be needed to realize the full potential of the script.

Lighting designer. Working alongside the director, the lighting designer creates mood, focus, rhythm, and illusion. Lighting design is far more than hanging and turning on lights, for its artistic nature is found within its ability to create dramatic focus through definition of the playing space. Lighting design is its own unique specialty, and many universities offer specialized training in the discipline. While a lighting design is a necessity, often set designers or technical directors have enough training in lighting to design and run a light plot. Indeed, often these positions are combined in a small scale production setting.

Sound designer. Some plays require a sound designer. Sound designers, under the director's guidance, create sound effects, record pre-show and show music, and create sound selectivity and balance. The artistry of sound design is very similar to that of lighting design in that it selectively focuses audible elements during a very specific dramatic moment. In musical theater productions, the sound designer must also balance the sound of the orchestra, the actors' speaking voices, the actors' singing, and the chorus' sound. In a small scale production, however, a good cassette recorder and a few well-placed speakers can perform adequately and convey the mood and focus necessary to the production. The real task in sound design is knowing what recording is right in capturing a specific mood or moment.

Makeup designer. Often the costume designer has some degree of training in make up design. Makeup, of course, can modify or highlight an actor's visage, thus defining the actor's portrayal of a specific character. Many actors have training in stage makeup, and, in a small scale production, usually makeup design is the purview of the costume designer, while makeup application is the actor's responsibility.

Properties designer. Properties design is one of the least appreciated but most important positions in theater. The job usually falls upon anyone who can be cajoled into the position. Properties design can range from an attentive attic scavenge hunt to fully designed and built pieces that are vitally important to the actor. Any producer should think twice before staging a props-heavy show.

Board operators. Sound boards and light boards need people to run them. Most boards in a small venture production setting can be operated with relative ease; however, finding a reliable person to operate the equipment can be difficult. Producers usually rely on volunteers or the stage manager to run the boards. Producers need not look for experience in equipment operation; rather reliability is the critical factor in the production setting.

Production Team Work: How to Get Everyone on the Same Page

Casting terrific actors, securing a wonderful director, and recruiting great design people is not enough. Either the producer or director must foster an environment wherein all production members are united in their effort to put on the best play possible. Most successful producers have discovered that following a few guidelines can greatly increase the odds that the team is pulling in a common direction, rather than in several directions. Take note of the Oscars, or Tonies, or Emmys. Most often when an actor or director or designer or producer wins, she spends her time at the microphone thanking the artistic and production team; "I couldn't have done it without Mr. X, Ms. Y, and my mother." Most athletes understand team concepts, and "Smith is not a team player," is a derogatory remark. So, a new venture producer can increase the chances of teamwork and keep the "Smiths" happy if she follows a few maxims.

Include everyone in brainstorming sessions and production meetings. Refer to the production as "our production," and goals as "our goals." Inclusion in planning and brainstorming fosters teamwork. Producers should invite everyone to brainstorming sessions; from the actors to the volunteer light board operator. If a truly original idea springs up, then the person who generated it has ownership of that idea and a much greater stake in seeing it through to completion. All-inclusive meetings, moreover, generate more ideas than does a limited, selective group. Even turtles and clams want to feel as if they are a part of the team, and maybe they will poke their heads out and offer a good piece of advice if provided with the opportunity to do so.

Expect and allow some disagreements. Do not impose "solutions" on the production staff. Disagreements can lead to discussion, and this should lead to solutions that are not imposed, but rather team-generated. Indeed, this concept fits the lateral management style popularized in the 1980's. Prior to the 1980s, management was regarded as a top-down delegation of responsibilities, with the top levels altogether removed from lower management. But in the 1980s, businesses realized that many workers had solutions to management problems and this realization changed their business practices. The new venture producer, too, can learn from American management and create a lateral style of team problem solving.

Avoid groupthink with reality checks. "Groupthink," a term coined by management guru Irving Janis, characterizes a phenomenon in which tightly knit groups can lose touch with reality through beliefs that, simply put, hold that they are invulnerable and better than they actually are. Outside opinions and a devil's advocate within the group are two measures that balance against a groupthink mentality.

Be willing to give up control. Leadership within the production team can, paradoxically, mean giving up some control.

Be honest. If a producer attempts to foster a productive teamwork setting, then that producer must be honest above all other attributes. This premise holds true for any level of producing. What goes around comes around. If a producer gets a reputation as being dishonest, that producer may make money, but he will have a difficult time recruiting new team members because the theater world is rather small and reputation is often linked to one's name.

Create an advisory board. An advisory board is not a board of directors (the governing body of nonprofit groups). An advisory board has no legal authority to run the production; rather they work as a team to provide advice to the producer on matters ranging from space to publicity to fundraising. Placing key production people on the advisory board along with a few people not directly involved with the production can confer a luster on the production effort. For example, one new venture New York producer created such a group and placed the names of the board members on the production's letterhead, which, in turn, lead to a favorable response among some publicity outlets because of familiarity with a few of the board members.

Evaluate the production as a team.

Offer each member a share in the profits. After the production expenses have been met, profits can then be divided among those people who own a share in the production. Even if the profits are modest, a share in them provides the team with a stake in the production that can lead to a greater personal investment of time and energy in the project. Many American companies, from Xerox to Ford, offer profit sharing among the rank and file employees because it nurtures employee dedication through product ownership. During Shakespeare's day companies were organized along a similar plan, with the key figures receiving a cut of the day's gate take. By extending such an offer, today's new venture producer makes a gesture to her team that heightens each team member's stature. Moreover, extending the offer won't cost the producer a dime from her personal assets.

Order a few t-shirts with the production title and the names of the artistic and technical teams members. This simple, meaningful gesture promotes group cohesion through a common identity. Theaters of all production levels do this. Besides, everyone likes a free t-shirt.

Avoid scheduling too many meetings. Producers should never schedule more meetings than necessary. Too many meetings can create group tension because of lost time.

Let the group reach the producer's conclusions. Many good producers *lead* their production team toward the goals they desire without imposing their will on the group. For example, allowing a designer to reach his own deadlines, assuming that they are reasonable, is a wise move because the designer will not view the deadlines as imposed but rather as self-generated. It also gives that designer a greater stake in meeting the deadlines because he reached them through his own logic. The producer's task, then, is to gently nudge the production team toward reasonable deadlines and schedules.

Insure that ideas are translated into action. For example, brainstorming sessions are relatively easy and can be rather enjoyable. But the best group decisions will mean nothing unless someone shepherds the ideas through to their completion. That someone is the producer. Circulating the ideas to the team, and then allowing the team to divide up responsibilities, best accomplishes this. Delegation of specific tasks to team members is the norm in a professional, paying environment, but in a new venture setting that affords little pay, allowing the team to "volunteer" for duties is less autocratic and it encourages a greater stake in the responsibility. Monitoring the progress of ideas into action is the producer's task. Well done is better than well said.

Summing Up: Producer's Points

• Design simplicity presents artistic challenges to the design team. A clean production concept means that designers must make less do more.

• While producing theater is a business, the producer does make *artistic* decisions when hiring the designers and technical staff.

• The producer or director should check references. Such screening can help the producer avoid costly mistakes.

• Increasing cohesion among the group will lend the production synergy, which it could not have had if people worked independently.

Moving On

Many new venture producers dread legal, insurance, and tax reporting issues. But such topics will only haunt the producer if he ignores them or pretends that if they don't exist, they will go away. In matters of the law, ignorance is not bliss; rather it can lead to bothersome predicaments that can jeopardize the production. What a new venture producer doesn't know can hurt him. The next chapter puts the producer in the know by taking away the apprehension from legal, tax, and insurance issues.

Chapter Eight

Legal Issues, Tax Law, and Insurance

Producers make agreements with people. They make agreements with actors, designers, graphic artists, theater owners, press agents, and the public. Agreements can be as simple as a handshake, and can be as complicated as those found within a twenty-page contract. Although not all agreements are legally binding contracts, legality is determined by a few essential contractual elements, rather than the outward appearance of a document. Indeed, the courts upheld the sale of an NFL football team even though the contract was scribbled on the back of a cocktail napkin. Oral contracts can also be enforceable if the agreement contains the definitive contractual points.

A valid contract is determined by:
- a valid offer;
- an acceptance;
- a consideration (or value);
- and legality.

For example, if a theater producer approaches a costume designer and asks her to design and build Hamlet's costume for a $300 fee, and if the designer agrees over a handshake and delivers the costume on time, there is a legally enforceable contract found within the handshake. If the producer fails to pay the designer $300, the designer could take the producer to court and sue for contract fulfillment. Nothing was signed, but a contract was formed between the parties because their agreement fulfilled the four key points. Obligations were created on both sides of the agreement, the nature of the contract was legal, and both parties were of legal age and presumably of sound mind when the deal was struck.

There are two types of contracts of which a new venture theater producer should be aware. The first is a *unilateral contract*. A unilateral contract is a promise for a specific action. For example, if a theater producer knows that his buddy John has a pick-up truck and that John has some time on his hands, the producer might say to John, "If you go across town and pick up the lighting instruments and deliver them to me in the next hour, then I'll pay you $20." John does not say a word, but hops in his truck, picks up the instruments, and delivers them to the producer within the hour. The producer then owes John $20 because he held up his end of a unilateral contract. John performed the action required by the contract and can expect his $20. A promise and an action, then, characterize a unilateral contract. The producer did not receive a promise from John, but rather an action.

Theater producers, however, will usually enter into *bilateral contracts* with people. A bilateral contract is characterized by a promise for a promise. In the earlier example, the producer *promised* to pay the costume designer $300 if the costume designer *promised* to design and build Hamlet's costume. Contracts with actors, designers, stage managers, and theater landlords are almost always bilateral contracts—a promise for a promise, an offer and acceptance, along with some consideration or value.

Besides an offer, acceptance, and consideration, contracts must be enforceable. For example, suppose a producer wishes to rent a theater space. The producer goes to the space, examines it, works out a contract (offer, acceptance, and consideration) with the assistant theater manager but later discovers that the assistant manager had no power to negotiate the lease. Then, the contract is not enforceable. For the contract to be legal, both parties must have the legal capacity to enter into the agreement. If the assistant theater manager was not acting as the theater owner's agent, then the assistant manager has no legal authority to enter into the contract and cannot bind the theater owner to the agreement. Moreover, both parties to the contract must be of legal age because a minor can take steps to disaffirm a contract. And it is a good idea not to sign contracts with insane people.

The subject matter of the contract must also be legal. For example, if a producer signs a contract with a theater owner to conduct a cash-bar fund-raiser, but the theater does not have the legal license to dispense alcohol, then the contract is not legal. Or, if a producer contracts with a composer for the right to use a piece of music, but the composer does not hold the copyright to the piece of music, then the contract is not legal. Or, in an extreme case, the producer purchases a sound board at an unbelievable price, but it turns out the sound board is "hot" property, then contract enforceability is highly unlikely.

To avoid problems, producers should put all contracts and agreements in writing. Without a written record, parties may very easily forget the terms of the agreement and disputes can arise. While oral contracts can be legal, it is a far better practice for the producer to secure all agreements in writing to avoid misunderstandings. Issues such as theater rental, advertising, and hiring key personnel should always be recorded in writing. In some states it is mandatory that rental agreements, contracts in which the consideration is greater than $500, and contracts that cannot be performed within a year, be placed in writing to be enforceable.

An attorney is not necessary for every contract. However, an attorney will examine a contract and look for contingencies that the parties did not, or could not, foresee. In other words, things can go very wrong, and an attorney will try to anticipate what could happen and protect her client from such circumstances. For example, if a producer puts down a deposit on a theater space and on opening night the space is found to be a fire hazard, then what happens? Is the rental deposit and rental money refunded to the producer? Is the fire hazard the producer's fault or the fault of the theater owner? How is the circumstance to be handled? Or, perhaps the producer signed a letter of agreement (a contract) with a director in a nonunionized situation and fires the director two weeks before opening night. How much payment can the director collect? Does the director receive full credit in the program for his artistic efforts? When a great deal of money is at stake, as in a Broadway production, an arbitrator or a court of law often decides these cases. People with the best of intentions on both sides of the contract cannot see all the possibilities; however an experienced lawyer will be able to write a contract that will protect the producer in the event of such calamities.

Letters of agreement are contracts. If the essential features of the letter include a valid offer, an acceptance, a consideration (or value), and legality, then a contract exists. Letters of agreement are important for the small producer because they clarify the terms and conditions of employment and can help avoid disputes that may arise. If the small scale producer relies on volunteers, she may still write letters of agreement, however, without consideration (payment), but they will not be binding contracts. With all key personnel, the producer should write letters of agreement that spell out the general understanding between the parties. Moreover, theaters, rental companies, and advertising agencies may expect the producer to sign contracts they draw up. It is important to recognize that everything in a contract or letter of agreement is negotiable. Everything. There is no such thing as a standard contract that is, in itself, set in stone.

Letter of Agreement with the Director

The letter of agreement should include:

- A payment schedule, if applicable
- Conditions for termination of service by either party as well as payment and program credit in the event of termination
- Clear statement of the director's responsibilities
- An understanding that artistic control is the province of the director
- The number of complimentary tickets under the director's control
- A statement regarding publicity and marketing requirements
- A statement regarding the control of the hiring of artistic personnel (actors and designers)
- A statement regarding the choice of script
- A statement regarding budget allocation and spending limits
- A statement regarding rehearsal hours and schedules
- A statement regarding complimentary tickets for agents and producers
- A statement regarding travel reimbursement
- An understanding of when script revisions terminate
- A beginning and an end date
- Signatures of both parties

Letter of Agreement with the Actors*

The letter of agreement should include the following:

- A payment schedule, if applicable
- Conditions for termination of service by either party, as well as payment and program credit in the event of termination
- A clear statement of the actor's responsibilities, including punctuality
- An understanding that artistic control is the province of the director
- The number of complimentary tickets under the actor's control .
- A statement regarding publicity and marketing requirements including the circulation of cast photographs
- A statement regarding rehearsal hours and schedules
- A statement regarding complimentary tickets for agents and producers
- A statement regarding travel reimbursement
- An understanding of when script revisions terminate
- A beginning and an end date
- Signatures of both parties

*Note that if the actor is a member of Actors' Equity, then specific rules apply.

Letter of Agreement with the Designers

The letter of agreement should include:

- A payment schedule, if applicable
- Conditions for termination of service by either party as well as payment and program credit in the event of termination
- A clear statement of the designer's responsibilities,

including building or overseeing the construction of the design
- An understanding that overall artistic control is the province of the director
- The number of complimentary tickets under the designer's control
- A statement regarding publicity and marketing requirements and the use of the design in publicity photography
- A statement regarding the control of the hiring of personnel (shop staff, running crews)
- A statement regarding the choice of script
- A statement regarding budget allocation and spending limits
- A statement regarding deadlines for initial design and completion of design
- A statement regarding complimentary tickets for agents and producers
- A statement regarding travel and out-of-pocket reimbursements
- An understanding of when script revisions terminate
- A beginning and an end date
- Signatures of both parties

Letter of Agreement with the Stage Manager*

The letter of agreement should include:

- A payment schedule, if applicable
- Conditions for termination of service by either party as well as payment and program credit in the event of termination
- A clear statement of the stage manager's responsibilities, including rehearsals and show duties
- A statement regarding the stage manager's role during production meetings

- An understanding that overall artistic control is the province of the director
- The number of complimentary tickets under the stage manager's control
- A statement regarding the control of the hiring of personnel (shop staff, running crews)
- A statement regarding the choice of script
- A statement regarding budget allocation and spending limits
- A statement regarding complimentary tickets for agents and producers
- A statement regarding travel and out-of-pocket reimbursements
- An understanding of when script revisions terminate
- A beginning and an end date
- Signatures of both parties

*Note that stage managers can belong to Actors' Equity, and certain rules apply to contractual agreements.

If a letter of agreement is breached, the small producer will probably not run to a court of law to recover damages. For example, if an actor drops out at the last minute, thereby breaking the letter of agreement, the small venture producer should grin and bear it and likely scramble with the director to find a replacement but will not threaten a lawsuit against the actor. It follows that if the payment is small, the recovery will be small, and the bad will created by a lawsuit is not worth the trouble.

The Need for an Attorney

There are, however, certain circumstances that necessitate contact with an attorney. These conditions include:

- If the producer is sued. Suppose the stage manager

falls from a ladder and breaks his leg. The stage manager can sue the producer to recover medical expenses and lost wages.

- If the theater owner breaks the rental agreement and thousands of dollars are lost. An attorney's services may be necessary to recover the deposit and rent and other damages.
- If the producer wants to incorporate her theater as a nonprofit organization.
- If the producer forms a production company with partners.
- If the producer signs a long-term lease or purchases a building.
- If the producer hires full-time employees.
- If the producer coproduces a large scale production with another producer.

What to Look For

Note that most of the above situations occur if the producer expands her operation into an ongoing theater venture. If the producer finds herself in a situation that necessitates an attorney's services, then the producer should:

- Look for both quality and price. A cut-rate lawyer might end up costing the producer more in the long run.
- Ask the attorney for a price quote in writing. Some attorney services, such as incorporation, often have a standard fee schedule.
- Ask for an itemized billing record. Attorneys almost always keep billing records based on an hourly rate, and an itemized invoice provides specifics as to the segment and subject of each hour.
- Don't stick with one lawyer if the services provided are inadequate.

Important Tax information

Producing theater is a business. Although the product is artistic, the IRS makes no special distinction for the new venture, for-profit theater producer apart from the mechanic or the insurance agent. It is best for the small, new venture producer to regard his business as a sole proprietorship, since the producer should only take steps to acquire nonprofit status if he can sustain the venture for a good period of time—a year or two at least. Subsequently, when the producer hires people to work for him, the producer has, in effect, hired employees. It makes no difference how small the business is, for if the hirees are classified as employees, then certain steps must be taken to satisfy the IRS. The popular press is full of stories detailing the embarrassment of the congressman or famous actor who forgot to withhold and report the nanny's wages! So beware.

Theaters, of course, have employees. If the hiree is considered to be an employee, then the theater must take a few important steps to satisfy the people at the IRS. The producer must fill out an SS-4 form and obtain an Employer Identification Number (EIN). This means that the established theater or producer must withhold payroll tax from every check issued to the employee. The theater must also make timely payments to the IRS from all withheld taxes. There is a mountain of paper work that accompanies the initializing of this procedure. Additionally, taxes must be withheld for social security, and state agencies often demand an additional piece of the action.

Is there a legal way out the paperwork blizzard for the small venture producer? The answer is yes. The small venture theater producer can consider the hirees to be "independent contractors," not employees. The semantic difference, however, is erroneous in the eyes of the IRS. If the set designer is considered to be an independent contractor, then:

- The producer is not required to withhold federal, state, and social security taxes.
- The producer need not offer any benefits to the independent contractor.

This does not mean, however, that a small producer is off the hook. The producer must file IRS Form 1099 detailing the amount of salary for every individual who receives more than $600. The good news is if no one on the production team is paid more than $600, then the producer need not worry about the IRS 1099. But if the producer pays her set designer $750, then the bad news is the independent contractor status becomes a very gray area. The IRS discourages such classifications because they feel that independent contractors tend to underreport their earnings, and subsequently short Uncle Sam a few dollars. Neither the duration of employment, nor the amount of pay (over $600) matters to the IRS in determining independent contractor status. To prove independent contractor status, the producer must argue three essential points.

1. The amount of direct supervision by the employer. If the producer hires a designer to design and build the sets, the producer generally does not give the designer specific instructions as to how to accomplish the task. Usually, designers have a good deal of creative freedom to design a set—and while the director may work closely with the designer, the director is technically not the employer. A similar argument can be made for actors and directors. A producer does not instruct actors how to act, nor should they instruct the director how to do his job. Within the parameters of a theatrical production, most employees pass the first hurdle of determination for independent contractor.

2. The number of employers. The IRS will look at the set designer and ask if the designer has other jobs. Most designers, actors, and directors do indeed have other jobs to pay their rent. Actors bartend, directors teach, designers might be office temporaries. If the producer can show that the artists have a number of different jobs, both in theater and outside theater, then the argument of independent contractor status is bolstered.

3. The place of employment. This is a bit tricky. Independent contractors usually do their work off-premise. In the case of a theater producer, the official place of employment would probably be the theater itself. The argument for the designer is strongest, since they actually do the design at home or in an office. What about actors, directors, and stage managers? The producer would have to make an argument that much of what is accomplished in the theater is the result of much work outside the theater. For example, actors spend time memorizing lines and doing character analysis work outside rehearsal, and the director spends a great deal of time away from the theater planning rehearsals and analyzing the script. The stage manager might be the most difficult case to make, but to do so would require a focus on planning activities performed away from the theater.

Don't panic. The truth is that the IRS probably won't look at a small producer because the money is not significant enough to merit their time. It is a precedent that the greater the amount of money involved in a business, then the greater the chance of an audit. If a producer is losing sleep over a hiree's classification, the producer can request IRS Publication 15, Circular Ɛ, Employer's Tax Guide, which sets down the classification guidelines. Moreover, the producer could fill out form SS-8, Determination of Employee Work Status, and send it in to the IRS for ruling on determination questions.

Insurance

What happens if a chair breaks and a patron sprains his wrist? What happens if an actor is injured during rehearsal? What happens if the box office computer is ripped off? If a calamity should occur, the producer can be held liable. Moreover, if the production is organized as a sole proprietorship, the producer can be held personally liable because the producer's personal assets, apart from the production, are not protected as they are in a corporation. While insurance itself cannot provide the all answers, it can protect the producer from personal financial liability and loss.

Almost every theater has some form of insurance. Producers and boards of directors take out insurance for three major reasons:

Theft. Theaters have a lot of expensive equipment, from the light board, to the audio speakers, to period swords, to the office computers. Because theaters tend to have a lot of traffic moving through them at all hours, they are often a tempting target for quick hands. Most theaters experience loss due to theft at some point in their existence. Unfortunately, often theater employees, or people with the right set of keys victimize theaters most often. Usually theaters have to provide an itemized list of equipment to the insurer and continually update their inventories. Theft insurance covers such losses by either insuring equipment at replacement cost or its depreciated value.

Property insurance. The life of many distinguished theaters ended in a fiery blaze, from Shakespeare's Globe to P. T. Barnum's American Museum Theatre to the Milan Opera House that burned a few years ago. Fire has been the nemesis of theater buildings for centuries. Of course, today innovations in architecture, public safety, and on-site fire marshals greatly reduce the number of tragedies, but property damage can still occur. Pipes can freeze and break, roofs can leak, and a car can ram through the lobby of a theater (as recently experienced by an Indianapolis theater). Property insurance provides a mechanism that protects the owner of the space from certain damages and calamities and protects the renter from loss of personal property. The best thing to do is to take a complete inventory of all property, determine values, and decide if each piece is worth insuring. Producers should then check to see that the theater policy covers items on the inventory list for the correct amount.

Liability. There are over 20 million lawsuits filed every year in America. The best playwright in the world couldn't come up with some of the real life reasons people take other people to court— from the football player who sued his university because they wouldn't let him be the starting quarterback to the lady who spilled coffee on herself and sued McDonald's because the beverage did not come with a warning label. She won her case, the football player didn't. A theater producer must be covered in the event of an unforeseen circumstance that gives rise to a lawsuit. Most accidents happen on stage and backstage. Theaters can be ripe grounds for accidents waiting to happen; with their shops filled with power tools and table saws, electrical cables running to and fro, and tall ladders that beckon a climber. If an accident happens, larger established theaters have insurance and worker's compensation plans in place, but because the small producer cannot afford worker's compensation insurance, the producer must carry enough liability insurance to cover accidents. The medical bills for one broken finger could put a small producer in a lot of *personal* debt.

Liability insurance protects the producer's assets when the producer is sued for something the theater did (or failed to do) that contributed to the injury or property damage of someone else. Liability coverage extends not only to paying damages but also to the attorney's fees and other costs involved in defending against the lawsuit— whether valid or not. The standard theater policy provides liability coverage, as does a separate policy known as a commercial general liability (CGL) insurance policy. Commercial liability insurance, whether purchased in a separate policy or as part of a standard business owners policy, will cover bodily injury, property damage, personal injury, or advertising injury. The medical expenses of a person or persons (other than employees) injured at the business, or as a direct result of the operations of the business, are also covered. Usually excluded from both types of liability insurance policies are suits by customers against a business for nonperformance of a contract and by employees charging wrongful termination or racial or gender discrimination or harassment.

Chances are that if the new venture producer rents an established theater, she will be covered under the established theater's insurance. Every producer should understand, however, that who and what the existing insurance covers is not the theater owner's decision, but rather it is a consequence of how the policy was written. In other words, a producer should read the policy and contact the insurer for clarification if there is any doubt as to limitations and exceptions in the policy.

If the new venture producer rents a nontraditional space, then the producer should contact insurers directly, explain the situation, and solicit price quotes. Existing theaters can guide the new venture producer toward insurers. Contact local theaters, including community theaters, to ascertain the name of their insurance company. Some companies specialize in performing arts insurance and may be willing to write a short-term policy to cover only one production. Moreover, loss of business property is usually reimbursed up to $250 for business property damaged or lost away from the premises. It's also important to know that a standard homeowner's policy includes no business liability coverage.

Important Considerations in Purchasing Insurance

All insurance premiums are based on risks. The insurance company evaluates the situation to determine the risk or potential for losses and bases its rates on the results. Therefore, deliberate steps the producer takes to lower the risks not only can help safeguard the production, but also may make the producer eligible for lower insurance rates. In evaluating risk, an insurance agent will consider if the producer has taken steps to:

- Maintain adequate lighting throughout the theater.
- Keep electrical wiring, stairways, scene shop, flooring, seats, and lobby in good repair.
- Install a sprinkler system, smoke and fire alarms, and adequate security devices. If a fire marshal is on staff, let the insurer know this.
- A policy of keeping only a small amount of cash in the cash register and removing the cash drawer after each performance.
- A policy of keeping good records of inventory, equipment purchases, and the like. Producers should consider keeping duplicate records of everything of value.
- A policy of making sure the staff knows how to properly use all necessary safety equipment, such as goggles, gloves, and respirators.
- A policy of making sure the staff knows how to properly use all equipment, and only trained staff be allowed to operate equipment.
- The producer may also wish to raise the deductible where appropriate to lower insurance premiums. How high to raise the deductible should be governed by how much the producer can afford to pay out of pocket. A producer should be careful not to raise it so high that she cannot cover a loss should it occur.
- Finally, producers should make sure the agent is familiar with theater and the risks inherent in it. The agent

should be able to advise the producer on risk management techniques to lower costs.

Summing Up: Producer's Points

- A valid contract is determined by: (1) a valid offer, (2) an acceptance, (3) a consideration or value, (4) and legality.

- Even though verbal agreements can be binding contracts, producers should put all agreements in writing to avoid factual discrepancies.

- Producers should write letters of agreement with all personnel, regardless of their position within the production.

- A new venture producer should consider the production effort to be a sole proprietorship if feasible. Income is reported as regular, personal income and is subject to taxation.

- If a producer pays his employees more than $600, then the producer must decide if he will pursue the independent contractor status for employees or if he will withhold tax.

- Insurance issues must be considered before a calamity occurs. Producers should not take chances and rely on providence to see them through the production.

Moving On

Box office and house management should not be arranged at the last minute, since what happens on the audience's side of the production is as important as that which happens on stage. Indeed, if patrons have a difficult time getting a ticket, all the effort on stage will be diminished by that difficulty. Besides, it is not much fun to act before empty seats or disgruntled people. Box office and house management are two areas where audience members interact with the production, and often a patron's mood will be tempered by her experiences with these managers.

Chapter Nine

Box Office and House Management

Suppose the producer has done everything right in choosing the play, hiring a director, and finding a space. The actors rehearse with dedication, the set designer has come up with a brilliant way to capture the play's given circumstances with a $200 budget, and the costume designer figured out a way to costume Hamlet from rag stock. However, if the box office is not properly set up, or if the theater house is not managed well, the entire production venture could collapse around the show's management. Patrons who have a difficult time getting tickets, or patrons who are not treated well by the front-of-house staff will be disgruntled patrons, a person no producer can afford. Literally.

Usually, patrons will have contact with the box office before all other production personnel. That initial contact is important for a number of reasons. First, it provides a mechanism whereby patrons can buy tickets or make reservations. Today, consumers expect ease when purchasing products or services. Credit cards, mail order, toll-free numbers, and the internet condition people to shop for tickets or products from their homes. People can, and do, buy Yankees World Series tickets from their homes in the Midwest, or purchase Broadway tickets before stepping onto an airplane in Arizona. Producers, then, must make it easy for a potential patron to secure a ticket via armchair shopping since most people will not go out of their way to make the *initial* contact with the ticket provider.

Second, box office staff can be a good marketing outlet. Not every customer is a realized customer, for some people will simply make a noncommittal phone call requesting information about the production. Perhaps they heard about the show, or saw a listing in the newspaper that sparked their curiosity enough to pick up the phone, but not enough to purchase a ticket outright. In other words, the sale must be closed. The box office staff or system that provides the patron with enough information about the production so that the consumer can make the decision to purchase is a necessity for every producer. If a caller gets someone on the phone that is indifferent toward the production, the sale of the ticket will likely falter at the point where it should be encouraged and facilitated. The very best box office worker is someone who artistically connects with the production, which enables him or her to convey enough enthusiasm for the production to close the sale to the wavering patron.

Third, a well-functioning box office makes it easier for the producer to realize money up front. At one time theater was a cash-and-carry business. For example, at Shakespeare's Globe, people expected to pay one penny, two pennies, or three pennies in exchange for *immediate* admission to the inn yard or one of the gallery boxes. Today, people expect to be able to make *advance* purchases for theater tickets. Advance purchases take away some of the hassles and uncertainties of ticket purchasing by allowing the patron to purchase a ticket for a future date. Advance sales also mean the producer realizes money sooner than she would if the point of purchase was only production night. Since the producer has already spent most of her money prior to opening night, an advance sales box office means that those advance sales can recoup the initial outlay of cash faster than a simple box office. On a much larger scale, Broadway producers count on advance sales of months worth of tickets to recoup initial production expenses and to generate bank interest on the advanced capital.

Box offices, like productions, can range from very simple to very complicated. Simple operations might include a dedicated answering machine and one person to manage the box office during performances. Advance box offices operate with networked computers, remote point-of-purchase locations, a paid staff, on-line credit card authorization, and, perhaps, a network link to national ticket distributors such as Ticker Master. The type of box office depends on the needs of the production, the long range needs of the producer, and the various ticket packages the producer offers to patrons. Of course, the simple operations require little money and set-up time, but the larger box office operations can become a substantial part of the producer's annual budget, or capital budget if the theater must renovate space and set up computers. A small venture producer should consider the simple, economic, yet efficient operation before purchasing a computer and box office software.

On Setting Up the Box Office

The basic box office set up. In a small venture production situation, the producer may not have funds set aside for box office operation. Moreover, the people involved with the production volunteer their time while continuing to hold down full time jobs, and it is unlikely they will be available to run a box office during performance days. In such a situation, most producers now opt for an "answering machine box office." An answering machine box office provides the basics; it dispenses information and takes reservations or even sells tickets. Most off-off Broadway theaters, in fact, set up this type of ticketing system. To set up an answering machine box office the producer must do the following:

- Purchase a good quality digital answering machine with remote functions. Digital machines do not use a micro-cassette to record the announcement and messages, so they tend to be more reliable and easier to use. It is important, however, to secure a machine with ade-quate message and recording times.
- The producer or box office manager records a message that details basic show information, performance times, ticket prices, and ticket availability information.
- A phone number is temporarily dedicated to the box office answering machine.
- Patrons are asked to leave their name, performance date, the number of tickets required, and a contact phone number, and, in some cases, a credit card number.
- The machine is checked frequently during the day. A machine with remote access can be checked by call-ing the machine and entering the code. Either the pro-ducer or box office manager keeps a master log of the names and reservations for each evening.
- If reservations exceed the number of seats, the mes-sage is immediately changed and patrons are notified that the theater cannot guarantee the caller a ticket on a specific night.
- Before the performance the answering machine box office log is brought to the theater, as it is the evening's reservation record.

Basic Ticketing Options

A ticket is a form of currency in that its exchange for admis-sion is guaranteed. Theaters began issuing tickets in 1703, and ever since tickets have been a convenient form of exchange for both patron and producer. Moreover, the ticket also provides tangible evidence that can be used in auditing and balancing the box office books. Ticket stock is, in itself, valuable, and major theaters guard their ticket stock almost as closely as the U.S. Treasury guards the paper used for printing money. In a small venture production setting where the run is limited and the reservations relatively few in number, the producer has options unavailable to the major producer.

The program-ticket. Many off-off Broadway theaters double the duty of the theater program to include ticketing. It works like this: the producer provides a specific number of programs to the box office manager. When patrons pay for admission, they receive a program that guarantees admission into the theater. The box office manager tallies the number of tickets sold (programs distributed to patrons) with their prices and balances the tally against the cash received. Although there is the possibility of a program being used twice, that is on different evenings, many theater choose this method of ticketing because it is economical. However, advance ticket sales are nearly impossible with this form of ticketing and multiple price categories are difficult to reconcile. Moreover, if fraud is a fear, then programs can always be stamped with a specific performance date.

Carnival tickets. Carnival tickets sell in large rolls, with about a thousand tickets per roll. Each ticket is numbered sequentially, and different-colored tickets can be purchased for specific performances or different price categories. Carnival tickets are available in either single ticket formats or double ticket formats with identical tickets printed side by side. Most theater producers purchase the double printed tickets because the second half is held by the theater and serves as an audit stub. As with program tickets, carnival tickets are not conducive to advance sales because the tickets lack specific dates and show time information.

Carnival tickets, however, are very cheap and can be purchased at most party supply stores.

Homemade tickets. A staff member can design tickets by computer, and they can be duplicated on a photocopier using card stock paper. The card stock is then cut into individual tickets. This method of ticketing is good if the performance run is limited and seating is not reserved. To counter fraudulent tickets, a special rubber stamp can be designed and employed on each ticket, giving the ticket a unique mark that cannot easily be duplicated. A laser printer and a simple graphic design program can produce a quality ticket.

Although all these ticketing alternatives are economical and easy to employ, they do have some drawbacks. None of these tickets allows for reserved seats, and this is a drawback because some patrons prefer to choose specific seats in advance. Moreover, all of the above tickets are normally used immediately prior to performance, which allows for short-term advance reservations, but not long-term advance sales. And, if measures are not taken, the tickets can be easily duplicated.

The Cash Box

The basic box office is not complete without cash for making change. The producer should purchase or borrow a good cash box, which should have separate compartments for bills of differing denomination and coins. The cash box should never be left unattended and should be removed from the theater or locked up after each performance. At the start, the cash box should be stocked with drawer money — money to make change. Once enough cash is generated through ticket sales the drawer money should be returned to the producer or whomever supplied the initial drawer money.

Reservations

Reservations are relatively easy to record. The problem occurs when tickets are set aside, and the patrons do not show up to claim them. Theaters have learned to deal with this problem through two means: first, securing reservations with credit cards, and second, not accepting reservations but rather selling the patron the ticket over the phone. Secured reservations require that the patron provide a credit card number to the box office staff, and if the patron does not cancel the reservation within a prearranged time, the patron is, nevertheless, charged for the tickets. Moreover, most established theaters have moved away from reservations altogether by requiring that the patron purchase the ticket with a credit card. Once purchased, the theater offers a liberal exchange policy for patron convenience. If a theater does not have credit card capabilities, reservations become risky when seats are held back and other customers turned away. The producer who accepts unsecured reservations plays a guessing game as to how many reservations will be picked up, how many will be left at the box office, and how many patrons to put on the waiting list. No one has come up with an exact formula for balancing out the unpredictable nature of human behavior. Experience is the best indicator in balancing this tricky situation. At some point, perhaps thirty minutes prior to curtain, all unsecured reservations should be released for general sale.

Box Office Reports

After the production begins, the box office manager or producer should balance the box office books. This is a simple procedure that balances the value of the number of tickets sold against the net cash realized.

Cash Value of Tickets Sold = Cash Box Money – Drawer Money

The cash value of the ticket may or may not be its face value. Producers allow for a certain number of complimentary tickets as well as a few discounted tickets for groups and senior citizens or students, perhaps.

Thus, it is important for the box office manager or producer to keep track of the number of tickets sold at their realized or net value. Of course, if all tickets are equally priced, there are no advance sales, and no complimentary tickets are provided, the task of balancing the box office is made easy. Reservations do not complicate the matter since the ticket is accounted for when it is sold.

If, however, tickets are sold in advance of the performance, then accounting procedures require a couple of additional steps. Rather than the nightly box office report, a daily report should be compiled. A daily box office report tallies ticket sales for each performance every day the box office makes a sale. At the conclusion of the production run, the "dailies" are merged into a production or show report that breaks down ticket sales by both day and performance. Moreover, if tickets are discounted, it is customary to also produce a price category report, which, you guessed it, breaks down sales according to the number of tickets sold in each price category. Price category reports are especially important if the market is price sensitive and the producer is planning to mount another show in the future.

Trustworthy Staff

Besides being a good sales person, the box office manager must be honest. Small venture productions lack the checks and balances of an established operation, and the temptation to pocket till money is always present. Most producers either work the box office themselves or ask a trusted colleague to staff the operation in their absence.

House Seats, Comps, and Press Tickets

All producers set aside a number of free tickets for special purposes. House seats were originally seats put aside for the landlord or theater owner. In a small production situation, however, house seats are tickets held out of the sale stock by the producer to cover unforeseen contingencies, such as a newspaper critic showing up unannounced, or an actor's mother who arrived after a three-hour drive. House seats should be made available for sale about half an hour prior to curtain time to realize any potential profit. Complimentary tickets or comps are free tickets designated by the producer to staff members or people who provided favors to the production. Usually artistic, design, and technical staff members each receive two comp tickets, which can be used at their discretion. Press tickets are seats set aside for reviewers or other members of the media who can provide production publicity. It is standard producing practice to make press tickets available, even though some journalists insist on paying for their seats. Another wise move is to provide a few free tickets to social service groups who help disadvantaged people. These moves not only "dress the house" (make attendance look good), but it also begins to establish a track record of social service involvement that will be important if the producer ever approaches government agencies for funding.

Advance Box Office Options

Credit card handling. Today people are accustomed to paying for products and services with credit cards. Most established theaters accept credit cards because patrons expect this service, and it enables phone ticket sales. How does a producer get approval for credit card handling? The producer should start at his local bank. The producer needs to fill out an application for credit card merchant status. If a producer is turned down at one bank, he should try again and again at other banks. After merchant status is obtained, the producer can process credit card orders received by phone or in person. It should be noted, however, that banks charge a processing fee that is usually about 5 percent of every transaction. Another option is to utilize an established theater's credit card system. If a new venture producer opts for this, then she should be very diligent in overseeing that her accounts are properly credited; such a set up is entirely controlled by the established theater's credit card system and initial deposits will be made to the established theater.

Preprinted tickets. Preprinted tickets add a professional face to the production effort. Preprinted tickets should be designed with a minimum of three perforated parts: the house stub, which is used to generate house counts; the box office stub, which is used in auditing and balancing the box office accounts; and the patron stub, which serves as evidence of the ticket purchase. Some pre-printed tickets have a fourth stub for exchanges.

Reserved seating. An advantage of professionally printed tickets is the unique information on each ticket. Reserved seating is one such advantage. If reserved seating is desired, the producer must furnish the ticket printer with a seating chart detailing every seat number and their location, as well as show date, time, and price. It follows that producers must have firm control on the arrangement and locations of theater seats before broaching this option, since the open nature of flexible seating does not lend itself to reserved seating tickets. Reserved seating is, of course, an expected feature of larger, established theaters, but generally patrons do not expect reserved seating in smaller production venues.

Computerized box office. A computerized box office is another feature of established theaters. While it would not be prudent for a small venture producer to invest in a computer system, it is possible that an established theater's computer system be made available to the small producer who rents the space. In this situation, the small producer must thoroughly familiarize herself with the system before agreeing to utilize it. A good idea is to program a mock show into the computer, evaluate the computer system with the mock production by using all the computer's features, and then delete the mock show before programming the actual production into the computer. If the new venture producer does not know the quirks of the box office software, then simple procedures such as ticket exchanges can become the producer's woe.

Ticketing services. Many large cities have ticketing services. These services handle all phases of ticketing by simultaneously selling a number of productions out of a central location, by providing information to patrons, by generating reports, and by making timely deposits to the producers. Many ticketing services are willing to work with small scale producers, and some such as Ticket Central in New York even specialize in modest productions. While such services provide more customer conveniences than a modest box office operation, they do charge a percentage of the revenue and do take away some control of box office operations. Ticketing services should be licensed and insured and have a list of references available upon request.

Preprinted ticket envelopes. Preprinted ticket envelopes provide patrons with a convenient way of carrying tickets, and furnish the box office staff with a quick way a recording information on the envelope. The envelope should contain blank spaces for the patron's name, phone number, credit card information, show date and time, and number of tickets in each price category, and amount of the total sale.

Hours and staffing. Advanced box office operations have a professional, often unionized, staff. Hours of operation are usually afternoons and two hours before curtain. Such arrangements are usually out of the reach of a small producer because of the staffing overhead.

House Management

The primary duties of the house manager are to ensure the safety and comfort of patrons. In a small production setting, this means checking for obstructions that could cause problems for patrons, such a cables strung across the floor or seats precariously balanced on risers. The house manager should not allow anything that could possibly cause a patron to trip, lose balance, or fall. Technical staffs are not always cognizant of patron safety and can unintentionally sacrifice safety for production technical elements. The house manager should view the house through the patron's eyes, noting anything that could be an obstacle between the patron, his seat, and the exits. The house manager should also develop an emergency plan in case a patron becomes ill or injured. First aids kits and emergency phone numbers should always be close at hand.

House managers also help to create theater atmosphere. Theaters, like people, can be laid back and relaxed, or formal and stiff. Most small venture producers want to create a relaxed atmosphere, one that is inviting and informal, one where blue jeans are the norm. The manner in which the house manager greets the patron subliminally conveys the tone of the evening. The house manager should always be polite, helpful, and appropriately dressed. House managers also oversee the concessions sold before, during, and after the production.

House Management Procedures

One Week Prior to Opening

1. Communicate with stage manager regarding:
- communication procedures during show between the house manager and stage manager
- running times of show acts
- late seating opportunities (breaks in the action).

2. Secure ushers if needed.

3. Check first aid kit for adequate supplies. Check fire extinguishers, noting locations. If not adequately charged, the producer should be notified.

4. Check with producer regarding theater programs.

5. Check seating arrangements (in a studio theater this does change frequently).

6. Check condition of the seats. If any are broken report this to the producer.

7. Check if actors have special entrances, or if the director has special house usage.

8. Ask the director if any special displays are required in lobby.

9. Check flashlights. A minimum of two should be in working order. If not, report this to the producer.

10. Check with stage manager regarding intermission times (number and duration).

One Hour Prior to Curtain

1. Check flashlights again. Two should be in working order.

2. Review all entrances and exits. None should be blocked.

3. Check with box office staff regarding wheelchair patrons and check seating arrangements for disabled patrons if appropriate.

4. Turn on all lobby lights.

5. Check condition of restrooms. If not well supplied, replace items.

6. Prepare to distribute programs.

7. If concessions are sold, make arrangements for a concessions cash box.

8. Walk through the house. All litter from floor and between the seats should be removed.

Forty-Five Minutes Prior to Curtain

1. Assign ushers and ticket taker(s) to posts. Familiarize the ushers with the house arrangements.

2. Instruct ushers regarding seating procedure.

Curtain Time and During Show

1. Communicate with the stage manager regarding a house hold. If a hold is necessary, set the hold time.

2. Once the house is in, notify stage manager to begin the show.

3. Once the show has begun, always remain near the theater in case problems arise.

4. Hold all latecomers until an appropriate seating time or allow patrons to take an empty seat near the back of the theater.

5. Be aware of disruptive patrons. Do not permit the use of cameras during the show. Do not permit children to disrupt the show. If a patron is being disruptive for any reason, the house manger should politely ask the patron to alter his or her disruptive behavior. If it continues, the house manger should ask the patron to stop the behavior or leave the theater. If it still persists, notify the patron that the police will be called. If the disruptive behavior continues, call the police or theater security. The house manager should never attempt to physically remove a patron from the theater. Always let the police handle out-of-control situations. This also reduces liability risk.

At Intermission

1. Check with concession sellers to see they are set up.

2. Open theater doors.

3. Two minutes prior to the start of the second act, give audience the "Two Minute Warning" by flashing lights or sounding a bell.

4. Notify stage manager that the house is in and the show can begin again.

After the Show

1. After the patrons have left, walk through the theater and collect programs.

2. Secure flashlights.

3. Secure cash box(es).

4. Turn off all lights and lock appropriate doors.

Summing Up: Producer's Points

- Patrons will have contact with the box office before all other production personnel, and such contact can help to market the play, as well as set the tone for the patron's experience.

- Producers can set up an answering machine box office for very little cost, which will provide the patron with necessary information and record reservations.

- Producers should exercise caution when working with another theater's credit card system, as money must be transferred from one theater to another.

- The primary duties of the house manager are to ensure the safety and comfort of patrons as well as creating a theater atmosphere fitting to the production.

Moving On

Selling the play is perhaps the greatest challenge facing the new venture producer. Since the new venture producer often does not have name recognition and a lot of money backing the production, marketing must take on a sharp focus as well as creative tactics in reaching the goal of putting people in the seats. The next chapter discusses several low-cost marking strategies that have proven to be effective for new venture producers.

Chapter Ten

Getting the Word Out: Marketing the Production

People are inundated with sophisticated marketing every hour of the day. One could regard television as a medium that creates a product that entices people to sit still long enough to watch the commercials. Radio, of course, peppers the airwaves with commercials, advertising everything from political campaigns to fast food restaurants. Highways are dotted with billboards, and advertising comes into people's homes via the internet and telephone. American companies have become very proficient at marketing their products by finding new ways of reaching people through sophisticated targeting backed up with huge advertising budgets. Indeed, marketing is considered to be the most important activity of most businesses, since maintaining viability without the customer is like acting in front of an empty house—it's not profitable and it's not much fun.

Marketing is everything that touches potential ticket buyers. Everything. From sales ads, to phone calls, to the appearance of the theater building, to the out-of-service water fountain, to the title of the play, to the publicly spoken opinions of the set designer. Many variables are thrown into the cauldron, creating stress and complicating marketing because diverse variables need to work together to create a coherent plan that motivates ticket sales. It is no coincidence that marketing managers of performing arts venues tend to burn out quickly—the cauldron doth boil over.

With multimillion dollar advertising campaigns surrounding people every which way, does the small venture theater producer have a chance at attracting an audience? Can small producers even compete against larger theaters with their extensive mailing lists, years of patron loyalty, and sophisticated print advertising? The answer is yes, but a few essential marketing premises condition patronage. Every producer must understand the cold, hard facts of marketing. They are:

The general populace does not give a darn about the production. A producer risking his own money on the production and artistic and technical staffs working hard to create art do not imply that people outside of the production will care about such work or the product created. It is not a question of apathy, but rather the way the general populace ranks their personal priorities. G. B. Shaw once said that the theater is always at a low ebb. In Shaw's time this was true, but today it is even more pertinent with competition rising from digitized entertainment that is easily accessible to most people. Moreover, today's audiences did not grow up with theater and are not in the habit of attending live dramatic productions. People are creatures of habit, and encouraging younger people to break away from ingrained behavior and consumer patterns is not accomplished with a singular theatrical production. Rather, it is a consequence of years of habitual theatergoing. Because most people do not establish theatergoing habits, they will not be predisposed to attending a play.

The producer asks a lot. The producer should consider just what marketing efforts ask of potential audience members. Consider this, a producer who puts forth a marketing effort says to the public that she has a product that is a better choice than that offered by popular media on a given night. In other words, a producer implies that the play is a better consumer choice than what television offers, better than what is on the video store shelves, better than the popular novel that might sit on the bedside table, or even better than a quiet evening at home. Marketing theater is an audacious act because the producer asks people to put aside easily accessible, and often free, forms of art and entertainment, leave their homes, drive down to the theater, and pay a ticket price that is three or four times that of a video rental. And that is asking a lot. To ask a lot of the public means that much should be offered in the way of artistic excellence, or intellectual stimulation, or imaginative dramatic worlds that beg audience participation. Being different is not enough.

Friends and family first. It is not an accident that Henry Ford sold his first few cars to his friends and neighbors, and it is not a coincidence that Colonel Sanders sold his first bucket of chicken in his own neighborhood. A small venture producer should learn from the Colonel's marketing moves and begin all efforts with her friends and neighbors. Family, friends, and neighbors have reason to be interested in the production because they know someone involved in it. Such personal eye-to-eye contact gives the producer enough of an emotional marketing hook to pull family, friends, and neighbors into the theater. Consider this: most parents go to a high school play because their son or daughter is involved in the production. Dance recital audiences are filled with proud parents, grandparents, and perhaps the performer's siblings. The same "grandparent" logic applies to the small venture producer in that she must spur interest among her own inner circle before expanding marketing efforts outward to the general public.

Marketing is a team effort. Everyone involved in the production must be a marketing manager. If marketing efforts are to be effective, the actors, designers, technicians, volunteers, even the ushers must take an active role in encouraging people to attend the show. Involvement of the producer's artistic, technical, and managerial colleagues effectively expands the circle of friends and family outward, creating a much greater central marketing target than if the producer were marketing alone. Subsequently, a sharp producer knows that marketing the marketers is his first priority, that is, selling the production staff on the merits of the production so that they will in turn sell the production to others. Nothing kills marketing more effectively than an actor, or designer, or manager who talks the production down to his own friends and family. Anyone who has been involved with theater long enough has experienced this very problem; the actor who is embarrassed about his work, the designer who holds a grudge against the producer, or the playwright who doubts his own script. These are all examples of marketing nightmares because if bad will is created, then the "inner circle" effectively diminishes with every offhand remark. Conversely, if the producer successfully rallies show participants, then the marketing reach will be greatly enhanced.

Be different: let the monkey go. A couple of generations ago, a young executive of the Ford Motor Corporation desperately wanted to get the attention of the executive board. The young executive entered the board meeting with a surprise, a live monkey, which he released in the boardroom during the meeting. Of course, as one might expect, the monkey romped about the room, crawled over board members, and generally stirred up a lot of chaos in a generally stuffy environment. The young executive was heard, and more importantly he was remembered. His name was Lee Iacocca, and he went on to become the chief marketing officer of the Ford Mustang, and later C.E.O. of the Chrysler Corporation. Iacocca's strategy was different: He did not sell his plans in a fashion expected by the board members. Consequently, his message stuck. A theater producer must also think of new ways to be heard and remembered by coming up with his own creative "monkey strategies" unique to each production. In a world in which people are inundated with marketing messages every day, the smart producer should make his marketing message new, fresh, and unconventional so that it has a chance to be remembered. A true marketing genius always puts an old message, "buy this," in a new package.

Know the product. To market a product or service, one must know the nature of the product or service. In the theater world, this is more difficult than it appears, since sometimes the nature of a play only reveals itself before an actual paying audience. This makes marketing a new play especially difficult: The very nature of the product changes before an audience. For example, it is very possible that the producer and artistic staff believe that they have a comedy on their hands, but before an audience, it may play like a serious drama, or vice versa. Moreover, in performance, other elements can emerge that no one expected; perhaps the players unearth a new theme or an actor in a supporting role steals the show. The producer must be sensitive to the mercurial nature of live theater as to not place all her marketing hopes on one or two strategies based upon a single preproduction belief. An astute producer also knows that the product might not be the play itself, but rather the actors may be the high selling point, or the special effects, or the music, or even the ambiance of the theater space itself. Knowing the essence of the total product and all its marketing angles creates a more diverse marketing environment, one richer in potential customers.

Success depends on the audience. A theater troupe traveled half way around the world to perform at the New York International Fringe Festival during the summer of 1998. The actors got into their costumes and applied their makeup, managers opened the house, and not one single person showed up. That performance was a failure, not because of anything artistic, but because of nonexisting marketing. Of course, this group was upset—they spent a lot of money and energy on the production. The troupe, though, failed to understand that marketing was entirely their responsibility, a point made by the Fringe Festival to every presenting group. The story illustrates an important point: If marketing fails completely, the production will die because success in theater is found not only on the stage, but also in the audience. Ultimately the audience is the only arbiter of popular success or failure; artists' opinions of their work, even if well founded, do not matter nearly as much as opinions from paying customers. Good producers have an uncanny ability to focus on the audience's side of the proscenium by understanding audience motivation in ticket buying and seeing the finished product through an audience member's eyes.

Be careful. The danger in marketing a small venture production is overspending on nonproductive strategies. Good marketing does not necessarily cost a lot of money, since it depends upon defining a unique marketing universe reached not only by financial means, but by creative means as well. Overspending on proven strategies appropriate to established theaters is tempting but probably counterproductive because established companies have marketing strategies built on their unique history. In other words, if it worked once for someone else, that does not mean it will work for another production in another time frame.

Selling the Play: The Marketing Plan

A marketing plan is a written statement that coordinates all marketing activities. Marketing plans for small venture theater productions should be written from the ground up; that is, marketing tactics should be connected first to the actual ticket buyers and then to means of reaching them. All marketing tactics have four elements: the target, the strategy, the timing of the strategy, and the cost.

The Target

The totality of all potential customers is the *marketing universe*. The marketing universe, however, is much too large and diversified to approach with one strategy. The marketing universe contains people of all different ages, economic backgrounds, geographic bases, and theater-going preferences. People within the marketing universe respond differently to marketing strategies because of their own individual preferences and habits. As such, marketing managers break up the marketing universe into *target markets*, which are smaller groups composed of individuals who share some common characteristics, whether it be age, demographics, affiliations with groups, or economics. Targeting allows the marketing manager to formulate plans for reaching a group of homogeneous people with a specific, custom-built strategy that appeals to the target group. A good real world example of targeting is the Coca-Cola Company's advertising campaign, which targets the general population in dozens of different ways and fashions television commercials specifically for each target. A Coca-Cola commercial on MTV does not look like a Coca-Cola commercial during "Sixty Minutes". The commercials are radically different because the targets are radically different. Theater producers, too, must target their potential audience into manageable units of potential ticket buyers. Typical targets include students, people who have previously purchased tickets, friends of the artists, and those interested in the subject matter of the play.

The Strategy

Once the marketing universe has been targeted, the next step is to formulate a strategy for encouraging members of the target group to purchase tickets. The strategy is often the most obvious component of the marketing plan; advertising, direct mail campaigns, or personal contact with potential patrons are all strategies. For example, if high school teachers comprise the target group, an appropriate strategy for reaching them might be a personalized letter from the producer. If the target group is high school students, the strategy might be a live presentation of a scene from the play. And, if senior citizens comprise the target group, perhaps the marketing strategy is to schedule a matinee at a convenient time. Marketing strategies, of course, vary widely according to the group or groups targeted. Marketing strategies are fine tuned by manipulating the four marketing variables, commonly known as the "four P's" in marketing circles. The four P's are: product, price, place, and promotional strategies.

1. Product. The product, predominately the play itself, is an important marketing variable. Many young producers do not realize this until it is too late to adjust marketing strategies. The play choice is, in fact, the single most important marketing variable because it largely defines the product being offered. New plays are inherently risky because there is no identifiable, recognizable name to connect to a target group. Under most circumstances, it is much easier to sell *A Streetcar Named Desire* than an unknown play because name recognition fosters familiarity—the product is of known quality and therefore easier to sell. Some plays and musicals have developed a kind of "brand loyalty" that the new play is hard pressed to meet. While the play is the primary product, other aspects of the production can also be sold as the product, such as a particular actor or director, or even food that is available at the production. If one considers that spectacle sells many Broadway musicals, the spectacle itself becomes the central product.

2. Price The ticket price is another variable in the marketing mix. Set the ticket price too high and many people view the production as too pricey, and if set too low, others may regard the production suspiciously and believe it to be substandard. Ticket price is an especially important marketing variable if the target group is price sensitive, such as students or senior citizens. When setting ticket prices, a producer should consider:

- The target group's price sensitivity.
- Similar caliber theaters' ticket prices. A producer should stay close to the structure of *comparable* theaters. A producer should never compare new venture theater with an established theater, however.
- Theater prices should have no relationship to movie ticket prices. Theater producers often make the mistake of assuming that they can charge higher prices than a movie theater by virtue of theater's live nature. This thinking, though, is wrong-minded because the average ticket buyer looks for an evening of entertainment or diversion, not necessarily the form that entertainment takes. Moreover, the cost of the production and its breakeven point makes absolutely no difference to the average ticket buyer.
- In most professional theaters ticket revenue comprises about half of their earned income. Very few theaters, save for Broadway venues, balance expense with only ticket revenue. If theaters were to balance expenses with only ticket revenue, theaters might price them-

selves out of business. Nonprofit theaters make up the balance with grants and contributions. The new venture, for profit producer, then, must budget conservatively.

- Free is not always a selling point. Although ticket price is a factor in consumer behavior, it is not the only factor. Free forms of entertainment and art can have a stigma attached, an implied capitalist notion that something of value costs money, and if the price is free, then the value of the art can be brought into question.
- Discounts work only if properly targeted. Price breaks must be well thought out and aimed at a specific group for a specific reason.

3. Place. As discussed in Chapter 5, the location of the theater building, the character of the theater building, and the timing of the production are all important marketing variables. As earlier outlined, the space for the performance carries with it many subjective characteristics that make an impression on a potential audience member. The timing of the production is also a critical marketing decision. For example, in New York it is almost suicidal for a small producer to open his production during the fall when Broadway and off-Broadway roll out their new shows because the larger budgeted productions will receive nearly every column inch of the newspaper's theater page.

Opening a small production in the summer can be risky because, traditionally, theaters are dark in the summer, and audiences may well be drawn to other outdoor activities. Opening a production in the dead of winter has its problems because, in the Midwest and Northeast, the winter weather can discourage people from attending. Also, the time of day matters, as senior citizen theatergoers prefer an earlier hour and cabaret hounds prefer late night theater spots. This mix of seasonality and performance hours should only be decided after considering the makeup of the potential ticket buyers. If timing is to be a true marketing variable, it must not be decided with solely the convenience of the performers and staff, but rather the preferences of the audience in mind.

4. Promotional strategies. Promotional activities make up the foundation of a marketing strategy. Most people consider promotion to be advertising, that is, billboards, flyers, brochures, radio ads, and the like. Promotional activities are the guts of the marketing strategy because promotional designs reach specific people and motivate them to open their wallets. Larger theaters employ an army of experts to design and place promotions where the ticket buyers will likely respond. In fact, promotion accounts for about 20 percent of many Broadway production budgets and forms one of the greatest expense items. Small producers without large budgets can promote, but they must target much smaller groups and encourage person-to-person contact. The latter portion of this chapter details promotional strategies that have proven to be effective for the modest production effort.

Timing of Promotions

Once an audience has been targeted and promotional strategies discussed, then scheduling or timing of promotions should be considered. Some promotional strategies hinge on a lengthy marketing campaign designed to slowly build interest in the production, and other strategies are timed to hit very close to opening night. A very common mistake that small venture producers make is to wait too long to implement their marketing plans. Often production marketing is an afterthought, only considered when panic over ticket sales rises to a level that demands the producer's attention. Good marketing strategy, though, takes time to formulate and is, itself, timed to reach the public in the most effective manner. For example, a postcard should be designed well in advance of the production and, if mailed out at the bulk rate, the inherent delay in delivery should be calculated into the overall timing of the marketing plan. The flip side of the timing coin is also tricky; if promotions hit too early, they can be forgotten and lose much of their punch. Or if promotions hit the public before the box office is set up, the producer is throwing money away and may well lose customers by unintentionally discouraging them.

Money

Money is the last variable in the marketing equation. A producer can approach the marketing budget two ways; either start with an overall marketing budget and allocate money to strategies, or he decides on specific strategies and builds the budget up to an aggregate amount. Either approach will work, but one must monitor the marketing budget to have planning and control value. After budgetary considerations, the cost of the promotion must balance against its anticipated effectiveness. All marketing managers search for promotional strategies that give them the best return on the marketing dollar. Marketing is made especially difficult because no one knows exactly which strategies will yield a cost-effective return. Old, proven, cost-effective strategies burn themselves out after a cycle because their newness and "stopping power" become dulled with repetition. Even the best advertising people play a guessing game when estimating cost effectiveness. The small venture producer can minimize promotional risks by avoiding costly, and sometimes conventional, strategies followed by other producers. If, for example, people are flooded with postcards advertising a production, it might be wise to try another approach that will appear innovative in the patron's mind.

Creating the Marketing Plan

To create the marketing plan, the producer should gather together the actors, designers, and managers associated with the production for a grand brainstorming session. Such brainstorming sessions generate marketing ideas and involve a number of people in the marking process. Marketing plans, unlike most play scripts, are best written with the contribution of many diverse opinions because marketing plans can be multifarious, with few options necessarily excluding others. In other words, as long as the ideas fall within budget and time parameters, the producer can try a lot of different things. The marketing effort is a kind of mirror to the production in that both efforts require a number of people working together to create and deliver a valued product. Moreover, the producer will later need members of the production team to carry out the ideas, since in new venture producing much of the marketing hinges on the personal contacts of people involved and to what extent they are willing to use their personal connections to sell the play.

Marketing objectives. All marketing plans must have objectives. In a diverse marketing context, such as in an established theater, setting marketing objectives can be difficult because marketing must simultaneously focus on season ticket sales and a number of distinct productions, and sometimes merchandised products such as t-shirts and gift items. In a single production setting, however, marketing objectives usually boil down to selling a specific number of tickets for the production. Period.

A sample single production marketing plan. It is impossible to provide a marketing plan if it does not relate to a production grounded in a specific context. Marketing plans spring from the play, the time, the cast, where it is produced, and who is doing the producing. As an example, however, let us assume a new play is being produced in Minneapolis, on the West Bank theater area of the university campus. The play in this fictitious example bears a striking resemblance to Beth Henley's *Crimes of the Heart* in that it is a story of how three sisters find love and reconciliation amidst a comic backdrop of gunshots, shrunken ovaries, and failed singing careers. The play will be presented in March in a 150-seat theater with a nonequity cast. The play is called *Heart Crimes*. Its author is also the producer.

Target audiences. The following marketing plan is just that—a plan. Plans should be evaluated and reevaluated before marketing action commences. Some strategies should be eliminated because of cost and time. Note that the next section discusses all the following items.

Habitual theatergoers

Strategy: Postcard mailing.
Timing: Start at least three months before opening night.
Money: Considerable, but variable depends on the printing costs and mailing list size. In this example, the mailing list has 500 names. The rough price estimate is $300 for black and white printing and postage.

Strategy: Advertisement in another theater's program.
Timing: Begin three months before opening night.
Money: Variable, but perhaps an exchange can be worked out.

Strategy: Internet advertising.
Timing: Begin three months before opening night.
Money: Little. But some computer skills are necessary.

Strategy: E-mail.
Timing: About a week before opening night.
Money: Little, if any.

New play lovers

Strategy: Announcement or posters and flyers at The Minneapolis Playwright's Center.

Timing: Begin three months before opening night.

Money: The cost of poster and flyers.

University and college professors

Strategy: Fax a copy of the press release to university and college theater departments.

Timing: A day or so before opening night.

Money: Little, if any.

University Students

Strategy: Ticket price discounts.

Timing: Set student prices before all advertising hits.

Money: No out of pocket or budgeted costs.

Strategy: Radio spots on the campus station.

Timing: Radio spots should run immediately before as well as during the production run.

Money: Radio costs vary according to the market reach of the station and the number of spots. In this example, $400 for fifteen radio spots.

Arts-appreciating people

Strategy: An advertisement in the Twin Cities *Reader*.

Timing: Start at least six weeks before opening night. Run the ad two times before the production opens.

Money: Variable, depending on ad size. In this example, the total cost is $600

Friends of the core group. That is, for example, friends of the actors and designers. And the friends' friends as well.

Strategy: A phone tree.

Timing: A week or so before the play opens.

Money: Free.

People met via face-to-face contact
>Strategy: Print business cards with production informa-
>tion.
>Timing: Begin three months prior to opening night.
>Money: About $100, but varies depending on quantity
>printed.

Word-of-Mouth Marketing
>Strategy: Complimentary tickets opening night to spe-
>cific people.
>Timing: A week or so before opening night.
>Money: No out of pocket costs.

Senior citizens
>Strategy: Live presentation.
>Timing: Begin two months before opening.
>Money: None.

The general public
>Strategy: Black and white posters.
>Timing: Begin three months before opening night.
>Money: Variable, depending on size, colors, and number
>reproduced. In this example the posters are 11 X 17
>photocopies. Cost $100.

Patrons who frequent the restaurant adjacent to the theater
>Strategy: Cooperative advertising with the restaurant.
>Timing: Begin two months before the production.
>Money: Low. The cost of duplicating flyers or posters.

Hotel guests staying near the theater
>Strategy: Contact the concierge, and make friends with
>the hotel staff.
>Timing: Begin a month before opening night.
>Money: None.

Direct Mail: The Postcard Mailing

Direct mailing can be a highly effective means to reach a potential audience. Below are some things to keep in mind.

Quality is important. Direct mail marketing success is entirely dependent on the quality of the mailing list and the design of the marketing piece. Mailing lists, like marketing strategies, should target specific groups with materials designed to entice that group into buying tickets.

It's quick and easy to produce. For example, one can produce postcards in a matter of days, and mail them out quickly after the printing.

Mailing lists can target a specific audience. In our example, the production *Heart Crimes* is a modern comedy. If another theater in Minneapolis has produced a similar show, chances are they will have a mailing list that was geared to that production. Indeed, theaters compile lists that are show specific; a *Sound of Music* list might share little with a *Buried Child* list, for example. Depending on the relationship with the established theater, their list could be borrowed or rented. Some theaters guard their lists like a Shakespeare first folio, while others are generous. Another negotiation point is the percentage of the total list borrowed. For example, a theater might be reluctant to loan out their entire list but may well rent out or exchange addresses within a specific zip code or two. Moreover, *Dramatics* magazine sells lists of high school thespians broken down by state and zip code for a very reasonable amount of money.

Mailing lists can be made. If a theater near the University of Minnesota produces *Heart Crimes*, then a mailing list of theater students can be compiled from the University directory. It would take more than a few hours for one individual to record the list, but a group working together could complete the job in a few hours. Also, a list of theater students at the local colleges could be gathered together from college directories and the personal contacts of people within the group producing *Heart Crimes*. It would also be possible to compile a theater faculty list from the college and university directories.

Lists can be traded. After establishing or acquiring a mailing list, it can be traded for other lists. Think of mailing lists as if they were baseball cards. An individual might have to pay for his packet of cards, but once acquired, the cards can be traded for others. Mailing lists, though, can be copied and then traded with no loss of players or contact names.

Direct mail is more immediate than other forms of advertising. A postcard or a letter almost always finds its mark because it is personally addressed and delivered to the target. Other forms of advertising, however, are more hit and miss. Radio and newspaper ads may or may not find their mark.

However, there are some draw backs to direct mailing:

It can be costly if the mailing is extensive. Although bulk rate is economical, the cost of printing and the cost of the mailing list must be considered in estimating the overall cost. The more items mailed, the greater the reach, but the greater the cost.

On average, direct mail provides about a 5 percent return rate. In other words, if 1000 postcards are sent out, and fifty people buy tickets, the direct mail campaign would be considered a success. This potential success must be weighed against the mailing costs.

People are inundated with tons of mail. It is interesting to note that in 1996 companies spent more money on direct mail advertising ($36 billion) than on television advertising

($31 billion), according to *Ad Age* magazine. Thus, there is the chance that the theater postcard will get lost amidst the other pieces of mail and end up in the bottom of the waste-basket without even a cursory glance. One woman's marketing strategy is another's junk mail.

Although a black and white design and reproduction is inexpensive, a full-color design can be costly. The national "1-800-POSTCARDS" printing firm has become very popular among small venture producers due to their pricing and quick turnarounds.

Advertisement in Another Theater's Program

This strategy has a clearly defined target group—theater-goers. It is much easier to cultivate someone who has demonstrated an interest in theater than it is to cultivate someone who has never set foot inside a theater. The cost of a theater program advertisement varies with its size and location. Of course, the wise producer will try to work out a trade, or at least a discount, with the theater's program editor. The advertisement must be well designed to be effective.

A good print advertisement should contain the following elements:

Stopping power. This is the attention-grabbing aspect to the ad. Some ads, by virtue of a slogan or image, draw the viewer in for a closer examination. Madison Avenue executives spend hours and days knocking around ideas that will grab the attention of the viewer. Look at national magazines and newspapers to see how the professionals design ads and slogans. Stopping power elicits emotion, curiosity, and surprise from the viewer because it presents information unconventionally and creatively. The musical *Rent* is advertised with the phrase "No Day But Today" because this copy captures the essence of the show and reminds potential patrons that *today* is the day to buy tickets.

Good, clear, succinct writing. Advertising copy nearly always sports muscular phrases that pack a punch and deliver a clear message.

Good visuals. Most ads contain one, clear, strong, attention-grabbing image. Many Broadway and off-Broadway plays have an immediately recognizable design at the center of the advertising effort—the cat's eyes, the helicopter, and the phantom's mask. Seemingly simple, these designs were created by professionals who undoubtedly spent numerous hours discussing concepts and rejecting faulty ideas.

A balance between words and imagery. Good print advertising results from a harmony between images and words. Images, of course, can be words. Consider the ad campaign for the Broadway play *Art*. The advertisements were visually striking but simple. The word *art* was displayed with red, green, and yellow hand-painted letters. The word-visual was brilliant, powerful, and it captured the essence of the play with three stokes of the painter's brush.

Posters and Flyers

Although poster design is similar to print copy design, there is one essential difference. In the poster design, the central image must do more work than print text because poster designs grab and hold attention of people in transit for only a few seconds. Posters are displayed in public places; streets, hallways, and grocery stores, whatever. A passerby is only going to glance at the poster for a brief moment or two, and the design will either capture his or her attention then, or it will be passed over along with the blizzard of other displayed images. The truth about posters and flyers is that they are lousy initial advertisements but great reminders.

Interestingly, many Broadway posters do not even contain basic information, such as date, time, and place. Such posters are designed to keep the production's central image alive in the viewer's mind, reminding her that the show is playing and it is time to get tickets.

With today's photocopier reproduction technology, the cost of posters and flyers has dramatically fallen from what it was just a few years ago. Color photocopiers do a nice job of reproducing a full color design on 11 X 17 paper for a very reasonable amount of money. Black and white reproductions are even more economical and can be very fetching if appropriately designed. The striking, stark, black image of the Shaffer play *Equus* (it looks like the knight chess piece) set against a white backdrop could be easily reproduced on a black and white photocopier. Moreover, the quality of paper is nearly irrelevant—posters are not designed to be souvenirs; rather they are cheap advertising designed to last a week or two. It's the nature of the business.

Internet Advertising

Web pages are growing like moss in a musty forest. Web addresses are seemingly everywhere; on television, in magazines, on billboards, printed on t-shirts, even on the side of blimps in illuminated lettering. What's next? Broadway shows have web pages, actors have web pages, birds and bees have web pages, so why not a new venture theater production! Not so fast.

Designing a web page and putting it on the net is the easy part. The hard part is making that web page work for the production to bring in ticket buyers. The internet will continue to expand, but its open availability and millions of web pages will make matching specific sites to potential customers a bit like finding a husband through an on-line chat room. A few web guidelines can effectively facilitate matching web sites to potential patrons.

Don't rent space on the net. Chances are you've already got it. Practically all on-line, e-mail services (AOL, Excite, HotMail) offer their customers space on the server to post personal home pages. Colleges and universities also make server space available to students and faculty members. Chances are good that someone on the production team is a student or subscribes to an on-line service and has internet space already set aside that is not being used. Moreover, a few web servers offer free home pages to anyone. Producers should conduct a web search under "Free Home Pages" to find such services.

Don't hire a professional designer. It is not cost effective. The production web page will only be up and running for a couple months or so, and a professionally designed site won't add much to ticket sales.

Do create a site loaded with interesting information about the production. Include information about the play, the actors, the director, and preproduction photographs if possible. The real value of a new venture production web site is that it provides the customer with far more information than could be squeezed onto an advertisement or poster.

Do include the web address on all marketing materials. People usually do not accidentally stumble onto a web site; rather they visit web sites promoted through comprehensive marketing efforts.

Link, and be linked. Include a good number of links to local theater web pages, and ask the web masters of other sites if they will add a link to the new venture production page.

Do include a number of relevant keywords in the software codes. Search engines lock onto keywords called metatags. Carefully chosen metatags will yield more hits and more exposure for the production since more people will find the web page.

Do include an e-mail link. Potential patrons can then receive answers to specific questions.

Check the page before posting it on the web. Have a friend look at it, run the links, and troubleshoot any problem areas.

E-mail

E-mail shares many of the same advantages as direct mail marketing, but there is one essential difference; e-mail is usually free. Marketers realize the potential of e-mail and consequently many people turn on their computers and find themselves flooded with tons of e-junk every day. The real challenge for the producer marketing via e-mail is to get the message noticed amidst the listings of other e-mails that sprang up overnight. Giving considerable thought to the e-mail subject tag meets this challenge best because the subject tag is displayed for the message receiver. A dull subject tag almost guarantees the message will be deleted without being read. An interesting, creative subject tag can get the producer's message onto the screen of a potential patron.

The e-mail message itself should be short, spunky, and to the point. Producers should be sure to get across date, time, place, who, and what information up front. Furthermore, e-mail lists are best compiled with the help of the entire production team. College and university directories can generate lists, and some on-line providers break down customers according to interests and hobbies. E-mail marketing is a no-lose proposition because it is free, relatively quick, and it can't hurt the marketing effort.

Fax Machine Marketing

The fax machine is a great tool for quickly getting out special information to a select number of people. Let us suppose that the newspaper ran a positive preview article about the upcoming production. Rather than hope that a particular person saw the preview article, the fax machine makes sure that article gets noticed. The fax machine is also a great device for communicating a good review to potential patrons. And usually someone on the production team has access to a fax at work. Its limitations are the cost of the fax and a list of approachable fax numbers.

A Print Advertisement

The same information about ad design applies here as it does with theater program advertising. But taking out an ad in a publication begs more research because the costs escalate and the target reach of the publication is not as narrowly defined as is a theater program. Producers should always take note of the following before placing an ad:

Check the publication's identity. A theater producer should know the character of the publication before placing an ad. Publications usually have very specific readerships, which form various target reaches. For example, the Twin Cities *Reader* appeals to a wide array of people, some of whom support the performing arts, and a smaller group that support live theater. The size of the readership target of theatergoers determines the cost effectiveness of the ad. As a prospective customer, a producer should ask the advertising account manager for detailed information about the readership. Some publications conduct circulation audits and have very specific readership information on file; others do not have readership profiles available. If not much publication information is available, it is a little like shooting an arrow at a target under a pitch-black sky— no one knows if the target was struck, or if the effort was simply a waste of energy and money.

Check deadline and closing dates. Producers must make certain that camera-ready art or computer disk ad copy is furnished to the publication by the deadline date.

Check cost. All publications have a rate sheet that varies by the size of the ad, the number of times the ad runs, and the number of colors in the ad.

Ticket Price Discounts

"How much is it?" "Is it worth it?" At the point of exchange, where money changes hands, and the patron secures a ticket, these questions are always asked, either implicitly or explicitly. "Is this play worth the price of a two-topping medium pizza?" This is where marketing gets tricky because it is not what the play is worth to the producer and actors; rather it is what the play is worth to a customer. "Would I rather see this play or do I have to buy a subway card?" Remember, marketing is the production seen through the patron's eyes. In setting ticket prices and discount structure, a producer should consider the following:

Is the target audience price sensitive? Ticket discounts provide incentive if the target group has thin wallets and are predisposed to attending theater. Drama students are one such group. Senior citizens, on the other hand, have come to expect ticket discounts, and many theaters consider meeting that expectation a necessity. Beware—price discounts rarely provide enough incentive to draw a *new* patron into a new theater, and a producer can lose money by steeply discounting tickets to people who would attend at the regular price. This leads to the second point:

A producer must understand what the patron is really buying before deciding on ticket prices. Patrons attend theater for a number of reasons, and, at times, the least important reason is the play itself. People attend established theaters to be seen with the in crowd or because it is politically wise to do so. In a new venture production setting, for example, the patron's ticket purchase may signal support of the effort itself, or support for a particular actor, not necessarily enthusiasm for the overall production. Such patrons would be relatively unaffected by price breaks because their ticket purchase is an act of support, not an exchange for an evening of theatricality.

A producer should set prices within the range of what is acceptable. If the going rate for small theaters is $10, then the new venture producer should set prices at $10 or slightly less because patrons expect to pay the small theater norm. Discounting too much is counterproductive and will not bring in many additional sales. The off-off Broadway theater community, for example, generally sets prices at about $12 per general public ticket, and $10 for students. Practically all productions fall within this range, whether they fall under the Equity Showcase Code (which provides ticket price parameters) or not.

The real price paid to attend theater is much more than the cost of the ticket. Producers should be aware that the $10 for the ticket must be tallied with the cost of transportation, dinner, and babysitter to get an accurate picture of what the evening costs the patron. The play ticket may be the best bargain in the deal.

Radio Spots

Radio is one of the best bargains available to the new venture theater producer. Radio has a reach comparable to newspapers and television, yet radio time sells for a fraction of other popular media. Radio advertising, moreover, can be targeted according to very specific demographics because radio stations program their material to please loyal listeners that fit specific profiles. For example, the hypothetical production of *Heart Crimes* will be staged near the University of Minnesota. The campus radio station would be a good, economical apparatus for reaching the twenty-something, university crowd. Radio spots can also run during very specific programs, such as an arts-related show that discusses campuswide events. Producers should understand the following points of radio advertising before buying airtime:

- Good radio ads create pictures in the listener's mind: good verbal imagery paints images that take hold and fire the listener's imagination and interest. For example, if the radio spot for *Heart Crimes* opened with a couple of gunshots and a voice saying, "I didn't like his stinking looks," then the listener will likely be engaged in the drama of the radio ad.

- Good radio ads use sound effects to capture the audience's attention.

- Repeat the name of the show, dates, and the box office number at least twice, preferably three times.

- Ask for a breakdown of the number of radio spots and placement before signing a contract. The number of people tuned into a station varies according the day of the week and the time. Running spots at off-peak times will not be nearly as effective as spots run during prime radio hours, which is usually morning and later afternoon when people commute to and from work.

A Phone Tree

A phone tree is a great stratagem for spreading the word of the production to friends, as well as friends of friends. It works like this: everyone involved with the production (everyone means everyone, from the producer to the volunteer assistant properties designer) compiles a list of ten friends or acquaintances. Each member of the production team calls ten people (branches out, if you will) and informs them of the production's dates, the place, etcetera, and invites the person to reserve tickets for the production. It is not a heavy-handed approach, but rather a soft-sell approach because the phone call is between friends and conveys information about the production first, and then casually invites the patron to make a reservation. If twenty people make ten phone calls, each to people they know, then the central core group of patrons expands. And that is payola to a producer. With any small venture production, a good percentage of the audience will be comprised of people who know people in the production. Friends. And friends of friends. The phone tree is an excellent way of conveying a personalized marketing message, which is a marketing strategy most difficult for the target to ignore. The phone tree works if:

- The producer gains the commitment from the entire production staff to make the phone calls in a timely manner.

- The producer organizes the calling list for those less organized.

- People loosely associated with the production are invited to join the phone tree marketing effort.

Distributing Business Cards with Production Information

Producers run into people during the course of the day; coworkers, the deli clerk, subway riders, people from the downstairs apartment, and others. Producers should always arm themselves with business cards that detail production information. People are accustomed to receiving business cards, and it is not an affront to hand them out if the conversation leads to such an offering. Moreover, the production team members should also have cards to distribute to their acquaintances. The cards themselves do a valuable service—they are like miniature billboards that contain the important information few people could retain through conversation.

- Business cards are relatively cheap.
- Business cards can be designed with a production logo as well as show information.
- People will customarily accept cards because the card is a soft-sell vehicle for information exchange.

Complimentary Tickets

Comp tickets help increase word-of-mouth marketing by providing key people with free seats. Folks who are noted for their connections and leadership in the local theater community would be prime targets for this strategy.

- Complimentary tickets must be valid only opening night. If word-of-mouth marketing hits too late, it is useless.
- Complimentary tickets should be used sparingly.
- Complimentary tickets should be assigned to a specific person and be nontransferable to a third party.

Live Presentations

Live presentations of a cutting from the play tend to work best in small communities. Live presentations and discussions often play well at senior citizen homes and schools because a ready-made audience is usually available. Cuttings should be relatively short, and a spiel on the play should either proceed the cutting or follow it. Producers following this marketing strategy should:

- Check with the actors regarding availability and willingness to present a scene or two from the play.
- Schedule the presentation well in advance and work with the venue's activities coordinator to secure an audience and space.
- Present an engaging cutting from the play that suggests a dramatic question.
- Always provide a postcard or flyer detailing production information.

Cooperative Advertising

Cooperative advertising is a gratis-for-gratis exchange that benefits both parties. Typical cooperative arrangements for theaters involve exchanging program ad space for permission to display promotions in another business. Cooperative arrangements can occur whenever a mutual benefit promotion can be established between the theater and business. Producers should look for tie-ins both in close proximity to the theater space as well as businesses that may be thematically connected to the play itself.

- Co-op ads are almost always a good bargain because, usually, no outlay of cash is required.

- Typical co-op ad arrangements involve a theater and local restaurants, print shops, and photographers. Some printers will run off free posters if the theater producer places the printer's logo on the poster and in the program. Photographers may discount their services in exchange for program advertising space. Co-op arrangements have also been successfully struck between theaters and flower shops, gas stations, laundromats, and even police stations.

- Co-op arrangements can also be made between theaters through the mutual promotion of upcoming productions of both organizations.

The Concierge Strategy

This is a good strategy if the show is being produced in a large city, such as New York. This marketing idea puts promotional material in the hands of hotel concierges in the hope that the word will spread to hotel guests that might be looking for entertainment off the beaten path. It's free and it can't hurt, so why not?

Summing Up: Producer's Points

- Marketing is everything that touches potential ticket buyers, from the character of the theater, to the design of ads, to the opinions of cast members. Producers should work hard to insure that such communications are all positive.

- The new venture producer must understand public perceptions about theater and the specific production before implementing marketing strategies.

- Producers must strive to involve the entire production team in marketing efforts since marketing is far more than a one person job and its effectiveness increases as does the number of people united in the effort.

- Producers must know exactly what aspect of the production they are selling to the public; what sells the play may not be the play itself.

- Producers must consider the cost of marketing and the timing of its implementation before enacting a strategy.

Moving On

The only thing better than a great marketing campaign is great *free* publicity. Indeed, publicity could be regarded as free marketing. But to acquire publicity, the producer must package the production to media editors as a timely and newsworthy event. The next chapter discusses placing the production in a wrapper that makes it attractive and irresistible to media gatekeepers.

Chapter Eleven

Creating a Buzz: Publicity

Publicity is a news story about the production broadcasted or disseminated through media outlets free of charge. Publicity is all around us. The movie review on television, the story in the paper about the new turbocharged sports car, the radio interview with the mystery writer, and the picture in the local paper of the champion cookie-seller Girl Scout are all forms of publicity. Publicity space, unlike paid advertising, is never guaranteed and both nonprofit and for-profit companies seek it. Everyone wants publicity because it is free advertising, and often the viewing public more readily notices publicity than paid marketing. A review of a theater production is a good example of publicity that often draws more attention than, say, a poster or a newspaper ad.

It is critical for the theater producer to understand that the production must be considered a newsworthy event by the editors or gatekeeps of the publicity media. If a producer fails to understand this point, all the press releases, slick photographs, press kits, and invitations to reviewers will likely not generate much coverage. The champion Girl Scout cookie seller is news because the Girl Scout set a record and also because a human interest story lurks behind the cookies. Likewise, the press reviews the sports car because the design is new, and such a story appeals to a substantial percentage of the paper's readership. Although some companies exert influence over media outlets to insure publicity (major film studios, for example) all publicity ultimately concerns itself with timely events believed to be important to the readership or viewers of the media outlet. The bottom line is this: if a producer wants to generate production publicity, the producer must focus on newsworthy angles or *create* newsworthy stories about the production. The fact that a play is being produced may or may not be news; it depends on the spin (angle) put on the story by the producer or publicist and the media outlet's audience proclivities.

What Is News? What's New Is News.

Where is the publicity sought? As a general rule, producers can expect that the smaller the city, the greater the publicity. For example, in large cities the competition for newspaper and television publicity spots is intense. In New York City, the vast majority of off-off Broadway productions do not receive coverage, and those that do get publicity usually have a press agent working contacts behind the scenes at media outlets. New York, Chicago, and Los Angeles host so many productions throughout the course of a year that a new play, or a new producing company, might not be deemed newsworthy because the newness is, ironically, commonplace. However, in small cities, the novelty of a new group producing live theater usually merits both newspaper articles and reviews. In medium-sized cities, such as Indianapolis, producers usually can count on an article or two in the local paper.

For a play to be received as newsworthy, two criteria must be met: first, the substance of the story must show some implicit connection to the media's audience, and second, that the story informs the audience of something noteworthy. For example, a story about a new play production will not have viability in a horticulture publication, unless the author, the actors, or the story line is connected to horticulture. If, however, the play centers on a missing, prize-winning orchid, then a chance exists that a horticulture publication would pick up the story as an amusing anecdotal piece. One editor's top story can wind up in the bottom of another's trash bin. This happens a lot. The chances of attaining publicity for a stage production, then, principally depend on matching the production with the mission and interests of the publications or media outlets.

Matching the Play and Players to Publicity Outlets

Producers should follow a few general rules before seeking publicity.

Read the publication every day for at least a month. Reading the publication gives the producer or publicity director a very good idea of the editorial interests of the publication. Some newspapers have a theater page, or a section of a page, that appears once a week, while others sporadically cover drama. Reading the publication for a month will also familiarize the producer with reviewers' bylines and preview writers. Producers should notice what type of material seems to interest the critic or what slants the preview articles generally take. This information will arm the producer with the insights necessary to approach the publication or specific journalist for production coverage.

Listen to and watch radio and television arts programs to discern content, frequency, and duration of such programs. The host of the program should be noted because approaching this individual is the best avenue to coverage.

Check the media guidebooks. Every sizable city has a media guidebook publication. Media guidebooks provide the reader with a detailed breakdown of every media outlet in the city. Most guidebooks provide contact names, addresses, and mission statements of media sources. Some theaters, in fact, develop in-house media guidebooks, and they serve as a wonderful resource for a new venture producer to borrow. If no media guidebook is available, then the producer can make one by diligently searching the phone book for print and electronic media contacts.

News does not always get noticed on its own merit, and at times a story must be presented to an editor as news even though its substance might not make earth-shattering press. *Before* approaching media outlets for publicity coverage, the producer should ask a few pertinent questions about her production to best present the story as newsworthy to a media gatekeeper.

Is it new? What is new about the production? Newness has an allure that many media outlets find attractive because newness makes news. A producer should look at all possible publicity angles to discover what is new about the production. Obviously, by their nature new scripts lend themselves to publicity because a production of a new voice in theater is often a noteworthy event. In most media outlets, new plays receive publicity coverage, especially if the playwright is connected to the production and a member of the local community. But if the script is a time-tested chestnut of a play, then the producer should search for another angle. Perhaps the production company itself is the news; that is, the fact that a new production company has come into being, or perhaps an actor lends the production some newness because of a unique quality. The space itself can be the story if the space has been converted into a theater, or perhaps a designer's personal story merits some publicity attention.

Is it significant? Producers should introspectively assess the significance of the entire production venture. If the play has a social or political message, then that message can be the springboard to publicity. Social commentary always attracts interest if presented on stage in a meaningful manner. The plays of Mac Wellman, Naomie Wallace, and Paula Vogel have garnered a lot of press coverage partially because of a significant social message at the foundation of the play. A social or political message provides the media outlet with a handle that focuses publicity along an identifiable angle. Moreover, if the city in which the play is being produced has experienced little live theater, then the very existence of theater can be a significant event in itself. The producer makes the production's significance apparent to the publicity gatekeepers by spelling out why the production is relevant to the media outlet's audience.

Will the play change the audience? If the play is significant, then it has the potential to change the audience. Change is always interesting because it comes with a highly personal price; perhaps change involves an adjustment of attitudes or a questioning of dearly held beliefs. Although personal change resulting from a stage production is impossible to gauge with any objectivity, the producer's publicity angle solely concerns itself with the *potential* for change. If the production implicitly asks the audience to question beliefs, then publicity can be created around that very questioning. Arthur Miller, in his essay *Tragedy and the Common Man*, wrote that at the core of modern tragedy is a deep questioning of social structures once believed to be unassailable. Such questioning, then, lends the play its significance in our popular media because it asks the audience to consider changing dearly held beliefs. And that is news.

What is the audience potential? Publicity editors usually show interest in the production's potential audience reach—the greater the audience promise, the greater the justification for press coverage because of a good number of readers. "It'll be standing room only!" A producer should not be modest when attracting publicity coverage; indeed, this is where optimism is truly justified. Besides, newspaper editors expect some hyperbole.

Is it current? The timing of the production's publicity must match the production, as well as the publication that carries the publicity. The producer or publicist must plan the timing months in advance to lend the publicity a current edge since the various media outlets have deadlines that vary as much as the makeup and nature of the outlets themselves. For example, radio and television publicity managers usually work rather fast since the currency of their media is immediacy between events and the public. Radio stations set up to cover events on a moment's notice and also have the capability of generating publicity sound bites within a couple of hours. This does not mean, however, that radio stations will avail themselves to covering a play on short notice simply because they have the capability to do so. Newspapers operate on a longer time frame, so publicity must be at the ready about a week before the production to be current. Also, newspaper publicity editors generally like to have photographs and artwork about five working days before the publications date, so photography arrangements must be made two to three weeks in advance. As mentioned before, magazines operate with much longer time frames and require publicity materials months in advance to be current with the publication date.

Is it close to home? The theater production must be within the audience reach of the publicity outlet or else publicity is useless to both the production and the media publicizer.

Is it well known? Anyone familiar with New York theater knows that the presence of a star actor creates a buzz around the production. Indeed, most Broadway productions publicize and market the attraction of a star actor or actors. Obviously, a small scale production cannot afford star power, but the smaller production can make use of local celebrities. If the production involves community personalities, then the chance of scoring significant publicity increases. A few years ago, a small theater in Minneapolis cast a news anchor in one of their productions. The play received gobs of publicity that focused on the presence of the anchorman on stage, which was apparently an irresistible story for the Twin Cities media people. As one might guess, the play sold out night after night. The hard truth of producing is that actors are not always cast for their artistic ability; rather they are sometimes cast because their name or presence will add a tremendous publicity factor to the production that may offset any artistic inadequacies. Film producers do this all the time.

Is it unusual? Productions that are downright bizarre garner a great deal of publicity. P. T. Barnum raked in lots of publicity with "productions" ranging from the presentation of George Washington's nurse (she was a fake), to the wedding of Tom Thumb and Mercy Bumpus, to the Swedish soprano Jenny Lind. Modern productions, too, can indulge in the unusual, such as a recent production in New York of *The Importance of Being Earnest* with an all-male cast, or the show *Hedwig and the Angry Inch*, the hit rock musical about the results of a transsexual operation that missed the mark by an inch. The unusual or bizarre makes for good press because people don't like to read stories about the commonplace. People are curious, and if a theater producer engages the reader's curiosity by presenting something unusual, then the publicity may work more effectively by virtue of its eye-opening slant.

Is there conflict? Conflict as considered in this chapter is not the dramatic conflict within the play, but rather conflict between the production and outside groups. While conflict can be distressing for the producer, it is also a great source of publicity. Most producers do not plan for protests, but if they should occur, a savvy producer will make the best of them by placing the substance of the conflict in publicity channels. A book that is banned or a play that is protested usually ends up finding its audience because the protesters actually publicize the play by the protest itself. During the 1980s a college in Indiana produced Caryl Churchill's *Cloud 9*. This play is somewhat controversial in that it portrays issues that surround racism and homosexuality with very graphic language and situations. The production of this play set off a small firestorm of protests because certain church groups felt that the play mocked bedrock community values. So, protesters showed up with picket signs, and shortly thereafter the press and local television reporters were on site asking questions and taking photographs. The result of this was, of course, a ton of free press and a sold-out run for the production because people wanted to see for themselves just what all the fuss was about. No local media reporter can resist a good protest because the protest itself hits on every single point previously outlined in this section.

Is there a human interest element? Human interest stories often hold prominent positions in local newspapers because the emotional element associated with such stories interests a good number of readers. A great grandmother returning to the stage after a fifty-year absence would merit a good position in a lot of local newspapers. If a cat was stuck in the lighting grid (who knows how it got there) and had to be rescued by the stage manager right before a show opened, it is safe to bet that incident would make the local newspaper especially if someone snapped a photograph of the cat being taken out of harm's way. Kids, dogs, and grandparents always make for good human interest stories.

On Newspaper Publicity

All newspapers care about news, and the goal of the publicity manager is to fulfill at least one of the above requirements to sell the story as newsworthy. The advantage of approaching newspapers for publicity is the localized nature of a media that focuses on the interests of a particular city. Interestingly, the smaller the city, the higher the percentage of regular newspaper readers. Newspapers usually allocate adequate space for most stories whereas radio and television outlets are always crunched for time, which often lends publicity a quick "sound bite" feel. The downside of newspaper publicity is that most people, in fact, do not read papers but rather scan them by picking off headlines, which can lead to stories being overlooked by a hurried readership. Also national demographic trends show that newspaper readership falls with reader age. In other words, young people do not frequently read newspapers, but many senior citizens devour them. Newspapers also have a relatively short life; in fact, they are relevant for only a few hours before the next paper is printed.

Publicity managers must also be savvy in knowing who to approach for newspaper publicity. Play dumb. One should approach the newspaper for information by first making a phone call. If one contacts a small or medium-sized paper, chances are one will get the publicity manager on the phone. One should ask the publicity manager (who may well be the managing editor) about guidelines for calendar listing, photograph formats, and publicity stories. If the newspaper has written guidelines, then one should personally drop by the office to pick up such guidelines from the publicity manager. The real agenda is not guidelines themselves, but rather the face-to-face meeting with the publicity manager. Even a brief, ten second meeting is worth the effort because it allows the newspaper to connect a story request with a specific person, which, in turn, builds contacts. As a matter of fact, any valid excuse one can use for dropping by the newspaper should be exercised because the real agenda is to build contacts with media members.

Previews and Reviews

There are two major types of newspaper publicity: the preview article and the review. The preview article appears a week or so before the play opens and is designed to generate interest in the production. Preview articles, unlike reviews, are not necessarily written by a newspaper critic. Indeed, theater producers often package preview articles and present them to newspapers as ready copy. Depending on editorial guidelines and staff size, some newspapers will run press releases in place of formal preview articles and, in fact, are very receptive to a well-written piece generated by the theater company itself.

Previews

Preview articles must meet five criteria to be favorably noticed by editors:

1. Follow a time-tested press release format of "hook-details-information." The hook is the opening sentence designed to grab the reader's attention. A good hook capsulates the essential points of the press release and presents them in a colorful fashion. For example, the sentence "On Thursday, January 22, the Cape Cod Players will present a new play by Boston playwright Kate McGinty" is rather boring. A better approach would be, "Insurance Agent or British Secret Service Operative?" This sentence hooks the reader by presenting a tiny slice of the play in a potent, punchy form alluding to the essence of the drama. The hook is the most difficult sentence to write because it must immediately grab the reader's attention and draw him into the body of the article. The details of a press release usually expand on the hook sentence by providing specifics about the event, such as what it is (a play) and what is noteworthy about the production. The information section of the press release provides who, when, and where information, as well as the box office essentials such as ticket prices and phone numbers.

2. The press release must be accurate. It is important that someone with knowledge of the production write the news release because well-intentioned writers can easily misconstrue information. At a very minimum, one should verify date, time, place, and box office accuracy. No producer can afford to overlook this point since a typo can lead to misdirected, disgruntled patrons.

3. The press release must be well written and conform to standard style. (See "Format Basics" on page 197.)

4. The press release must be newsworthy and free of hard-sell points. Press releases which push selling points rather than newsworthy angles will likely find the bottom of a trash can. Directly approaching the target audience with offers related to ticket purchases characterizes hard sell. Soft-sell marketing creates interest tangentially by spinning off a story related to the production but not by forcing the issue of ticket sales through, for example, specific discounts within a time frame.

Reviews

Reviews are perhaps the most critical form of publicity any producer receives; however, they are also the least controllable. A review in *The New York Times* of an off-off Broadway production is akin to winning the lottery; one hears about such things, but they rarely happen. Major newspapers are tightly constrained by space, so drama editors will focus coverage on productions that have the best chance of reaching a good number of people, and usually such productions are the big ticket shows. A critic's allegiance is to her readership, not the community of theater producers. Medium-sized and smaller newspapers are generally far more receptive to reviewing small scale productions because of the novelty of the event. Also, a smaller market paper might well have a drama critic who needs and appreciates review opportunities. When approaching a newspaper for a review, a producer should:

1. Complementary tickets. Always offer complimentary tickets for the reviewer and a guest.

2. Opening night. Encourage the reviewer to attend the opening night production or a preview production. If the review is to have a positive publicity effect, then it must appear in the paper quite soon after the production opens. While some producers might discourage a critic from attending and reviewing a final dress performance because of the lack of an audience dynamic, other producers feel that a critic's presence at a preview performance is justified because the review should appear a day or two earlier, thus enabling timely publicity.

3. Reminders. Remind the critic of the production dates a week or so in advance.

4. Criticism. Never criticize the critic. Conventional theater wisdom holds that even a bad review is better than no review because being ignored means that in an editor's eyes, the production does not merit coverage and lacks significance.

5. Reviewers. Ask a specific reviewer to cover the production, preferably one who is receptive to small venture productions.

Some theaters have found creative ways to interest editors in publishing production reviews. The Actors' Theater of Louisville, for example, works with underserved youth through local schools. ATL provides these youth groups with complimentary tickets and encourages the students to review the production. The ATL staff reads the reviews and then sends them to the local newspaper, where many of them have been published. The theater gets press coverage through multiple reviews, the newspaper receives theater reviews from unique and often insightful perspectives, and the students reap a good deal of satisfaction from their published work. Everybody wins. It's a fine idea that could work elsewhere.

About Calendar Listings

Most newspapers offer free calendar listings that publish artistic events in and around town in an abbreviated, alphabetized, and categorized layout. The theater producer must, however, keep two considerations foremost in mind when planning calendar listings: first, the submission deadline, and second, the listing format. All newspapers have submission deadlines for calendar listings and they are usually set a week to ten days before the publication date of the specific issue. It behooves a producer to gather deadline dates well in advance of submitting calendar events. Most newspapers also have specific preferred formats for submission regarding the listing of date, time, place, and ticket information. Most calendar editors find it irksome to have to search through a submission for pertinent information, and some will ignore submissions if not properly formatted. Additionally, some newspapers will print a sentence or two about the production. If this is the case, the producer must write pertinent, punchy, catchy sentences that will grab the reader's attention, much akin to a press release's opening sentence.

Magazine Publicity

The number of magazines that specifically target a city's population grew tremendously during the 80s and 90s. Indeed, many cities now boast magazines that cover artistic and cultural events and local issues such as restaurants, real estate, and city personalities. Magazines are good publicity outlets; however, a number of special considerations must be tended to before approaching magazine editors.

Always consider the magazine's target audience's interests before all else. National magazines are tailored to very specific audiences, and if the publicity article does not meet the magazine's readership needs, there is little likelihood of publication. The same logic applies to local magazines. The producer must always search for a connection between the production and readership of the local magazine. Indeed, the actual production might not be the publicity story, rather it may be wise to present a feature story that focuses on a human interest element since feature stories are to magazines what news is to newspapers.

Magazines favor feature stories. A feature differs from a news release in a number of key aspects.

- Features are more like fiction stories in that they place the climactic point near the end, rather than up front.
- Features usually focus on human interest angles that augment the story line with an emotional element.
- The most common feature profiles a specific individual.
- Features usually have a timeless quality in that a feature could be run within a relatively large publication time frame window. However, the timeliness of the feature story from the producer's point of view should be solely fixed on the relevance to the production itself.

A magazine staff writer need not write the feature. Most magazines have an open submission policy, which means that they will consider stories written by freelance writers. As in any publicity situation, the producer must insure that the story be factually sound and provide the reader with an intriguing spin on the production.

Research the magazine's editorial staff. Magazines usually have a number of associate editors working under the editor-in-chief. Producers should read a few back issues to determine interests of individual editors to discover if a particular editor is predisposed to theater productions and what angle defines the theater stories. One must respect editorial predilections because a story's inclusion in a publication is truly often due to the subjective likes and dislikes of a particular editor.

Approach the magazine at least four months before the magazine publication date. Four months is not an exaggeration, since magazines are highly stylized, glossy publications that demand far more preparation time than the average newspaper. Magazines need considerable time between the actual publication date and in-press dates.

Consider approaching newsletters and church bulletins. In a larger framework, one can consider newsletters and church bulletins as a close cousin of magazines. Many companies and even small businesses circulate newsletters to their employees and customers. If the producer, or another individual associated with the production, has any connection to the newsletter publisher, then asking for a mention or a small feature is entirely appropriate. Likewise, churches will often publicize events connected to or sponsored by congregation members. Such publications have a very narrowly defined audience, and as such, the reach of publicity is highly localized.

On Photography Issues

A good picture is worth a thousand . . . dollars. Photography is critical to any form of print publicity. Photography has the unique ability to capture the reader's attention with just a glance. A good photograph's impact is immediate because a picture tells a story and involves the viewer's emotions. The casual reader is likely to look at the pictures in a newspaper or magazine, yet be unlikely to read the majority of articles. There are several photography issues that all producers must understand.

A photograph should capture what the production actually looks like. A photograph is a window through which the viewer glimpses a moment of the production. In the past, now, and probably in the future, a few, somewhat unethical producers provide photographs which do not even remotely represent their productions. The classic example would be a provocative photograph that displays scantily clad women (or men) in seductive poses. The photograph implies that the viewer will "get" the image if he buys a theater ticket; when this does not materialize, the patron often feels cheated, which sets a bad precedent for any producer. Such scenarios do happen with surprising frequency.

Theater photography should capture an action. This does not necessarily imply a physical action, since the subject's demeanor and facial expressions can express mental action. Action of some sort, though, is critical because a static photograph that appears posed is dull to the viewer because nothing of interest is happening. Producers should consider the play's climactic moment, or a turning point in the script, and attempt to capture that moment of action.

Photographs should be kept relatively simple. Some of the most effective publicity photographs use only two actors. In fact, it is a mistake to use more than three actors because the photograph's emotional effectiveness is dissipated when the focus disperses among a number of actors. "Keep it focused" is advice to be heeded by the photographer and producer.

The subjects should be kept close together. A theatrical publicity photograph does not capture actual life, but rather it approximates stage life, an artistically designed product. In actual life, when people engage in conversation there is usually a distance between people that is known as personal space. If this space is violated, people usually feel uncomfortable. On stage, and especially on film, however, actors routinely violate such personal space for artistic effect, which often appears natural to the audience member watching the action from a distance. The photographer, too, must not approximate real life, but artistic life by keeping the subjects close together so that they appear to be engaged in some critical activity. A photograph must be "blocked" for the "newspaper stage" that is, perhaps, four square inches in all its grandeur.

The eyes have it. Good publicity photography often captures the glimmer in the actors' eyes because in the subjects' eyes the viewer can see the most potent expression of humanity in all its emotionally complex forms. If one considers the photographs that have made an impression on viewers, many have captured the essence of the subjects through the eyes of the subject, such as the publicity photography of plays ranging from *A Streetcar Named Desire* to *Burn This*. The photographs of Jessica Tandy's Blanche DuBois or John Malcovich's Pale are so memorable because each character's demeanor and action is so well expressed by an image that connects the viewer to the actor's eyes and visage.

Good publicity photography also presents a situation that captures the actor's reaction to the situation. If a publicity photograph sets up an actor appearing to be caught in a situation, whether it be one of danger or absurdity, the viewer of the photograph will be drawn to the actor placed in the predicament, not the other actor forcing the action. Most people will empathize with the victim because the image of the victim draws sympathy from the situation and curiosity from the actor's reaction to the viewer.

Publicity photography should always be shot with a sophisticated 35 mm camera. In the hands of a competent photographer, 35 mm cameras provide higher resolution and sharper focus than a simple, fixed lens camera. Additionally, many newspaper photographers freelance, and this provides the producer with an opportunity not only to hire a good photographer, but also to make a connection with the local newspaper.

Producers should have a competent photographer shoot the publicity pictures. A good photographer knows how to compose a picture, with line, balance, angle, and contrast. Indeed, contrast is vital in publicity photography since nothing dampens the effect of a photograph faster than muted contrast. For example, an actor sporting a dark suit against a dark background is usually a bad choice because the subject of the photograph and the background will morph and mask the actor.

A plain background is usually preferred by professionals because publicity photographs shot on set can obfuscate the subject of the photograph by drawing attention and focus away from the actors and to the set. The function of the background is to provide contrast with the subject and to focus the viewer's eyes on the actors.

Producers should keep up with the changes in technology. A few years ago, newspapers preferred an 8 X10 photograph. Now, most newspapers prefer color slides because technology has developed which enables high-quality reproductions of slide images on newspaper stock. In the future, newspaper will prefer digital photographs, not actual prints or slides, but photos saved on computer disk in PICT, TIFF, or JPG formats. Digital technology exists now, and most photographs are digitized in prepress operations, but today most papers and magazines still prefer color slides.

Producers should use color film, especially if the photograph will appear in a magazine. Color, of course, adds vibrancy to publicity photography, and editors can run a color photograph as either black and white or color. Providing them with a choice is advisable, but color does add to the cost of publicity photography.

Approaching Radio and Television Stations

The world rapidly changes with the onset of digital technology. For the theater producer this means that the next few years will create new publicity outlets that will provide wider access to traditionally "unapproachable outlets," such as television. The number of local stations and public access stations is indicative of the proliferation of television stations, which have grown tremendously and will continue to grow in the foreseeable future. Indeed, many television markets now find stations operated by colleges and universities, as well as public access channels operated by cable providers, and even local high schools have channels in some communities. Such local stations, which can now be seen in hundreds of communities, are always scouting for suitable material because they have a tremendous amount of airtime to fill. Small, local stations often repeat stories in order to fill their allotted airtime, while larger stations may run a piece once or twice. Moreover, stations with a local flavor are approachable and often receptive to local projects.

Naturally, the reach of a local station cannot compare with a national station, but most theater producers have a very specific and very limited target audience that does indeed match up well with the reach and target audiences of local stations. In spite of the poor quality of many public access programs, a producer should still approach such stations because the reach of even local television is tremendous and such publicity is very cost efficient to generate. Indeed, most Americans receive their news via television, and television works as a particularly effective media for reaching younger people who may not be regular newspaper readers.

Television Stations

Producers should keep up with rapidly changing technology. Videotape and video cameras were a miraculous innovation compared with the cumbersome nature of film. However, just as video supplanted film in the television industry, digital technology will replace video's analog technology. Digital cameras now on the market provide the user with moving images of astonishing resolution and editing capabilities that far exceed traditional videotape. Although digital technology is not yet the industry standard, it will soon become the standard when broadcast facilities become fully digitized and home televisions become digital receptors. The cost of digital cameras will fall, as supply of such units grows and competition among manufacturers intensifies.

Producers should think in visual terms when approaching local stations for publicity. It is always appropriate to ask a station to send a camera crew to record the publicity segment, but the reality is that stations may not have the staff or the time to fulfill such a request, especially a local access station. In such an instance, the next best alternative is to shoot a segment of video or digital tape that the station can air. Producers should try to secure an experienced camera operator, which is really not difficult to do in most communities. If the station agrees to run a segment on the production, they will edit the tape to fit the publicity segment or feature story. In other words, a producer should err on the side of bounty, not frugality.

Producers should turn off stage lighting and turn on simple white work lights. Colored lights may look great on stage when properly designed and focused, but on videotape, stage lighting often comes across as a streaky distortion. The quality of the tape matters, as does its audio.

Producers should focus on what is newsworthy. Watch local stations for a week to accurately discern what type of publicity stories are covered and who covers them.

Producers should be aware that some television stations will reject a publicity piece if the piece has been advertised in print media.

Producers should work with the director and actors in accommodating television publicity.

Producers should strive to approach the right person. Pitching the publicity story to a television producer who has covered similar events in the past is far more useful than approaching the station with a "To Whom It May Concern" letter, which will likely be filed in the trash can.

Radio Stations

Radio publicity differs, of course, from television because the media is aural, not visual. Successfully securing radio publicity, then, largely depends on the quality of the text of the public service announcement (P.S.A.). Like television, the world of radio broadcasting has changed; because more and more organizations seek publicity, the nature of the P.S.A. has changed from what once was a standard 60- or 30-second release to today's 15- or 10-second release.

Furthermore, as competition for publicity spots grows, and as radio stations fall under the control of multi-media organizations that are bottom-line oriented, the resulting crunch can seem daunting to the small scale theater producer. Radio stations usually reserve morning drive and evening drive prime times for revenue generating advertising, which means that P.S.A.s are often run at off-hours. Nevertheless, radio P.S.A.s are free, and approaching a station can be worthwhile if the producer follows a few guidelines. Write the P.S.A. with the active, not passive, voice. Read it out loud, not only to time it, but also to test its phonetic friendliness.

Get to the point fast. Considering that most P.S.A.s are now only 10 or 15 seconds, it is vital that the first sentence not only grab the reader or listener, but it must also contain some practical information. One of the most common mistakes is to present a P.S.A. that is simply too long. Program directors are far more likely to trash a long P.S.A. because they don't have the time to edit it. Another option is to present the station manager with a couple of different P.S.A.s, each of a different length.

Highlight a newsworthy angle. The producer should listen to the station to discern what material the program director considers to be a newsworthy announcement. Most radio announcements focus on a local angle for a local listenership. The closer a P.S.A. connects to the hometown target listener, the better the chance that the station will run it.

Avoid writing a P.S.A. that is too self-serving. A P.S.A. is not a "personal service announcement,"; a P.S.A. that catches the eye of a program manager will likely be an announcement that somehow serves the public by announcing information beneficial to the public. Placing the focus of the P.S.A. solidly on public benefits will make the P.S.A.

more competitive against the dozens or hundreds of other announcements received by the station.

Submit the P.S.A. to the "program director." Better yet, if possible, address it to the specific individal wo is the program director.

Format Basics

P.S.A.s and press releases should follow a format that has become standardized through years of industry practice. Failure to follow simple guidelines will brand the announcement as the product of an amateurish organization. All P.S.A.s and press releases should contain the following elements:

- Announcements should be printed on letterhead stationary, or at a minimum, photocopied from letterhead stationary. If a producer cannot afford to have stationary printed, most home computers are capable of generating basic designs that should serve the purpose.

- Place contact information at the beginning of the announcement. Contact information should include the writer's name, a phone number where he or she can be reached, and an e-mail address if appropriate.

- The tag line "FOR IMMEDIATE RELEASE" follows the contact information.

- The number 30, flanked by two hyphens, is the last item on the announcement. It should appear: -30- . The number 30 means that nothing else follows. It is also common for broadcast media announcements to end with: ###.

The Press Kit: Pulling It All Together

A press kit is a folder organized to present the production in a professional fashion to a perspective media contact. Press kits have become standard practice in performing arts management. Press kits are, indeed, flashy calling cards that anyone with a little ingenuity and creativity can make. Press kits begin with a folder, much like the folder many people used in grade school or high school. Press kit folders tend to be a bit glossier than the standard dull-finish folders found in discount stores and they often have a business card pocket. Also, a production photo or logo properly affixed to the front can personalize the folder. One can purchase the folder at a good stationary store or photocopying/printing business. The appearance of the folder counts for a lot since it, in part, represents the production's professionalism.

In the right pocket, the producer should place the following:

- Biographies of key personnel, including the playwright, actors, and designers.

- Head shots of all actors. Production publicity can extend beyond the production itself by promoting the actors. Actors, of course, have an interest in the production as well as any individual publicity they may garner.

- A cast photograph.

- Any published publicity that involves the artistic personnel including past productions.

In the left pocket, the producer should include:

- Show information, such as press releases and public service announcements.

- A synopsis of the play.

- Preproduction publicity photographs detailing scenes from the play.

- Any published publicity that involves the play.

One should usually hand the press kit to the targeted editor or station manager, rather than mail it out. It is yet one more opportunity for the producer to make a person-to-person contact.

On Press Agents and Publicity

Press agents, sometimes referred to as press representatives, facilitate publicity for a fee. A press agent is usually an individual who has worked in the media, knows the slants of various publications, is familiar with the likes and dislikes of editors, follows the ever-changing trends in digital and broadcast media, and understands timing and publicity packaging. Most importantly, however, a press agent must maintain her connections to media gatekeepers because publicity, like many production elements, is partly judged on the agent's subjective appeal. In other words, it is vital for the agent to be known in the business.

Connections to publicity gatekeepers make the press agent's job nearly indispensable in large cities characterized by intense competition for publicity hits. If one considers, for example, New York City with its hundreds of performing arts events that occur every week, balanced against the relatively limited amount of publicity space in print media, then one can rightly conclude that the press agent is necessary in securing a good probability (not the certainty) of publicity. In large cities, then, the press agent must be well connected, and a producer who hires a press agent really pays for the agent's connection to big city editors. Moreover, it follows that press agents thrive in media metropolises where competition for publicity is intense; in New York, Chicago, and Los Angeles, for example. In these cities, producers often regard the press agent's fee as necessary as money spent on actors or space rental, but in smaller cities, an astute producer can fulfill many of the press agent's functions by himself forming contacts with media people and professionally representing the production as press worthy to smaller town editors who may be more receptive to a producer's publicity pitch.

If a producer opts for a press agent's services, then finding the right agent becomes a priority since a press agent who lacks either interest or experience will prove to be frustrating to both sides of the producer-press agent relationship. Finding the right press agent, that is one willing to take on the producer's project for an agreeable fee, can be quite a task, but it can be smoothed if the producer follows a few guidelines.

Producers should begin the search by targeting those agents who have successfully represented similar plays. In New York, for example, it would probably be a waste of energy to approach a press agent specializing in off-Broadway musicals if the production was an off-off Broadway straight play with a modest budget. Press agents, just like critics, tend to specialize in a couple of areas—unionized press agents primarily specialize in Broadway productions, and some agents have found a niche in off-Broadway, and others thrive on the challenges of promoting off-off Broadway productions. Also, press agents tend to have their likes and dislikes regarding the style and sense of the play, thus, finding an agent who truly likes the production on paper is crucial in the agent's willingness to accept the project. The producer, then, should ask herself which press agents have successfully promoted similar plays produced in like venues. Sleuthing the answer to this question depends on asking other producers about their experiences with press agents; that is, did the press agent produce a good amount of specific publicity hits? The best source of information about a press agent is those people who have employed the agent in the past.

Finding the right press agent can also be accomplished by researching old playbills/programs. Most likely, even small venture productions would list the press agent in the program. Most theaters have an archive file (which may be a large cardboard box stuffed in a closet) and locating an old program shouldn't be that difficult. Obviously, actors and others keep programs for their personal archives, which can also be a source of information and an avenue of discovery. It pays to keep old programs since they can be a valuable resource years later.

The press agent, unlike most associated with a production, can demonstrate an objective record of accomplishment. While the work of the artistic staff is somewhat subjective (such as the director's exact contributions), the number and kind of publicity hits a production garnered can quantify the press agent's performance. If, for example, the press agent was able to place a preview article in the *Village Voice* (the leading New York weekly newspaper) that article is tangible and specific, and it is not a matter of opinion. Conversely, if a press agent fails to place the production in the media, save for a calendar listing or two, that too is a specific result. Moreover, reputable press agents will have a portfolio of publicity they have placed, as well as a record of broadcast media hits. The producer should request and review these records, and if a press agent cannot produce a track record of accomplishments, it would then be wise for a producer to look elsewhere.

Does the press agent want to read the play? Very few reputable agents would take on a project sight unseen. Most experienced agents will want to read the script before agenting the production to discover a) if the play dovetails with their interests, b) if the production lends itself to established publicity channels, and c) if the play is worthy of a major publicity push. When a well-established agent represents a play, she puts her reputation on the line because to secure publicity an agent will often vouch for the production's stage worthiness. In the publicity field, agents stake their reputations on every production represented because publicity is often secured by making personal appeals to media editors. In other words, a press agent often vouches for a production to publicize it, and an agent who is lukewarm about the venture may not generate much publicity. It follows that an agent who accepts the project without reading the script is likely one who will not be personally committed, and the publicity may suffer.

Also, a good agent will ask a producer numerous questions regarding publicity expectations, that is, what type of publicity and the frequency and timing of expectations. While a reputable press agent will attempt to place publicity for his client, a reputable agent will rarely make promises. Producers, then, should be wary of a press agent who promises a number of publicity hits because the agent is a facilitator, not an editor with gatekeeper authority. A good press agent will also inquire about the production's budget, venue, show dates, and the experiences of others on the production team. A reputable press agent will straightaway search for possible publicity angles arising from the production team's connections to newsworthiness. It's second nature for a good agent to do so.

How much does the agent charge? Producers should be aware that some press agents charge a service fee as well as an expense fee. The service fee covers what the agent does, and the expense fee covers the costs of doing business (such as mailings, photocopying, and photo reproductions). Expense fees are legitimate if presented in an upfront manner. However, some agents charge exorbitant expense fees that rack up hundreds of dollars beyond the normal service fee. A producer should always ask about expense fees and, if they exist, negotiate a cap on such fees to avoid unforeseen charges.

If a producer cannot afford a good agent, then the best alternative is for the producer to act as his own agent by following the guidelines set forth through the first part of this chapter. One can make a professional-appearing press package and present it to the media gatekeepers and, with a lot of polite persistence, some publicity may follow.

Another way of hiring a press agent for a reasonable amount of money is the freelance option. Major press agents often work in association with other agents, much like a small law firm with partners and associates. It is a widely known and poorly kept secret that young, associate agents accept freelance work on the side. If a producer wishes to negotiate a freelance arrangement, then the producer would be wise to approach the agent directly, not through normal office channels. Associate agents may be willing to accept such an arrangement for a reasonable amount of money since (let's face it) most associate agents eventually want to establish their own clientele before hanging out a shingle. The ethical ramifications of the freelance arrangement fall back on the agent, and it is their option to refuse the offer.

Summing Up: Producer's Points

- The production must be considered a newsworthy event by the editors or gatekeepers of the publicity media.
- Producers must match the production to the slant of specific publicity outlets.
- If the production has the potential to change its audience, then editors will be more likely to favorably view a publicity request.
- If the production has a human interest angle and can

appeal to a good number of people, then editors will be more likely to favorably view a publicity request.

- In approaching a magazine for publicity, producers should always consider the publication's target audience as well as the publication date of the magazine.
- A press kit is a folder organized to present the production in a professional fashion to a perspective media contact.
- The next few years will create new publicity outlets that will provide wider access to traditionally "unapproachable outlets," such as television.
- The format of the press release, P.S.A., or calendar listing is important to media gatekeepers.
- Connections to publicity gatekeepers make the press agent's job nearly indispensable in large cities characterized by intense competition for publicity hits.

Moving On

Sometimes great things come in small packages. Indeed, some modest productions have transferred to higher levels of professionalism, and at times actors are discovered in modest settings. The next chapter discusses how new venture producers can begin to form relationships with people who can take the play and careers to the next step.

Chapter Twelve

Moving On

Stories come across from time to time about the Broadway play with very modest beginnings, or the film star who was discovered in an off-off Broadway production that played in a grungy little theater. While such scenarios can happen—that is, plays can transfer to higher levels of production, and actors are sometimes "discovered"—such tales have untold stories involving years of associations, friendships, and mutual trust between artists, producers, and agents. This chapter discusses the first steps in building associations with others in the profession. Efforts to build affiliations with professionals relate to many basic marketing principles, but one key difference exists; the target market (those agents and producers who can move plays and careers) is very specific, down to a particular face and phone number.

How to Find Producers and Agents

A new venture producer should make the obvious moves in finding producers and agents; that is, asking others in the field for names and contacts. Finding producers can require a little detective work by backtracking old programs and talking to theater owners and artistic directors. Of course, cities in which the nonprofit theater model dominates would likely have few producers of the for-profit ilk and the very possibility of quickly transferring a play to a higher production standard locally may be a moot point.

However, one can usually find agents in any decent-sized city. Apart from asking others for agents' names, there are two other good sources of information. The first is Actors' Equity Association. AEA maintains a database of agents who represent actors, broken down regionally. Access to this information is open to any member of AEA, so maintaining ties with an AEA member, whether cast in the production or not, is a wise move. Another terrific source of information is a state's film commission. Most states have an office (often a branch of the state's commerce department) that serves as an information source to producers who film in that particular state. Although film directors and casting agents generally cast the major roles out of Los Angeles or New York, they usually hire extras locally because it is economically practical to do so. Subsequently, local governments created film commissions to establish immediate contact between film producers and local agents and actors. State film commissions exist to help producers and to bolster commerce in their particular states, and in response to this mission they often provide the names of agents at no cost to those who inquire.

Once a producer selects a target of agents and producers, the next step is to attract those people to the production. There are five "P's" of courting agents and producers. They are: Professionalism, Politeness, Persistence, Patience, and Petit fours.

Professionalism. means efficaciousness in all matters. For example, if one initially approaches an agent by letter, the letter should be produced on letterhead stationary and be free of grammatical errors. New venture producers should promptly return agent's or producer's phone calls, offer complimentary tickets, and use punctuality as the watchword in all matters. Professionalism means never burning a bridge between oneself and an agent or producer because in the small world of theater, burned bridges can leave one on the outside.

Politeness. Polite manners should extend beyond agents and producers to their associates and secretaries. Human nature dictates that it is easier to say no to a rude person than it is to someone who is consistently polite.

Persistence. Coupled with politeness is persistence. Indeed, a fine line separates persistence and becoming a nuisance, and walking that line is an art in itself. Agents and producers, however, expect persistence from potential clients, so polite persistence simply comes with the territory. For example, most people in the profession will return a phone call once but will not put themselves out to return a call. Persistence means redoubling an initial effort that fails to make the appropriate connection. An opportunity to follow up on contacts also is facilitated by faxing copies of reviews and articles to agents and producers immediately after their appearance in newspapers. While the fax conveys information about the production, it covertly reminds the agent or producer to drop by and have a look for herself.

Patience. Not every effort will yield results within a short amount of time. Patience means not expecting or demanding payoffs that quickly follow initial contact efforts. How does patience balance against persistence? No one has an exact answer, but the standard of reasonable time applies. Afford producers and agents enough time to respond to a request before contacting them. The amount of time is completely subjective, but one may safely assume that more than one phone call a day borders on impolite behavior.

Petit Fours. Food goes a long way in enticing people to attend a production. A new venture producer who encourages agents and producers would do well to provide a reception following the performance because the reception serves not only an enticement, but also provides a forum during which those present can make new contacts and associations. In other words, the reception provides a ready-made reason to stay in the theater and network. Many of the prestigious east coast theater training programs wine and dine agents before and after they present their students at the annual spring showcases in New York. The receptions are, in fact, a major drawing card and the schools put out lavish spreads to attract top-notch agents. On a smaller production level, a reception need not break the producer's wallet, for a wine and cheese spread won't be too dear and it will serve the basic function of holding people so that conversations can occur that may lead to future associations.

Recent Changes

The paid workshop performance has recently become acceptable in New York and Los Angeles. The name is misleading because the actors or the playwright do not get paid; rather agents are paid to attend the performance in return for their consideration of accepting new clients. It typically works like this; a number of actors will pool their money and invite a handful of agents to attend a workshop performance for a lump sum of money. The agents do not obligate themselves to accept any of the actors as clients, but many actors justify the expense because without the payment to agents, they may not even get consideration for representation. It is not a question of ethics; rather it is a reflection of the ever-changing and highly competitive nature of the business of acting.

Associations With Television Producers

Small venture producers should also consider that their product could interest film and television producers. With the oncoming digitalization of America, the number of local television opportunities will expand, as will the number of national carriers. On a local level, television producers will have hundreds of hours of airtime to fill and, as such, will need more broadcastable product than currently available. Even skeptics admit that the face of broadcasting will change and more airtime will open up at the local television level, time which actors and playwrights can fill with products produced at the local level. The possibility exists, then, for theater producers to offer their shows as marketable products for local television. Of course, the playwright holds the script filming rights, and, as such, a producer must secure permissions before any filming can commence. Whereas only a slim possibility of making money on such a venture exists, the associations that can develop may prove to be of value down the road.

The Final Word

Viability in the theater world depends on knowing people. The theater world from the outside looks like a Brinks armored truck with its bullet-proof glass, metal armor, and at least the potential for some money inside (who knows exactly what's in those trucks anyway—is it coming or going)? Every year actors trek to large cities armed with glossy head shots (now more aptly described as half-body shots) and a monologue or two locked away in long-term memory, and playwrights shoot off scripts to theaters from coast to coast. These are worthwhile and necessary activities for both actors and playwrights, but in themselves they are not enough. Breaking into the profession is based on talent and the realization of the old cliché — "it's who you know." The academic model based in training and study only partially captures the attributes necessary for viability in the profession.

That's both good news and bad news. It's bad news because it can seem like a catch-22—how can one get to know people without first making an artistic breakthrough and how can one make a breakthrough without first knowing people? This puzzles hundreds of actors and playwrights every year. The good news is that producing theater leads to connections with others in the profession. At every step of producing theater, opportunities shine for reaching out to others who have traveled down the road before, and most people are generous and willing to share their experiences with the new venture producer. Even an activity as mundane as budgeting provides an opportunity for sharing preproduction planning with others, and that can result in fraternity with others in the profession—being on the inside.

And that's the raison d'être of this book. The relationships that develop throughout the producing project, often unforeseen at the onset, may turn out to be rewarding both in the short term and long term. The more associations built and maintained, the better the chances for an actor or playwright to remain viable, that is, on the inside of the profession. And that's what producing at the small venture level is all about—creating opportunities for oneself and others that can pay off in both the present and the future.

BIBLIOGRAPHY: The Producer's Library

General Books on Producing Theatre

Alberts, David. *Rehearsal Management for Directors.* Portsmouth, NH: Heinemann, 1995.

Apple, Jacki. *Doing it Right in L.A.: Self-producing for the Performing Artist.* Los Angeles: Astro Artz, Fringe Festival, 1990.

Ball, David. *Backwards and Forwards: A Technical Manual for Reading Plays.* Carbondale: Southern Illinois University Press, 1983.

Bayer, William. *Breaking Through, Selling Out, Dropping Dead.* New York, N.Y.: Limelight Editions, 1989.

Beck, Roy A. ... [et al.]. *Play Production Today.* 4th ed. Lincolnwood, Ill., U.S.A.: National Textbook Co., 1989.

Chater, Kathy. *Production Research: An Introduction.* Oxford ; Boston: Focal Press, 1998.

Condee, William Faricy. *Theatrical Space: A Guide for Directors and Designers.* Lanham, Md.: Scarecrow Press, 1995.

Cohen, Edward M. *Working On a New Play: A Play Development Handbook for Actors, Directors, Designers & Playwrights.* New York: Limelight Editions, 1995.

Farber, Donald C. *From Option to Opening: A Guide to Producing Plays Off-Broadway.* 4th ed., New York: Limelight Editions, 1988.

Farber, Donald C. *Producing Theatre: A Comprehensive Legal and Business Guide.* Rev. ed. New York: Limelight Editions: 1987.
Frome, Shelly. *Playwriting—A Complete Guide to Creating Theater*; with a foreword by Kenneth Pickering. Jefferson, N.C.: McFarland, 1990.

George, Kathleen. *Playwriting: The First Workshop*. Boston: Focal Press, 1994.

Green, Joann. *The Small Theatre Handbook: A Guide to Management and Production; text illustrations by Leo Abbett*. Harvard, Mass.: Harvard Common Press, 1981.

Grote, David. *Staging the Musical: Organizing, Planning, and Rehearsing the Amateur Production*. Englewood Cliffs N.J.: Prentice-Hall, 1986.

Heniford, Lewis W. *1/2/3/4 for the Show: A Guide to Small-cast One-act Plays*. Lanham, Md.: Scarecrow Press, 1995.

Holtje, Adrienne Kriebel. *Putting On the School Play: A Complete Handbook*.West Nyack, N.Y.: Parker Pub. Co., 1980.

Johnston, Chris. *House of Games: Making Theatre from Everyday Life*. New York, N.Y.: Routledge, 1998.

Kahn, David. *Scriptwork: A Director's Approach to New Play Development; With a Foreword by Lanford Wilson*. Carbondale, Ill.: Southern Illinois University Press, 1995.

Kissel, Howard. *David Merrick, The Abominable Showman: The Unauthorized Biography*. New York: Applause, 1993.

Koster, Robert. *The On Production Budget Book*. Boston: Focal Press, 1997.

Langley, Stephen. *Theatre Management and Production in America: Commercial, Stock, Resident, College, Community, and Presenting Organizations*. New York: Drama Book Publishers, 1990.

Lee, Robert L. (Robert LeRoy). *Everything About Theatre: The Guidebook of Theatre Fundamentals*. Colorado Springs, Colo.: Meriwether Pub., 1996.

Leon, Ruth. *Applause New York's Guide to the Performing Arts*. New York: Applause Theatre Book Publishers, 1991.

Levison, Louise. *Filmmakers and Financing: Business Plans for Independents*. 2nd ed. Boston: Focal Press, 1998.

Litherland, Janet. *Broadway Costumes On a Budget: Big-time Ideas for Amateur Producers*. 1st ed. Colorado Springs, Colo.: Meriwether Pub., 1996.

Morrow, Lee Alan and Pike, Frank, eds. *Creating Theater: The Professionals' Approach to New Plays*. New York: Vintage Books, 1986.

Pike, Frank & Thomas G. Dunn. *The Playwright's Handbook*. Rev. ed. New York: Plume Book, 1996.

Rodgers, James W. *Play Director's Survival Kit: A Complete Step-by-Step Guide to Producing Theater in any School or Community Setting*. West Nyack, N.Y.: Center for Applied Research in Education, 1995.

Rosso, Henry A. *Achieving Excellence in Fund Raising: A Comprehensive Guide to Principles, Strategies, and Methods*. foreword by Robert L. Payton. San Francisco: Jossey-Bass Publishers, 1991.

Schlaich, Joan, ed. ... [et al.]. *Dance: The Art of Production*. 3rd ed. Hightstown, N.J.: Princeton Book Co., 1998.

Singer, Dana. *Stage Writers Handbook: A Complete Business Guide for Playwrights, Composers, Lyricists, and Librettists*. New York: Theatre Communications Group, 1997.

Schneider, Richard E. *The Theater Management Handbook*. Cincinnati, Ohio: Betterway Books, 1999.

Swanson, Dwight. *The Play Book: A Complete Guide to Quality Productions for Christian Schools and Churches*. Glen Rose, Texas: Promise Productions, Inc., 1995.

Telford, Robert S. *Handbook for Theatrical Production Managers: A Community Theatre System That Really Works*. New York: S. French, 1983.

Williamson, Walter. *Behind the Scenes: The Unseen People Who Make Theater Work*. New York: Walker, 1987.

Wright, Michael. *Playwriting-in-Process: Thinking and Working Theatrically*. Portsmouth, N.H.: Heinemann, 1997.

Books on Budgeting

Baker, Sunny. *On Time/On Budget: A Step-by-Step Guide for Managing Any Project*. Englewood Cliffs, N.J.: Prentice-Hall, 1992.

Chadwick, Annie. *Showbiz Bookkeeper: The Tax Record keeping System for Professionals Working Arts*. New York: Theatre Directors Pub., 1992.

Eisen, Peter J. *Accounting the Easy Way*. 3rd ed. Hauppauge, N.Y.: Barron's, 1995.

Jay, Ros. *Marketing On a Budget*. Boston: International Thomson Pub. Europe, 1998.

Kremer, John. *High-Impact Marketing On a Low-impact Budget: 101 Strategies to Turbo-charge Your Business Today*. Rocklin, Calif.: Prima Pub., 1997.

Label, Wayne. *10 Minute Guide to Accounting for Non-accountants*. New York: Macmillan, 1998.

Lawrence, Judy. *The Money Tracker: A Quick and Easy Way to Keep Tabs on Your Spending*. Dearborn, 1996.

Lawrence, Judy. *The Budget Kit: The Common Cent$ Money Management Workbook*. 2nd ed. Chicago, Ill.: Dearborn Financial, 1997.

Lewis, James P. *Project Planning, Scheduling & Control: A Hands-on Guide to Bringing Projects In On Time and On Budget*. Rev. ed. Chicago, Ill.: Irwin, 1995.

Muckian, Michael. *The Complete Idiot's Guide to Finance and Accounting*. New York, N.Y.: Alpha Books, 1998.

Rice, Craig S. *Marketing Without a Marketing Budget: How to Find Customers Yesterday, On a Shoestring, Without Fouling Up Your Schedule Any Worse Than It Already Is*. Holbrook, Mass.: B. Adams, 1989.

Tracy, John A. *Accounting for Dummies*. Foster City, Calif.: IDG Books Worldwide, 1997.

Turk, Frederick. *Financial Management Strategies for Arts Organizations*. New York: America for the Arts, 1986.

Wehle, Mary M. *Financial Management for Arts Organizations*. Cambridge, Mass.: Arts Administration Research Institute, 1975.

Williams, Paul B. *Getting a Project Done On Time: Managing People, Time, and Results*. New York: AMACOM, 1996.

Books on Fund-Raising

Allen, Nick, ed. *Fundraising On the Internet: Recruiting and Renewing Donors online*. Berkeley, Calif.: Strathmoor Press, 1996.

Blasius, Chip. *Earning More Funds: Effective Proven Fundraising Strategies for All Non-profit Groups*. B.C. Creations, 1995.

Burlingame, Dwight. *Critical Issues in Fund Raising*. New York: John Wiley and Sons, 1997.

Burke, Mary Ann. *Creative Fund-Raising*. Menlo Park, Calif.: Crisp Publications, 1993.

Edles, L. Peter. *Fundraising: Hands-on Tactics for Nonprofit Groups*. New York: McGraw-Hill, 1993.

Flanagan, Joan. *The Grass Roots Fundraising Book: How to Raise Money In Your Community*. Chicago: Contemporary Books, 1992.

Freedman, Harry A. *The Business of Special Events: Fundraising Strategies for Changing Times*. Sarasota, Fla: Pineapple Press, 1998.

Grace, Kay Sprinkel. *Beyond Fund Raising: New Strategies for Nonprofit Innovation and Investment*. New York: John Wiley and Sons, 1997.

Henley, Michael J. *Fund Raising & Marketing In the One-Person Shop: Achieving Success With Limited Resources*. Minneapolis, Minn.: Development Resource Center, 1997.

Hopkins, Karen Brooks. *Successful Fundraising for Arts and Cultural Organizations*. 2nd ed. Phoenix, Ariz.: Oryx Press, 1997.

Johnston, Michael W. *The Fund Raiser's Guide to the Internet*. New York: John Wiley and Sons, 1998.

Keegan, P. Burke. *Fundraising for Non-Profits*. New York: Harper Perennial, 1994.

Klein, Kim. *Fundraising for Social Change*. 3rd ed. Inverness, Calif.: Chardon Press, 1994.

Kuniholm, Roland. *The Complete Book of Model Fund-Raising Letters*. Englewood Cliffs, N.J.: Prentice-Hall, 1995.

Lewis, Herschell Gordon. *How To Write Powerful Fund Raising Letters*. Chicago: Pluribus Press, 1989.

Panas, Jerold. *Born to Raise*. Chicago, Ill.: Pluribus Press, 1988.

Poderis, Tony. *It's a Great Day to Fund-Raise: A Veteran Campaigner Reveals the Development Tips and Techniques That Will Work for You*. Cleveland, Ohio: FundAmerica Press, 1996.

Reiss, Alvin H. *Don't Just Applaud, Send Money: The Most Succesful Strategies for Funding and Marketing the Arts*. New York: Theatre Communications Group, 1995.

Rosso, Henry A. *Achieving Excellence in Fund Raising: A Comprehensive Guide to Principles, Strategies, and Methods*. San Francisco: Jossey-Bass Publishers, 1991.

Warwick, M. *999 Tips Trends and Guidelines for Successful Direct Mail and Telephone Fundraising*. Berkeley, Calif: Strathmore Press, 1995.

Warwick, Mal. *How to Write Successful Fundraising Letters*. Berkeley, Calif.: Strathmoor Press, 1994.

Books on Theater Space

American Theatre Planning Board. *Theatre Check List: A Guide to the Planning and Construction of Proscenium and Open Stage Theatres With Drawings by Ming Cho Lee*. Middletown, Conn.: Wesleyan University Press; Scranton, Pa. , 1969.

Breuel, Brian H. *The Complete Idiot's Guide to Buying Insurance and Annuities*.New York, N.Y.: Alpha Books, 1996.

Bury, Don. *The Buyer's Guide to Business Insurance*. Grant's Pass, Ore.: Oasis Press/PSI Research, 1994.

Corry, Percy. *Planning the Stage*. London: Pitman Publishing Co., 1961.

Diamantes, David. *Fire Prevention: Inspection and Code Enforcement*. Albany: Delmar Publishers, 1998.

Elder, Eldon. *Will It Make a Theatre: Find, Renovate & Finance the Non-Traditional Performance Space*. New York: ACA Books , 1993.

Halfmann, Janet. *Theaters*. Mankato, Minn.: Creative Education, 1999.

Izenour, George C. *Theater Technology*. 2nd ed. New Haven: Yale University Press, 1996.

McAuley, Gay. *Space In Performance: Making Meaning In the Theatre*. Ann Arbor: University of Michigan Press, 1999.

New York City Fire Law Handbook: Title 15, Fire Prevention and Control, and Title 27, Chapter 4, Fire Prevention Code (of the New York City administrative code). Binghamton, N.Y.: Gould Publications, 1987.

Reid, Francis. *Stages for Tomorrow: Housing, Funding, and Marketing Live Performances*. Boston: Focal Press, 1998.

Russell, David. *Insuring the Bottom Line: How to Protect Your Business From Liabilities, Catastrophes, and Other Business Risk*. Santa Monica, Calif.: Merritt Pub., 1996.

Stollard, Paul. *Fire From First Principles: A Design Guide to Building Fire Safety*. 3rd ed. New York: E & F Spon, 1999.

Books on the Producing Team

Alberts, David. *Rehearsal Management for Directors*. Portsmouth, N.H.: Heinemann, 1995.

Brem, Caroline. *Are We On the Same Team? Essential Communication Skills to Make Groups Work*. Allen & Unwin, 1995.

Buerki, F. A. *Stagecraft for Nonprofessionals*. A new edition revised and updated by Susan J. Christensen. Madison, Wis.: University of Wisconsin Press, 1983.

Clark, I. E. *Stagecrafters' Handbook: A Guide for Theatre Technicians*. 3rd ed. Studio City, Calif.: Players Press, 1995.

Cohen, Robert. *Acting Professionally: Raw Facts About Careers in Acting*. 5th ed. Mountain View, Calif.: Mayfield Pub. Co., 1998.

Cunningham, Glen. *Stage Lighting Revealed: A Design and Execution Handbook.* Cincinnati, Ohio: Betterway Books, 1993.

Gillette, J. Michael. *Theatrical Design and Production: An Introduction to Scene Design and Construction, Lighting, Sound, Costume, and Makeup*. 3rd ed. Mountain View, Calif.: Mayfield Pub. Co., 1997.

Glenn Alterman, ed. *The Job Book: 100 Acting Jobs for Actors*. Lyme, N.H.: Smith and Kraus, 1995.

Glerum, Jay O. *Stage Rigging Handbook.*: 2nd ed. Carbondale, Ill.: Southern Illinois University Press, 1997.

Hays, David. *Light On the Subject: Stage Lighting for Directors and Actors —And the Rest of Us*. New York: Limelight Editions, 1989.

Henry, Mari Lyn. *How To Be a Working Actor: The Insider's Guide to Finding Jobs In Theater, Film, and Television*. 3rd ed. New York: Back Stage Books, 1994.

Holt, Michael. *Stage Design and Properties*. Phaidon Press, 1995.

Ionazzi, Daniel A. *The Stagecraft Handbook*. Cincinnati, Ohio: Betterway Books, 1996.

Kayser, Thomas A. *Building Team Power: How to Unleash the Collaborative Genius of Work Teams*. Burr Ridge, Ill.: Irwin Professional Pub., 1994.

Kelly, Thomas A. *The Back Stage Guide to Stage Management*. 2nd ed. New York: Back Stage Books, 1999.

Lord, William H. *Stagecraft 1: A Complete Guide to Backstage Work*. 2nd ed. Colorado Springs, Colo: Meriwether Pub., 1991.

Luere, Luere, ed. *Playwright Versus Director: Authorial Intentions and Performance Interpretations*. Westport, Conn.: Greenwood Press, 1994.

Luere, Jeane and Berger, Sidney, eds. *The Theatre Team: Playwright, Producer, Director, Designers, and Actors*. Westport, Conn.: Greenwood Press, 1998.

Miller, James Hull. *Stage Lighting In the Boondocks: A Layman's Handbook of Down-to-Earth Methods of Lighting Theatricals With Limited Resources*. 4th ed. Colorado Springs, Colo.: Meriwether Pub., 1995.

Moran, Linda. . . . [et al.]. *Keeping Teams On Track: What To Do When the Going Gets Rough*. Chicago: Irwin Professional Pub., 1996.

O'Neil, Brian. *Acting as a Business: Strategies for Success*. Portsmouth, N.H.: Heinemann, 1993.

Stephen A. Schrum, ed. *Theatre in Cyberspace: Issues of Teaching, Acting and Directing*. New York: P. Lang, 1999.

Stern, Lawrence. *Stage Management*. 6th ed. Boston: Allyn and Bacon, 1998.

Vilga, Edward. *Acting Now: Conversations On Craft and Career*. New Brunswick, N.J.: Rutgers University Press, 1997.

Young, James Webb. *A Technique for Producing Ideas*. Lincolnwood, Ill.: NTC Business Books, 1997.

Books on Theater Law and Taxes

Adams, Paul. *155 Legal Do's (and don'ts) for the Small Business*. New York: John Wiley & Sons, 1996.

Hanlon, R. Brendon. *A Guide to Taxes and Record-Keeping for Performers, Designers, and Directors*. New York: Drama Book Specialists, 1980.

Herrick K. Lidstone, ed. *A Tax Guide for Artists and Arts Organizations*. Mass.: Lexington Books, 1979.

Hummel, Joan M. *Starting and Running a Nonprofit Organization*. 2nd ed. Minneapolis: University of Minnesota Press, 1996.

Jarvis, Susan S. *Basic Law for Small Businesses*. Minneapolis/St. Paul: West Pub. Co., 1997.

Litwak, Mark. *Contracts for the Film & Television Industry*. 2nd ed., expanded. Los Angeles: Silman-James Press, 1998.

Litwak, Mark. *Litwak's Multimedia Producer's Handbook: A Legal and Distribution Guide*. 1st ed. Los Angeles: Silman-James Press, 1998.

Mancuso, Anthony. *How to Form a Nonprofit Corporation*. 4th ed. Berkeley, Calif.: Nolo Press, 1997.

Morgan, Patricia T. *Tax Procedure and Tax Fraud In a Nutshell*. 2nd. ed. St. Paul, Minn.: West Group, 1999.

Nicholas, Ted. *The Complete Guide to Nonprofit Corporations*. Dearborn, Mich.: Enterprise, 1993.

Pinson, Linda. *Keeping the Books: Basic Recordkeeping and Accounting for the Small Business Plus Up-to-Date Tax Information*. 4th ed. Chicago: Upstart Pub. Co., 1998.

Taubman, Joseph. *Performing Arts Management and Law*. Law-Arts Publishers, 1972.

Tyson, Eric. *Taxes for Dummies*. IDG Books Worldwide, 1998.

Volunteer Lawyers for the Arts. *To Be or Not to Be: An Artists Guide to Not for Profit Incorporation*. Volunteer Lawyers for the Arts Pub., 1986.

Books on Box Office and House Management

Apperson, Linda. *Stage Managing and Theatre Etiquette: A Basic Guide*. Chicago: Ivan R. Dee, 1998.

Beck, Kirsten. *How to Run a Small Box Office*. New York: Alliance of Resident Theaters, 1980.

Turk, Frederick. *Financial Management Strategies For Arts Organizations*. New York: Americans for the Arts, 1986.

Books on Marketing

Adkins, Val. *Creating Brochures & Booklets*. Cincinnati: North Light Books, 1994.

Arntson, Amy E. *Graphic Design Basics*. 3rd ed. Fort Worth, Texas: Harcourt Brace College Publishers, 1998.

Bacon, Mark S. *Do-It-Yourself Direct Marketing: Secrets for Small Business*. 2nd ed. New York: John Wiley & Sons, 1997.

Bjorkegren, Dag. *The Organization of Art: Management Strategies for the Arts-Related Business*. London and New York: Routledge, 1996.

Grant, Daniel. *The Business of Being an Artist*. Rev. ed. New York: Allworth Press, 1996.

Hahn, Fred E. *Do-it-Yourself Advertising and Promotion: How to Produce Great Ads, Brochures, Catalogs, Direct Mail, Web Sites and more*. 2nd ed. New York: John Wiley & Sons, 1997.

Hatch, Denison. *Method Marketing: How to Make a Fortune by Getting Inside the Heads of Your Customers*. Chicago, Ill.: Bonus Books, 1999.

Hiam, Alexander. *Marketing for Dummies*. Foster City, Calif.: IDG Books Worldwide, 1997.

Hofacker, Charles F. *Internet Marketing*. Dripping Springs, Texas: Digital Springs, 1999.

Kotler, Philip, and Scheff, Joanne. *Standing Room Only: Strategies for Marketing the Performing Arts*. Boston, Mass.: Harvard Business School Press, 1997.

Levinson, Jay Conrad. *Guerrilla Marketing Excellence: The 50 Golden Rules for Small-business Success*. Boston: Houghton Mifflin Co., 1993.

Levitt, Theodore. *The Marketing Imagination*. New York: Free Press, 1986.

Melillo, Joseph. *Market the Arts*. New York: Arts Action Issues, 1995.

Peithman, Stephen, and Offen, Neil, eds. *The Stage Directions Guide to Getting and Keeping Your Audience*. Portsmouth, N.H.: Heinemann, 1999.

Pinskey, Raleigh. *101 Ways to Promote Yourself*. New York: Avon Books, 1997.

Ries, Al and Trout, Jack. *The 22 Immutable Laws of Marketing: Violate Them at Your Own Risk!* New York: Harper Collins, 1994.

Ritchie, Karen. *Marketing to Generation X*. New York: Lexington Books, 1995.

Russell, James. *Screen and Stage Marketing Secrets*. James Russell Pub, 1998.

Sargeant, Adrian. *Marketing Management for Nonprofit Organizations*. New York: Oxford University Press, 1999.

Schulberg, Pete. *Radio Advertising: The Authoritative Handbook*. 2nd ed.Lincolnwood, Ill.: NTC Business Books, 1996.

Shaw, Lisa Angowski Rogak. *1,001 Ways to Market Yourself and Your Small Business*. New York: Berkley Publishing Group, 1997.

Smith, Bud E. *Marketing Online for Dummies*. Foster City, Calif.: IDG Books Worldwide, 1998.

Sugarman, Joseph. *Advertising Secrets of the Written Word: The Ultimate Resource On How to Write Powerful Advertising Copy From One of America's Top Copywriters and Mail Order Entrepreneurs*. Las Vegas, Nev.: DelStar, 1998.

White, Sarah. *The Complete Idiot's Guide to Marketing Basics*. New York: Alpha Books, 1997.

Wilson, Jerry. *Word of Mouth Marketing*. New York: John Wiley & Sons, 1994.

Books on Publicity

Borden, Kay. *Bulletproof News Releases: Practical, No-Holds-Barred Advice for Small Business From 135 American Newspaper Editors*. Marietta, Ga.: Franklin-Sarrett Publishers, 1994.

McArthur, Nancy. *How To Do Theatre Publicity*. Bevea, Ohio: Good Ideas Company, 1978.

McIntyre, Catherine V. *Writing Effective News Releases: How To Get Free Publicity For Yourself, Your Business, or Your Organization*. Colorado Springs, Colo.: Piccadilly Books, 1992.

O'Keefe, Steve. *Publicity On the Internet: Creating Successful Publicity Campaigns on the Internet and the Commercial Online Service*. New York: John Wiley & Sons, 1997.

Peithman, Stephen. ed. *The Stage Directions Guide to Publicity*. Portsmouth, N.H.: Heinemann, 1999.

Pinskey, Raleigh. *You Can Hype Anything*. Secaucus, N.J.: Carol Pub. Group, 1995.

Pinskey, Raleigh. *101 Ways to Promote Yourself*. New York: Avon Books, 1997.

Saffir, Leonard. *Power Public Relations: How To Get PR To Work For You*. Lincolnwood, Ill.: NTC Business Books, 1993.

Solano, Sheila. *You and the Media: A "How-To" Publicity Handbook for Non-profit Organizations*. OTR Publications, 1990.

Wade, John. *Dealing Effectively With the Media*. Los Altos, Calif.: Crisp Publications, 1992.

Wilcox, Dennis L. *Public Relations: Strategies and Tactics*. 5th ed. New York: Longman, 1998.

Yale, David R. *The Publicity Handbook*. Lincolnwood, Ill. : NTC Business Books, 1991.

Yale, David R. *Publicity and Media Relations Checklists: 59 Proven Checklists to Save Time, Win Attention, & Maximize Exposure with Every Public Relations & Publicity Contact*. Lincolnwood, Ill.: NTC Business Books, 1995.

Yudkin, Marcia. *6 Steps to Free Publicity and Dozens of Other Ways to Win Free Media Attention For You or Your Business*. New York: Plume, 1994.

Books on Agents and Producers

Callan, K. *Directing Your Directing Career: The Resource Book and Agent Guide for Directors*. Sweden Press, 1993.

Callan, K. *The New York Agent Book*. Sweden Press, 1997.

Callan, K. *The Los Angeles Agent Book*. Sweden Press, 1998.

Cohen, Robert. *Acting Professionally: Raw Facts About Careers In Acting*.: 5th ed. Mountain View, Calif.: Mayfield Pub. Co., 1998.

Henry, Mari Lyn. *How To Be a Working Actor: The Insider's Guide to Finding Jobs In Theater, Film, and Television*. 3rd ed. New York: Back Stage Books, 1994.

Hurtes, Hettie Lynne. *The Back Stage Guide to Casting Directors*. New York: Watson-Guptill Publishers, 1998.

Joseph, Erik. *The Glam Scam: Successfully Avoiding the Casting Couch and Other Talent and Modeling Scams*. Los Angeles: Lone Eagle Pub. Co., 1994.

Kondazian, Karen. *The Complete Actors Encyclopedia of Casting Directors*.Los Angeles, Calif.: Lone Eagle Pub., 1999.

O'Neil, Brian. *Acting as a Business: Strategies for Success*. Portsmouth, N.H.: Heinemann, 1993.

O'Neil, Brian. *Actors Take Action: A Career Guide for the Competitive Actor*. Portsmouth, N.H.: Heinemann, 1996.

Searle, Judith. *Getting the Part: Thirty-three Professional Casting Directors Tell You How to Get Work In Theater, Films, Commercials, and TV*. New York: Limelight Editions, 1995.

Small, Edgar. *From Agent to Actor: An Unsentimental Education, Or What the Other Half Knows*. Hollywood: S. French, 1991.

The Little Black Book:
Useful Contacts for Theater Producers

Alabama

Showbiz Theatrical Service
2960 Old Shell Road, Mobile, AL 36607
(334) 473-2053

United Stage Equipment Inc
110 Short Street Southeast, Hartselle, AL 35640
(256) 773-2585

Alaska

DLS Supply
530 West 72nd Avenue, Anchorage, AK 99518
(907) 522-4660

Arizona

Arizona CINE Equipment
2125 East 20th Street, Tucson, AZ 85719
(520) 623-8268

Arizona Professional Sound
1035 South Tyndall Avenue, Tucson, AZ 85719
(520) 884-8550

Creative Designs In Lighting
1900 East Indian School Road, Phoenix, AZ 85016
(602) 248-7822

Illumination Station
7th Street & East Monroe Street, Phoenix, AZ 85034
(602) 307-9592

JR Russell Systems
4800 South 36th Street, Phoenix, AZ 85040
(602) 276-4800

Marich Associates
1920 East Rio Salado Pkwy, Tempe, AZ 85281
(480) 303-9482

Performance Systems
1033 South Tyndall Avenue, Tucson, AZ 85719
(520) 629-0295

Rhino Staging Productions Inc
600 West 1st Street, Tempe, AZ 85281
(480) 894-6131

Sets Etc
7232 East 1st Street, Scottsdale, AZ 85251
(480) 949-8610

Snellstrom Lighting-Entrtn
PO Box 27812, Tucson, AZ 85726
(520) 747-2279

Sonora Theatre Works Inc
210 West 5th Street 2, Tucson, AZ 85705
(520) 620-0846

Sunbelt Scenic Studios Inc
8980 South McKemy Street, Tempe, AZ 85284
(480) 598-0181

Wig-O-Rama
98 East Congress Street, Tucson, AZ 85701
(520) 882-8003

Arkansas

Golden Grotto
1717 Stadium Boulevard, Jonesboro, AR 72401
(870) 935-8336

Spectrum Production & Service
13401 Chenal Pkwy, Little Rock, AR 72211
(501) 228-9999

Stageworks
1510 Main Street, Little Rock, AR 72202
(501) 375-2243

Theater Group Corporation
2024 Arkansas Valley Drive, Little Rock, AR 72212
(501) 223-3529

California

20th Century Props
11651 Hart Street, North Hollywood, CA 91605
(818) 759-1190

A1 Dance & Theatrical
22120 Redwood Road, Castro Valley, CA 94546
(510) 537-8288

American Fencers Supply Company
1180 Folsom Street, San Francisco, CA 94103
(415) 863-7911

Anchor Rigging Corporation
4632 1/2 Hollywood Boulevard, Los Angeles, CA 90027
(323) 661-1029

Ariel Theatrical Warehouse
Fort Ord, Seaside, CA 93955
(831) 884-9823

Art Deco LA Prop House
7007 Lankershim Boulevard, North Hollywood, CA 91605
(818) 765-5653

Arts Information Hot Line
644 South Figueroa Street, Los Angeles, CA 90017
(213) 688-2787

Assigned Seating
102 California Avenue, La Puente, CA 91744
(626) 333-4464

B & R Scenery
3675 Old Conejo Road, Newbury Park, CA 91320
(805) 498-6581

Bay Theatrical
455 Reservation Road, Marina, CA 93933
(831) 443-5773

Black Point Productions
201 Channel Drive, Novato, CA 94945
(415) 897-7482

Black Sheep Enterprises
15745 Stagg Street, Van Nuys, CA 91406
(818) 909-2299

Branam Enterprises Rigging
13345 Constable Avenue, Granada Hills, CA 91344
(818) 368-9793

Burman Industries Inc
14141 Covello Street Building 10C, Van Nuys, CA 91405
(818) 782-9833

California Seating
12455 Branford Street, Arleta, CA 91331
(818) 890-7328

California Stage & Lighting
3211 West Macarthur Boulevard, Santa Ana, CA 92704
(714) 966-1852

California Theatrical Supply
132 9th Street Fl 2, San Francisco, CA 94103
(415) 863-9236

Center Stage
895 Jackson Street 301, Napa, CA 94559
(707) 255-1895

DeClercq's Theatrical Spec
724 Kevin Court, Oakland, CA 94621
(510) 633-5110

Dongjin Wig Industry Company Limited
1107 North Western Avenue, Los Angeles, CA 90029
(323) 461-8332

EC Prop Rentals Inc
6905 Beck Avenue, North Hollywood, CA 91605
(818) 764-2008

Edwin Shirley Staging
956 Seward Street, Los Angeles, CA 90038
(323) 461-2182

Entertainment Equipment Corporation
6363 Santa Monica Boulevard, Los Angeles, CA 90038
(323) 871-2194

Film Actors Workshop
2050 South Bundy Drive, Los Angeles, CA 90025
(310) 442-9488

Gil Draper Props
2595 Fair Oaks Avenue, Altadena, CA 91001
(626) 797-5411

Gimmicks Unlimited
16214 Arrow Highway, Irwindale, CA 91706
(626) 338-0773

GLB Manufacturing
22313 Meekland Avenue, Hayward, CA 94541
(510) 889-7795

Goodies Props
9990 Glenoaks Boulevard B, Sun Valley, CA 91352
(818) 252-1892

Grosh Scenic Studios
4114 West Sunset Boulevard, Los Angeles, CA 90029
(323) 662-1134

H & H Specialties Inc
2214 Merced Avenue, South El Monte, CA 91733
(626) 448-8538

Hair Unlimited
36 North Euclid Avenue C, National City, CA 91950
(619) 264-2222

Halgo Specialties Company
16760 Stagg Street 209, Van Nuys, CA 91406
(818) 786-4436

Harlequin's Theatrical Supply
17 West Gutierrez Street, Santa Barbara, CA 93101
(805) 963-1209

Hollywood International
11319 Vanowen Street, North Hollywood, CA 91605
(818) 752-0900

Lamplighters Music Theatre
2885 Adeline Street, Oakland, CA 94608
(510) 832-7351

Legend Productions
782 Park Avenue, San Jose, CA 95126
(408) 279-3533

Lentor Production
9540 Pathway Street, Santee, CA 92071
(619) 448-1170

Lewis Studio Equipment
350 East Todd Road, Santa Rosa, CA 95407
(707) 585-6228

Lexington Scenery & Props
10443 Arminta Street, Sun Valley, CA 91352
(818) 768-5768

Liberty Theatrical Decor
22313 Meekland Avenue, Hayward, CA 94541
(510) 889-1951

Luners Professional Sound & Lighting
534 North Milpas Street, Santa Barbara, CA 93103
(805) 963-7756

Majestic Productions West
2335 University Avenue, San Diego, CA 92104
(619) 291-1010

MGI Studio Backdrops
2565 3rd Street 319, San Francisco, CA 94107
(415) 647-7424

Musson Theatrical Inc
890 Walsh Avenue, Santa Clara, CA 95050
(408) 986-0210

Norsaco Products
16760 Stagg Street 209, Van Nuys, CA 91406
(818) 780-3326

Oakland United Studios
724 Kevin Court, Oakland, CA 94621
(510) 633-5110

Omega Cinema Props
5857 Santa Monica Boulevard, Los Angeles, CA 90038
(323) 466-8201

Pantechnicon
941 Berryessa Road B, San Jose, CA 95133
(408) 453-8000

Peterson Lighting Productions
4897 Mercury Street, San Diego, CA 92111
(619) 277-0260

Phoebus Lighting
2800 3rd Street, San Francisco, CA 94107
(415) 550-0770

Phoenix Productions
2415 De La Cruz Boulevard, Santa Clara, CA 95050
(408) 970-8802

Production Fabrics
7528 Clybourn Avenue, Sun Valley, CA 91352
(818) 767-8278

Production Logic Inc
2468 Teagarden Street, San Leandro, CA 94577
(510) 352-1131

Retro
1908 Hyperion Avenue, Los Angeles, CA 90027
(323) 662-4021

Richard The Thread
8320 Melrose Avenue, Los Angeles, CA 90069
(323) 852-4997

RLH Enterprises
9775 Glenoaks Boulevard B, Sun Valley, CA 91352
(818) 768-8608

Rosebrand Textile Inc
10856 Vanowen Street, North Hollywood, CA 91605
(818) 505-6290

S & K Theatrical Drapery
7313 Varna Avenue, North Hollywood, CA 91605
(818) 503-0596

SL Service
1824 Castillo Street, Santa Barbara, CA 93101
(805) 687-6765

Sacramento Theatrical Lighting
950 Richards Boulevard, Sacramento, CA 95814
(916) 447-3258

San Diego Opera Scenic Studio
3064 Commercial Street, San Diego, CA 92113
(619) 232-5911

San Diego Stage & Lighting Inc
2030 El Cajon Boulevard, San Diego, CA 92104
(619) 299-2300

Sets Etc
81 Bluxome Street, San Francisco, CA 94107
(415) 512-7833

Show Biz Drapery Enterprises
15541 Lanark Street, Van Nuys, CA 91406
(818) 989-5005

ShowBiz Enterprises, Inc.
15541 Lanark Street, Van Nuys, CA 91406
(818) 989-5005

Showboy Original Dancewear
34 South 15th Street, San Jose, CA 95112
(408) 295-2891

Sound & Light Source Inc
3429 East Street 18, North Highlands, CA 95660
(916) 334-1888

Stage Door Lighting
9080 Activity Road B, San Diego, CA 92126
(619) 586-1334

Stage Lights
14948 Avenida Venusto Suite 21, San Diego, CA 92128
(619) 487-5195

Stage Lights.com
14948 Avenida Venusto, Suite 21, San Diego, CA 92128
(619) 487-5195

Stage Rigging Inc
913 Tanklage Road, San Carlos, CA 94070
(650) 595-2716

Stagecraft Studios
1854 Alcatraz Avenue, Berkeley, CA 94703
(510) 653-4424

Stages Unlimited
175 West Julian Street, San Jose, CA 95110
(408) 298-7146

Stembridge Rentals Inc
431 Magnolia Avenue, Glendale, CA 91204
(818) 246-4333

Stroup Studios
6310 Nancy Ridge Drive 107, San Diego, CA 92121
(619) 587-9809

Surplus City
4514 Pacific Heights Road, Oroville, CA 95965
(530) 534-1454

T & S Rigging
2355 Chain Drive, Simi Valley, CA 93065
(805) 520-9499

Technical Directions Special
Bellflower, CA 90706
(562) 920-2332

Technical Show Management Inc
3797 Old Conejo Road, Newbury Park, CA 91320
(805) 499-0097

Tegtmeier Associates Inc
PO Box 776, Menlo Park, CA 94026
(650) 324-4335

That's Sew Business
744 G Street 205, San Diego, CA 92101
(619) 544-9663

The Armour Store
5178 Acuna Street, San Diego, CA 92117
(619) 505-9761

Theater Specialty Products
1320 Simpson Way, Escondido, CA 92029
(760) 739-1521

Theatre Company
1400 North Benson Avenue, Upland, CA 91786
(909) 982-5736

Theatre Products International
19151 Parthenia Street, Northridge, CA 91324
(818) 886-8611

Theatrical Hair Goods Company
130 9th Street, San Francisco, CA 94103
(415) 626-6966

Theatrical Resources
6880 Beck Avenue, North Hollywood, CA 91605
(818) 765-0965

Theatre Service & Supply
9582 Topanga Canyon Boulevard, Chatsworth, CA 91311
(818) 701-4475

Theatrical Specialties
4211 Verdant Street, Los Angeles, CA 90039
(818) 244-2232

TPS Inc
4452 Park Boulevard, San Diego, CA 92116
(619) 293-0756

Triangle Scenery Drapery Company
1215 Bates Avenue, Los Angeles, CA 90029
(323) 662-8129

Ukiah Theatrical Supply
154 Freitas Avenue, Ukiah, CA 95482
(707) 462-5031

Upstage Design & Rental
2105 Camino Vida Roble, Carlsbad, CA 92009
(760) 438-2565

Upstage Parallel
1955 Blake Avenue H, Los Angeles, CA 90039
(323) 478-7012

Valley Theatre Fabrications
7013 Darby Avenue, Reseda, CA 91335
(818) 705-7544

Victorville Stage & Prop
16040 Tokay Street, Victorville, CA 92392
(760) 241-0744

Ward Rigging
11211 Rugh Street, Garden Grove, CA 92840
(714) 636-4866

West Coast Theatrical
4671 Alger Street, Los Angeles, CA 90039
(818) 240-8797

World of Magic
PO Box 4575, Santa Barbara, CA 93140
(805) 966-6666

Colorado

Barbizon Light of The Rockies
2390 Syracuse Street, Denver, CO 80207
(303) 394-9875

Berland Technical Service
229 Vallejo Street, Denver, CO 80223
(303) 744-3500

Chair Rental Stage Company
2675 South Tejon Street, Englewood, CO 80110
(303) 936-0794

Corona Stage Lighting
3110 North Stone Avenue B, Colorado Springs, CO 80907
(719) 473-8748

Diana Did-It Designs Inc
1839 East Harmony Road, Fort Collins, CO 80528
(970) 226-5062

Dincler's Fabrics
109 Broadway Avenue, Pueblo, CO 81004
(719) 542-1574

Five Star Decor
2637 Durango Drive, Colorado Springs, CO 80910
(719) 390-0255

Just Imagine Playwear
180 Clearwater Road, Carbondale, CO 81623
(970) 963-3306

Karen's Costume Creations
518 West 24th Street, Pueblo, CO 81003
(719) 544-9608

Life of The Party Costumes
137 South College Avenue, Fort Collins, CO 80524
(970) 484-5433

Lighting Services
241 South Cherokee Street, Denver, CO 80223
(303) 722-4747

Maniac Productions
633 Sunnyside Street, Louisville, CO 80027
(303) 661-0920

Opera Shop Inc
2570 31st Street 11, Denver, CO 80216
(303) 455-1888

Pioneer Drama Service
7076 South Alton Way B, Englewood, CO 80112
(303) 779-4035

Professional Staging
5889 Greenwood Plaza Boulevard, Englewood, CO 80111
(303) 773-3808

Scarlett's Costume Closet Inc
121 West Monroe Drive A, Fort Collins, CO 80525
(970) 223-1992

Scenic Production Inc
PO Box 480414, Denver, CO 80248
(303) 455-5014

Scenographics-David Barnes
999 Tejon Street, Denver, CO 80204
(303) 260-7050

Stageco US Inc
8745 Vollmer Road, Colorado Springs, CO 80908
(719) 495-9497

Tankersley Enterprises
5225 West Warren Avenue, Lakewood, CO 80227
(303) 716-0884

Tankersley Enterprises
5255 West Warren Avenue, Denver, CO 80227
(303) 716-0884

Theatrix Inc
1630 West Evans Avenue C, Englewood, CO 80110
(303) 922-0505

Connecticut

All Media
128 Green Pond Road, Sherman, CT 06784
(860) 350-4120

All That Jazz
136 Simsbury Road, Avon, CT 06001
(860) 674-9987

Atlas Scenic Studios Limited
46 Brookfield Avenue, Bridgeport, CT 06610
(203) 334-2130

Cheney Design
115 Bruce Avenue, Stratford, CT 06615
(203) 386-0089

Collinsville Audio Supply
10 Front Street, Collinsville, CT 06022
(860) 693-8815

Connecticut Stage & Movie Supply
143 Whiting Street, Plainville, CT 06062
(860) 747-1232

Drobka Scenic Inc
456 Tolland Street, East Hartford, CT 06108
(860) 528-5184

New England Sound & Light
459 Washington Avenue C, North Haven, CT 06473
(203) 239-5553

Performance Audio
PO Box 2547, Westport, CT 06880
(203) 227-9599

Scenic Art Studios Inc
15 Chapel Street, Norwalk, CT 06850
(203) 838-6262

Show Lighting Corporation
20 Willard Avenue, Berlin, CT 06037
(860) 828-1633

Show Motion Inc
2 Meadow Street, Norwalk, CT 06854
(203) 866-1866

Silver Knight Studio
1084 East Broadway, Milford, CT 06460
(203) 874-8022

Stage Lighting Rental Service
201 Front Street, New Haven, CT 06513
(203) 787-9417

Theatrix Inc
Service available in your area.
(413) 323-7803

United Staging & Rigging Inc
15 Chapel Street, Norwalk, CT 06850
(203) 854-5820

Delaware

DSL Sound
Willow Grove Road, Camden Wyoming, DE 19934
(302) 697-7515

Leon's Inc Custom Interiors
203 North Dupont Highway, New Castle, DE 19720
(302) 328-1560

Light Action Inc
486 First State Boulevard, Newport, DE 19804
(302) 995-7055

Main Light Industries
402 MECO Drive, Wilmington, DE 19804
(302) 998-8017

Weber Prianti Scenic Studio
408 MECO Drive A, Wilmington, DE 19804
(302) 998-7567

Willow Lane Theaterical Supply
1509 Philadelphia Pike, Edgemoor, DE 19809
(302) 792-1883

Washington D.C.

Backstage Inc
2101 P Street Northwest, Washington, DC 20037
(202) 775-1488

Theatrical Technicians Inc
2700 Connecticut Avenue Northwest, Washington, DC 20008
(202) 332-4907

Florida

Adam & Eve Prop Rentals
528 16th Street, West Palm Beach, FL 33407
(561) 655-1022

ASI Production Service Inc
10101 General Drive, Orlando, FL 32824
(407) 240-8080

Asolo Scene Shop
1337 Manhattan Avenue, Sarasota, FL 34237
(941) 366-7771

Bay Stage Lighting Company Inc
310 South Macdill Avenue, Tampa, FL 33609
(813) 877-1089

Brent's Music Headquarters
1936 Courtney Drive, Fort Myers, FL 33901
(941) 936-6909

Choice Wigs
3060 Northwest 79th Street, Miami, FL 33147
(305) 693-1448

Coconut Grove Playhouse Shop
4238 Northwest 37th Avenue, Miami, FL 33142
(305) 633-7467

Dancer-XISE
8498 Southwest 24th Street B, Miami, FL 33155
(305) 225-7377

Dancing Light Photographic
1419 Clearlake Road, Cocoa, FL 32922
(407) 639-0180

Demetrio Scenery Inc
569 West 28th Street, Hialeah, FL 33010
(305) 883-1891

Design Line Inc
9700 Solar Drive, Tampa, FL 33619
(813) 626-5991

Design Source International Inc
13201 Northeast 16th Avenue, North Miami, FL 33161
(305) 893-3430

Effects Manufacturing
1555 Sunshine Drive, Clearwater, FL 33765
(727) 446-2647

Freckles Costume Rentals
5509 Roosevelt Boulevard, Jacksonville, FL 32244
(904) 388-5541

Hayes Equipment & Supply Company
PO Box 593866, Orlando, FL 32859
(407) 857-6810

Heritage Product Resources Inc
2225 East Edgewood Drive 3, Lakeland, FL 33803
(941) 667-1996

Hile's Curtain Specialties
4504 Town North Country Boulevard, Tampa, FL 33615
(813) 886-5464

Interamerica Stage Inc
220 Coastline Road, Sanford, FL 32771
(904) 761-5478

International Cinema Equipment
100 Northeast 39th Street, Miami, FL 33137
(305) 573-7339

Jack Link & Associates Production
1729 Cogswell Street, Rockledge, FL 32955
(407) 636-7231

Jupiter Scenic
603 Commerce Way West, Jupiter, FL 33458
(561) 743-7367

Kenney Drapery Associates
13201 Northeast 16th Avenue, North Miami, FL 33161
(305) 895-2224

Make Believe Costumes
9717 Beach Boulevard, Jacksonville, FL 32246
(904) 645-6337

Martin Professional Inc
3015 Greene Street, Hollywood, FL 33020
(954) 927-3005

Miami Stagecraft Inc
2855 East 11th Avenue, Hialeah, FL 33013
(305) 836-9356

Mr & Mrs Wig
376 Miracle Mile, Coral Gables, FL 33134
(305) 445-3454

Murphy Lighting Systems
622 Virginia Drive, Orlando, FL 32803
(407) 895-7475

Norcostco
442 North Shore Drive, Sarasota, FL 34234
(941) 359-9972

On Location Props & Scenery
9056 Northwest 41st Street, Miami, FL 33178
(305) 477-3138

Orlando Opera Company
1111 North Orange Avenue, Orlando, FL 32804
(407) 426-1717

Orlando Theatrical Supply
2400 East Colonial Drive 28F, Orlando, FL 32803
(407) 895-5555

Phoenix Star International Inc
1715 Independence Boulevard B7, Sarasota, FL 34234
(941) 351-5094

Piper Productions Inc
4560 36th Street, Orlando, FL 32811
(407) 426-7387

Props Warehouse
6541 Powers Avenue, Jacksonville, FL 32217
(904) 443-0003

Scenic Prop Stage Furniture
8034 Northwest 103rd Street 16, Hialeah, FL 33016
(305) 823-0490

Scenic Technologies Aprg Company
1000 Universal Studios Plaza, Orlando, FL 32819
(407) 903-1132

Scenicworks
7343 Presidents Drive, Orlando, FL 32809
(407) 851-9876

Schuler Packaging & Design
401 East Oak Ridge Road, Orlando, FL 32809
(407) 857-7216

Seaside Music Theater
348 2nd Street, Holly Hill, FL 32117
(904) 257-5299

Sew Biz
159 North Central Avenue East, Oviedo, FL 32765
(407) 366-6763

Stage Equipment & Lighting Inc
12250 Northeast 13th Court, North Miami, FL 33161
(305) 891-2010

Stage Equipment & Lighting
4600 36th Street, Orlando, FL 32811
(407) 425-2010

Sunshine Scenic Studio
1370 4th Street, Sarasota, FL 34236
(941) 366-8848

Tvp-Theatre & Video Products
921 Northeast 79th Street, Miami, FL 33138
(305) 754-9136

Vanco Lighting Service
1902 Cypress Lake Drive 100, Orlando, FL 32837
(407) 855-8060

VIKI Parkes' Stars-Tomorrow
2395 Tamiami Trail, Port Charlotte, FL 33952
(352) 624-5485

What's New
1935 Rain Forest Trail, Sarasota, FL 34240
(941) 379-8803

Zebedee Productions
231 Southwest 5th Court, Pompano Beach, FL 33060
(954) 942-0044

Georgia

Adres Prolyte Products
2338 Rowland Avenue, Savannah, GA 31404
(912) 964-5845

ASI Production Service
3700 Wendell Drive Southwest 25, Atlanta, GA 30336
(404) 505-7876

Atlanta Rigging & Staging Inc
1465 Howell Mill Road Northwest, Atlanta, GA 30318
(404) 355-4370

Bairstow Lifting Products Company
1785 Ellsworth IND Boulevard Northwest, Atlanta, GA 30318
(404) 351-2600

Capital City Supply Company
2140 James Jackson Pkwy Northwest B, Atlanta, GA 30318
(404) 792-8424

Current Events
1119 Logan Circle Northwest, Atlanta, GA 30318
(404) 355-4664

Custom Rigging Systems
12 Church Street, Ellaville, GA 31806
(912) 937-5050

Full Circle Lighting Inc
1360 Logan Circle Northwest, Atlanta, GA 30318
(404) 355-1655

Herschel Harrington Scenic Inc
132 10th Street Northeast, Atlanta, GA 30309
(404) 892-0065

Laser & Lighting Design Inc
4744 North Royal Atlanta Drive F, Tucker, GA 30084
(770) 493-9525

Lucky Star Productions
626 Valley Brook Road, Decatur, GA 30033
(404) 294-7002

Performer's Technologies Ear
155 Little John Trail Northeast, Atlanta, GA 30309
(404) 892-0660

Propper Source
1194 Huff Road Northwest, Atlanta, GA 30318
(404) 352-8700

Rich Scenery & Lighting
1354 Talbotton Road D, Columbus, GA 31901
(706) 327-8020

Showmasters Theatrical
4153 Lawrenceville Highway Northwest, Lilburn, GA 30047
(770) 491-0200

TTE Scenic Studios
7575 Ponce DE Leon Circle B, Atlanta, GA 30340
(770) 840-0483

Unique Wigs & Supplies
10479 Alpharetta Street, Roswell, GA 30075
(770) 552-5811

Wig Plaza
820 Ralph David Abernathy Southwest, Atlanta, GA 30310
(404) 752-8949

Hawaii

Act 1 Theatre Design & Productions
47-765 Ahuimanu Loop, Kaneohe, HI 96744
(808) 239-6455

Attco Inc
2855 Koapaka Street, Honolulu, HI 96819
(808) 836-1191

JD Productions
99-1269 Iwaena Street 4, Aiea, HI 96701
(808) 485-0590

Lahaina Towne Costume
1340 Front Street, Lahaina, HI 96761
(808) 667-6013

MDI Productions
3122 Huelani Drive A, Honolulu, HI 96822
(808) 988-6116

Pacific Stage & Lighting Group
2224 Alahao Place 203, Honolulu, HI 96819
(808) 845-6668

Standing Ovation
3880 OMAO Road, Koloa, HI 96756
(808) 742-9216

Idaho

Rocky Mountain Audio-Visual
3601 Chinden Boulevard, Boise, ID 83714
(208) 336-7655

Illinois

Abbott Theatre Equipment Company
430 Country Club Drive, Bensenville, IL 60106
(630) 860-2121

Art Drapery Studios
630 West Lake Street, Chicago, IL 60661
(312) 332-1603

Atlas Bleachers & Stages
11040 South Langley Avenue, Chicago, IL 60628
(773) 785-5401

Becker Studios Inc
2824 West Taylor Street, Chicago, IL 60612
(773) 722-4040

Brent Theatrical Lighting Company
12 Whippoorwill Road, Springfield, IL 62707
(217) 546-9608

Center Stage
497 South Route 59, Aurora, IL 60504
(630) 851-9191

Chicago Canvas & Supply Company
3719 West Lawrence Avenue, Chicago, IL 60625
(773) 478-5700

Chicago Hair Goods Inc
2405 North Milwaukee Avenue, Chicago, IL 60647
(773) 384-1474

Chicago Scenic Studios Inc
1711 West Fullerton Avenue, Chicago, IL 60614
(773) 348-0115

Chicago Spotlight Inc
1658 West Carroll Avenue, Chicago, IL 60612
(312) 455-1171

Cine-Way Service Company
7200 North Claremont Avenue B, Chicago, IL 60645
(773) 764-6093

Costume Shop
643 Center Street, Waukegan, IL 60085
(847) 336-2299

Costume Trunk
710 West Main Street, Peoria, IL 61606
(309) 637-4234

Custom Wigs Limited
4065 North Milwaukee Avenue, Chicago, IL 60641
(773) 777-0222

Designlab Chicago
806 North Peoria Street, Chicago, IL 60622
(312) 738-3305

Dimatronics Inc
6207 Commercial Road, Crystal Lake, IL 60014
(815) 455-4400

Diversitronics Inc
231 Wrightwood Avenue, Elmhurst, IL 60126
(630) 833-4495

GPC Cinema Service
112 Gerry Steven Court, Bensenville, IL 60106
(630) 616-0959

Grand Stage Lighting Company
630 West Lake Street, Chicago, IL 60661
(312) 332-5611

Hawkeye Scenic Studio
4121 North Ravenswood Avenue, Chicago, IL 60613
(312) 421-6737

Katem Theatricals Inc
241 South Madison Avenue, La Grange, IL 60525
(708) 354-3303

Klein David M
20 North Wacker Drive, Chicago, IL 60606
(312) 750-1779

Kling Theatrical Shoe Company
218 South Wabash Avenue 816, Chicago, IL 60604
(312) 427-2028

Kobotech Inc
28 East Jackson Boulevard 520, Chicago, IL 60604
(312) 786-0075

La Brosse Limited
2603 West Barry Avenue, Chicago, IL 60618
(773) 478-7077

Lighting Control Systems
420 Westminster Drive, Burr Ridge, IL 60521
(630) 654-0700

Major Dimming Service
Industrial Drive, Cary, IL 60013
(630) 801-1718

Matthews Owens Studio
735 West Division Street, Chicago, IL 60610
(312) 943-0213

Millennium Events
3355 North Drake Avenue, Chicago, IL 60618
(773) 509-0987

Motion Unlimited
218 South Wabash Avenue, Chicago, IL 60604
(312) 922-3330

North-West Drapery Service Inc
4507 North Milwaukee Avenue, Chicago, IL 60630
(773) 282-7117

Propabilities Inc
1513 North Elston Avenue, Chicago, IL 60622
(773) 278-2384

Scott U Adam Theatrical Supply
1805 South Allport Street, Chicago, IL 60608
(312) 738-0134

SGA Production Staging
103 West Main Street, St Charles, IL 60174
(630) 513-6812

Stage Dynamics
5645 North Ravenswood Avenue, Chicago, IL 60660
(773) 275-4600

Technical Theater Service
2208 Cornell Avenue, Montgomery, IL 60538
(630) 801-1718

Z Antiques & Props
3065 North Rockwell Street, Chicago, IL 60618
(773) 583-0505

Indiana

Audio Service Company
2207 South Michigan Street, South Bend, IN 46613
(219) 287-2111

Glamoure Costume Shop
105 State Street, Hammond, IN 46320
(219) 932-8910

Indianapolis Stage Sales
905 Massachusetts Avenue, Indianapolis, IN 46202
(317) 635-9430

IPA Production Service
4215 Lafayette Road, Indianapolis, IN 46254
(317) 291-3608

McGuire Scenic Inc
2118 Brookside Avenue, Indianapolis, IN 46218
(317) 267-9925

Merrill Stage Equipment
6520 East Westfield Boulevard, Indianapolis, IN 46220
(317) 255-4666

Michele's Stitch N Tyme
14 West Delaware Street, Evansville, IN 47710
(812) 423-0238

Mr Scary Productions
9212 South Old State Road 37, Bloomington, IN 47403
(812) 824-8935

Stage Technology Inc
6425 English Avenue, Indianapolis, IN 46219
(317) 357-6977

Studio One Theatrical Service
25833 State Road 2, South Bend, IN 46619
(219) 232-9084

Iowa

Blackhawk Lighting Company
2515 Dean Avenue, Des Moines, IA 50317
(515) 262-8083

Dowry Costumes & More
2100 Leech Avenue Fl 3, Sioux City, IA 51106
(712) 255-8007

Globe Theatrical Supply
813 Pearl Street, Sioux City, IA 51101
(712) 255-0972

River Cities Sound & Lights
1025 West 4th Street, Davenport, IA 52802
(319) 323-7398

Sound Concepts
837 3rd Avenue Southwest, Cedar Rapids, IA 52404
(319) 366-7357

Theatrical & Industry Design
Bettendorf, IA 52722
(319) 355-6126

Theatrical Shop
145 5th Street, West Des Moines, IA 50265
(515) 274-3661

Kansas

Class Act Lighting & Sound
2324 East Douglas Avenue, Wichita, KS 67214
(316) 265-1286

E P Systems
3060 South 24th Street, Kansas City, KS 66106
(913) 677-6771

High Performance Sound & Light
691 East 90th Avenue North, Belle Plaine, KS 67013
(316) 263-3399

Mc Daniel Grip & Lighting Inc
359 West 29th Street North, Wichita, KS 67204
(316) 838-1100

National Cinema Supply Inc
8246 Marshall Drive, Lenexa, KS 66214
(913) 492-0966

P & D Magic Palace
3658 Southwest Topeka Boulevard, Topeka, KS 66611
(785) 267-3699

Shot In The Dark Productions
319 Maple Lane, Wichita, KS 67209
(316) 946-9644

Systems & Products Engineering
709 North 6th Street, Kansas City, KS 66101
(913) 321-3978

T & M Stage Supplies
602 South Volutsia Street, Wichita, KS 67211
(316) 685-8822

Theatrical Services Inc
128 South Washington Street, Wichita, KS 67202
(316) 263-4415

Wig Shoppe
218 South Edwards Street, Wichita, KS 67213
(316) 263-7440

Kentucky

Costume Gallery
638 Monmouth Street, Newport, KY 41071
(606) 655-9419

Hadden Theatre Supply Company
10201 Bunsen Way, Jeffersontown, KY 40299
(502) 499-0050

River City Productions
6261 Saddle Ridge Road, Burlington, KY 41005
(606) 371-2561

Theatre House Inc
400 West 3rd Street, Covington, KY 41011
(606) 431-2414

Louisiana

Event Lighting Inc
4400 Poche Court West, New Orleans, LA 70129
(504) 254-4411

New Orleans Opera Association
3020 Lausat Street, Metairie, LA 70001
(504) 833-0110

Pyramid & Company
5620 Salmen Street, New Orleans, LA 70123
(504) 522-3947

Stage-Right Productions Inc
8468 Paris Avenue, Baton Rouge, LA 70814
(225) 929-7625

Maine

High Output Inc
101 John Roberts Road 17, South Portland, ME 04106
(207) 761-2828

Moonlighting Production Service
80 2nd Street, South Portland, ME 04106
(207) 767-6177

Maryland

Atlantic Stage Lighting
11 Egges Lane, Catonsville, MD 21228
(410) 525-2525

Baltimore Stage Lighting Inc
10 Azar Court, Baltimore, MD 21227
(410) 242-3322

Baron Stage Curtain Equipment
2617 East Fayette Street, Baltimore, MD 21224
(410) 327-6962

Bash Lighting Service
8900 Yellow Brick Road, Baltimore, MD 21237
(410) 391-8001

Burn Brae Productions
14719 Baltimore Avenue A, Laurel, MD 20707
(301) 317-1377

Cannon Stage Lighting Inc
6707 Dogwood Road, Baltimore, MD 21207
(410) 298-0636

Commercial Sound & Music
85 East Mechanic Street, Frostburg, MD 21532
(301) 689-9505

Crew Works Inc
2701 Saint Paul Street, Baltimore, MD 21218
(410) 235-2037

Electrol Engineering Inc
500 Bynum Road A, Forest Hill, MD 21050
(410) 638-9300

Killowatt Crew Lighting Service
7737 Race Road, Jessup, MD 20794
(410) 799-2929

Kinetic Artistry Inc
7216 Carroll Avenue, Takoma Park, MD 20912
(301) 270-6666

Maryland Stage Lighting
21406 Manor View Circle, Germantown, MD 20876
(301) 972-2252

Metro Technical Service Inc
8659 Cherry Lane, Laurel, MD 20707
(410) 792-9416

Parlights Stage Lighting
16 West 13th Street, Frederick, MD 21701
(301) 698-9242

R & R Lighting Company
813 Silver Spring Avenue, Silver Spring, MD 20910
(301) 589-4997

Roadworx Total Production Service
9300 Martin Luther King Jr Highway,
Lanham Seabrook, MD 20706
(301) 429-0101

Sound Ideas In Sound Engineering
2002 West Street A, Annapolis, MD 21401
(410) 266-9794

Theatre Service & Supply Corporation
1792 Union Avenue, Baltimore, MD 21211
(410) 467-1225

Theatrical Drape Rentals
10 Woodlawn Avenue, Baltimore, MD 21228
(410) 788-4662

Walsh Systems Inc
11519 Mapleview Drive, Silver Spring, MD 20902
(301) 774-6004

Massachusetts

Charlie's Music
14 Plant Road, Hyannis, MA 02601
(508) 771-2307

High Output Inc
184 Everett Street, Allston, MA 02134
(617) 787-4747

Keystone Productions Inc
12 Walnut Hill Park, Woburn, MA 01801
(781) 938-9191

Klondike Sound Company
37 Conte Drive, Greenfield, MA 01301
(413) 772-2900

Limelight Productions
471 Pleasant Street, Lee, MA 01238
(413) 243-4950

Major Theatre Equipment Corporation
190 Dorchester Avenue, Boston, MA 02127
(617) 464-0444

Marlborough Theatrical Technology
136 Main Street, Marlborough, MA 01752
(508) 485-9745

Merrimack Valley Staging Technology
15 Middle Road, Haverhill, MA 01830
(978) 372-8541

Planning Stage
219 Lynn Fells Pkwy, Melrose, MA 02176
(781) 662-3939

RNR Lighting
1211 Massachusetts Avenue, Arlington, MA 02476
(781) 643-4426

Roctronics Lighting & Effects
100-Abi Rocktronics Park, Pembroke, MA 02359
(617) 354-4444

Scenic Art Studios
568 West Union Street, East Bridgewater, MA 02333
(508) 378-7028

Scenic Brands Company
16 Rustic Street, Newton, MA 02458
(617) 244-9388

Starfire Swords Limited
235 Main Street, Carver, MA 02330
(508) 866-9188

Theatrical Arts
450 Harrison Avenue, Boston, MA 02118
(617) 292-2100

Theatrix Inc
636 Daniel Shays Highway, Belchertown, MA 01007
(413) 323-7803 http://www.theatrix.net

Walker Specialties Inc
99 Mahler Road, Roslindale, MA 02131
(617) 524-0700

Michigan

Advanced Lighting & Sound
433 Elmwood Drive, Troy, MI 48083
(248) 589-2842

Blickle Design
447 East D Avenue, Kalamazoo, MI 49004
(616) 349-4286

Cinema Film Systems/Tasa
3820 North Big Spring Drive Southwest, Grandville, MI 49418
(616) 249-9400

Complete Production Systems
212 South Wagner Road 3, Ann Arbor, MI 48103
(734) 995-5686

Corporate Sound Inc
4870 West River Drive Northeast F, Comstock Park, MI 49321
(616) 785-8580

Costume Gallery
4106 Page Avenue, Michigan Center, MI 49254
(517) 764-5893

Costume Rental Service
2442 North Grand River Avenue, Lansing, MI 48906
(517) 321-6672

Fantasy Attic Costumes
305 South Main Street, Ann Arbor, MI 48104
(734) 665-2680

Grand Stage
2743 Coolidge Highway, Berkley, MI 48072
(248) 546-4740

Great Lakes Access Inc
1925 Century Avenue Southwest, Grand Rapids, MI 49509
(616) 248-5438

Levitation Staging Inc
845 Chestnut Street Southwest, Grand Rapids, MI 49503
(616) 742-1174

Mavri Inc
6568 Center Industrial Drive, Jenison, MI 49428
(616) 669-9700

Northwest Studios Inc
36415 Groesbeck Highway, Clinton Twp, MI 48035
(810) 792-1380

Odyssey Lighting
1203 Butterworth Street Southwest, Grand Rapids, MI 49504
(616) 454-4700

On Stage Visuals
420 Baker Street, Lansing, MI 48910
(517) 393-7800

Pegasus Lighting & Stage Equipment
20570 West 8 Mile Road, Southfield, MI 48075
(248) 353-6130

Performance Sound Lighting
41560 Schoolcraft Road, Plymouth, MI 48170
(734) 513-4000

Professional Audio Inc
2825 Dormax Street Southwest, Grandville, MI 49418
(616) 538-8585

Sound EFX
763 West Franklin Street, Jackson, MI 49201
(517) 783-5955

Sound EFX Production
1115 North Washington Avenue, Lansing, MI 48906
(517) 487-6868

Stage Lighting & Sound Inc
616 Portage Street, Kalamazoo, MI 49007
(616) 343-3787

Technology FX
42319 East Ann Arbor Road, Plymouth, MI 48170
(734) 207-0088

Theatricks
1505 Plainfield Avenue Northeast, Grand Rapids, MI 49505
(616) 363-4259

Waco Stage Equipment
7801 Herbst Road, Brighton, MI 48114
(810) 229-6834

Minnesota

A-1 Costume Fabric Shop
729 Hennepin Avenue, Minneapolis, MN 55403
(612) 339-2793

Accent Store Fixtures Inc
835 East Hennepin Avenue, Minneapolis, MN 55414
(612) 379-2788

Audio Professionals
13 Columbia Avenue Southeast, St Cloud, MN 56304
(320) 253-3460

Don-Murnane Wigs
3710 Central Avenue Northeast, Columbia Heights, MN 55421
(612) 781-3161

Dynamic Smart Lights
783 Raymond Avenue, St Paul, MN 55114
(651) 644-2111

Gopher Stage Lighting Inc
2839 11th Avenue South, Minneapolis, MN 55407
(612) 871-0138

Hollywood Props
2912 North 2nd Street, Minneapolis, MN 55411
(612) 252-7852

Invincible Costume/Theatrical
512 Germain Mall, St Cloud, MN 56301
(320) 253-2240

Northwestern Costume-Norcostco
3203 Highway 100 North, Minneapolis, MN 55422
(612) 533-2791

Scaffold Service Inc
2525 Wabash Avenue, St Paul, MN 55114
(651) 646-4600

Schuler & Shook Inc
123 North 3rd Street 210, Minneapolis, MN 55401
(612) 339-5958

Stage & Studio Inc
PO Box 202, Dayton, MN 55327
(612) 537-8111

Stage One Supply Inc
1209 Old Highway 8, New Brighton, MN 55112
(651) 604-0691

Staging Concepts Inc
7500 Boone Avenue North 101, Brooklyn Park, MN 55428
(612) 337-5339

Twin Cities Magic & Costume
241 7th Street West, St Paul, MN 55102
(651) 227-7888

Voss Lighting
2031 Oakcrest Avenue, Roseville, MN 55113
(612) 339-5066

Westech Theatre Service
4029 20th Avenue South, Minneapolis, MN 55407
(612) 728-9640

Mississippi

Pickett Theater & Stage Supply
145 Fairmont Plaza, Pearl, MS 39208
(601) 664-0604

Thomas Audio Service
878 Foley Street, Jackson, MS 39202
(601) 354-9050

Missouri

A To Z Theatrical Supply & Service
307 West 80th Street, Kansas City, MO 64114
(816) 523-1655

Allied Theatre Crafts Inc
8600 Northeast Underground Drive P110, Kansas City, MO 64161
(816) 421-3980

Aries Audio & Lighting Company
4940 Northrup Avenue, St Louis, MO 63110
(314) 664-6610

Associated Theatrical Contractors
241 South Union Avenue, Springfield, MO 65802
(417) 862-4725

Bad Dog Grip & Electric
335 Leffingwell Avenue, Kirkwood, MO 63122
(314) 966-1016

Dancers Depot
1344 North Highway 7, Blue Springs, MO 64014
(816) 224-1913

Freelance Theatrical Studios
7222 Richmond Place, St Louis, MO 63143
(314) 647-8392

Freelance Theatrical Studios
3632 Windsor Place, St Louis, MO 63113
(314) 531-1946

Harvest Productions
7024 Universal Avenue, Kansas City, MO 64120
(816) 483-3889

Illumination Technology Service
130 Syminton Place, Hollister, MO 65672
(417) 337-5533

Illusions Unlimited Productions
3020 Little Blue Expressway, Independence, MO 64057
(816) 795-7400

Jim Renner Stage Service
3225 Meramec Street, St Louis, MO 63118
(314) 481-5950

Kansas City Scenery
1409 Murray Street, Kansas City, MO 64116
(816) 421-7707

On Your Toes
590 West Pacific Street, Branson, MO 65616
(417) 336-2675

Production Support Service Inc
1511 Washington Avenue R, St Louis, MO 63103
(314) 241-2066

Production Support Service
472 Tumulty Drive, Ballwin, MO 63021
(314) 394-1257

Prop Source Inc
1136 Washington Avenue Fl 7, St Louis, MO 63101
(314) 231-7767

Rent-A-Stage
520 Northeast 41st Street, Kansas City, MO 64116
(816) 455-2400

Sect Theatre Supplies Inc
406 East 18th Street, Kansas City, MO 64108
(816) 471-1239

Stage Call Inc
9845 Street Charles Rock Road 107, St Ann, MO 63074
(314) 890-2352

Technical Productions Inc
1693 South Hanley Road, St Louis, MO 63144
(314) 644-4000

Theatreworks
115 Industrial Park Drive, Hollister, MO 65672
(417) 332-1821

Montana

Sunshine Productions
2015 6th Avenue North, Great Falls, MT 59401
(406) 452-0307

Nebraska

Bobby's Dancewear & Supplies
14508 West Center Road, Omaha, NE 68144
(402) 393-1177

Comprehensive Design Solutions
3520 Cleveland Avenue 6, Lincoln, NE 68504
(402) 464-8080

Heartland Scenic Studio Inc
1308 Jackson Street, Omaha, NE 68102
(402) 341-9121

Omaha Stage Equipment Inc
3873 Leavenworth Street, Omaha, NE 68105
(402) 345-4427

Theatrical Media Service Inc
8942 J Street, Omaha, NE 68127
(402) 592-5522

Nevada

A & D Scenery Inc
3200 Sirius Avenue F, Las Vegas, NV 89102
(702) 362-9404

Cob Scaffolding
4825 Alto Avenue, Las Vegas, NV 89115
(702) 651-3350

Creative Illusions
4405 East Sahara Avenue 21, Las Vegas, NV 89104
(702) 641-6644

Desert Specialty Rigging Supply
5800 South Valley View Boulevard 107, Las Vegas, NV 89118
(702) 798-5559

Diamond Stage Designs
3170 West Pyle Avenue, Las Vegas, NV 89139
(702) 897-0569

DTR Entertainment Illusions
6290 Harrison Drive, Las Vegas, NV 89120
(702) 798-6559

Eagle Scaffolding & Equipment
3629 West Hacienda Avenue, Las Vegas, NV 89118
(702) 740-4041

Flying by FOY
3275 East Patrick Lane, Las Vegas, NV 89120
(702) 454-3300

FOY Inventerprises Inc
3275 East Patrick Lane, Las Vegas, NV 89120
(702) 454-3500

Magic Ventures
3518 West Post Road, Las Vegas, NV 89118
(702) 897-1224

Mobile Stage Xpress
749 Veterans Memorial Drive, Las Vegas, NV 89101
(702) 229-4616

Protech Theatrical Service Inc
3431 North Bruce Street, North Las Vegas, NV 89030
(702) 639-0290

Pyritz Pyrotechnics Inc
3300 Sunrise Avenue 103, Las Vegas, NV 89101
(702) 453-0808

S & K Theatrical Draperies Inc
6130 West Flamingo Road, Las Vegas, NV 89103
(702) 220-9301

Scenic Technologies
6050 South Valley View Boulevard, Las Vegas, NV 89118
(702) 942-4774

Sierra Lighting Service
2450 Valley Road 5, Reno, NV 89512
(775) 322-9427

Spider Staging Corporation
125 East Reno Avenue, Las Vegas, NV 89119
(702) 798-9691

Thoughtful Designs
6050 South Valley View Boulevard, Las Vegas, NV 89118
(702) 942-4567

ZFX Illusions Inc
1729 Stocker Street, North Las Vegas, NV 89030
(702) 399-8300

New Hampshire

Costume Gallery
11 1/2 East Broadway, Derry, NH 03038
(603) 434-0627

Mikan Theatricals
86 Tide Mill Road, Hampton, NH 03842
(603) 926-2744

New Jersey

Acadia Scenic
130 Bay Street, Jersey City, NJ 07302
(201) 653-8889

Anything But Costumes
111 Mine Street, Flemington, NJ 08822
(908) 788-1727

Anything But Costumes
44 Tisco Avenue, High Bridge, NJ 08829
(908) 638-9036

At-A-Glance Costumes
611 Main Street, Boonton, NJ 07005
(973) 335-1488

Avask Inc
75 West Forest Avenue, Englewood, NJ 07631
(201) 567-7300

Circuit Lighting Inc
299 US Highway 22, Green Brook, NJ 08812
(732) 968-9533

Logical Lighting & Sound Company
47 Junard Drive, Morristown, NJ 07960
(973) 267-7336

Mc Manus Enterprises
Atlantic City, NJ 08401
(609) 345-3345

Nelson Enterprises
942 State Route 122, Frenchtown, NJ 08825
(908) 996-3939

Prism Production Service
1333 Essex Street, Rahway, NJ 07065
(732) 574-1290

Special Projects Workshop
356 Glenwood Avenue, East Orange, NJ 07017
(973) 676-5555

Starlite Productions
2 Keystone Avenue Building 43, Cherry Hill, NJ 08003
(609) 489-9000

New Mexico

Costume Salon
631 Old Santa Fe Trail 3, Santa Fe, NM 87501
(505) 988-9501

Hogle's Theatrical Supplies
3212 Richards Lane B, Santa Fe, NM 87505
(505) 424-7435

Joy's Costumes
510 West 7th Street, Clovis, NM 88101
(505) 763-3344

Professional West Productions
224 Paseo Del Volcan Southwest, Albuquerque, NM 87121
(505) 831-0249

Quickbeam Systems
3716 High Street Northeast, Albuquerque, NM 87107
(505) 345-9230

New York

14th Street Stage Lighting Inc
431 West 14th Street 203, New York, NY 10014
(212) 645-5491

Adirondack Scenic Inc
20 Elm Street, Glens Falls, NY 12801
(518) 761-3335

Albany Theatre Supply Company
443 North Pearl Street, Albany, NY 12204
(518) 465-8894

Altered Image Studio
54 Franklin Street, New York, NY 10013
(212) 406-1192

Altman Stage Lighting Company
57 Alexander Street, Yonkers, NY 10701
(914) 476-7987

Applied Audio
2 Townline Circle, Rochester, NY 14623
(716) 272-9280

Associated Drapery & Equipment
40 Sea Cliff Avenue, Glen Cove, NY 11542
(516) 671-5245

Belle Lighting Company
313 Halstead Avenue, Mamaroneck, NY 10543
(914) 698-8782

Benjamin Warren's Props
690 East 137th Street, Bronx, NY 10454
(718) 665-3100

Bernhard Link Theatrical Inc
320 West 37th Street Frnt, New York, NY 10018
(212) 629-3522

Bestek Lighting & Staging
98 Mahan Street, West Babylon, NY 11704
(516) 643-0707

Bestek Lighting & Staging
353 Lexington Avenue 1522, New York, NY 10016
(212) 490-1163

BMI Supply
571 Queensbury Avenue, Queensbury, NY 12804
(518) 793-6706

Brighton Sound
315 Mount Read Boulevard, Rochester, NY 14611
(716) 328-1220

C-FEX Inc
23 Grattan Street, Brooklyn, NY 11206
(718) 628-7726

Camel Traders
57 Central Avenue, Schenectady, NY 12304
(518) 377-1196

Capital Scenic Inc
55 West Railroad Avenue, Garnerville, NY 10923
(914) 429-4800

Costume Armour Inc
2 Mill Street, Cornwall, NY 12518
(914) 534-9120

Daddy-O Productions
207 Flushing Avenue, Brooklyn, NY 11205
(718) 625-2135

Darrow Harry
355 South End Avenue, New York, NY 10280
(212) 912-1427

Dazian Fabrics
423 West 55th Street Fl 10, New York, NY 10019
(212) 307-7800

Delphi Studios Inc
207 Flushing Building 292 103, Brooklyn, NY 11205
(718) 522-2702

Drapekings
64 North Moore Street 2W, New York, NY 10013
(212) 219-2109

Drapery Industries Inc
180 Saint Paul Street, Rochester, NY 14604
(716) 232-2080

DTS Lighting & Scenic
37 Fulton Street, White Plains, NY 10606
(914) 949-1216

Eclectic Encore Properties Inc
620 West 26th Street Fl 4, New York, NY 10001
(212) 645-8880

Eric Winterling Inc
145 West 28th Street Fl 4, New York, NY 10001
(212) 629-7686

Erskine-Shapiro Theatre Technology
37 West 20th Street 703, New York, NY 10011
(212) 929-5380

Excel Lighting Productions
312 West 47th Street, New York, NY 10036
(212) 957-1777

Fashion Award
1225 Broadway Fl 2, New York, NY 10001
(212) 683-2767

Feller Precision Inc
62 Closter Road, Palisades, NY 10964
(914) 359-8116

Feller Precision Inc
377 Western Highway, Tappan, NY 10983
(914) 359-9431

Four Star Lighting Inc
30 Warren Place, Mt Vernon, NY 10550
(914) 667-9200

Goddard Design Company
51 Nassau Avenue, Brooklyn, NY 11222
(718) 599-0170

Grace Costumes Inc
250 West 54th Street 502, New York, NY 10019
(212) 586-0260

GSD Productions Inc
270 Duffy Avenue M, Hicksville, NY 11801
(516) 933-6200

Hoffend & Sons Inc
66 School Street, Victor, NY 14564
(716) 924-3770

Hoffend & Sons Inc
1160 Pittsford Victor Road C, Pittsford, NY 14534
(716) 381-6060

Hudson Scenic Studio Inc
1311 Ryawa Avenue, Bronx, NY 10474
(718) 589-7600

Independent Theatrical Installation
4171 State Route 5 and 20, Canandaigua, NY 14424
(716) 394-4220

Indigo Productions
2820 Bailey Avenue, Buffalo, NY 14215
(716) 836-2930

Industrial Supply Company
4730 Vernon Boulevard, Long Island City, NY 11101
(718) 784-1291

J Romeo Scenery Studio
115 Jackson Road, Hopewell Jct, NY 12533
(914) 226-6602

James Donahue Sets & Props
143 Roebling Street Fl 5, Brooklyn, NY 11211
(718) 388-9175

Karma Productions Inc
630 9th Avenue 303, New York, NY 10036
(212) 245-0650

L & M Sound Design
11 Rochelle Street, Staten Island, NY 10304
(718) 979-4213

Largent Studios
130 Bayard Street, Brooklyn, NY 11222
(718) 302-1941

Licensed Pyrotechnics
15 Moffitt Boulevard, East Islip, NY 11730
(516) 277-3390

Light Craft Professional
45 Edison Avenue, West Babylon, NY 11704
(516) 752-7574

Lincoln Scenic Studio Inc
560 West 34th Street, New York, NY 10001
(212) 244-2700

Lite-TROL Service Company
485 West John Street, Hicksville, NY 11801
(516) 681-5288

LKM Fabrication
Route 28 North, North Creek, NY 12853
(518) 251-3544

Majestic Theatrical Draperies
701 East 132nd Street, Bronx, NY 10454
(718) 401-3651

Manko Seating Company
50 West 36th Street, New York, NY 10018
(212) 695-7470

Michael-Jon Costumes Inc
411 West 14th Street, New York, NY 10014
(212) 741-3440

Miss Jezebel's Prop Rentals
9 West Merrick Road, Freeport, NY 11520
(516) 546-4352

Mood Fabric
250 West 39th Street Fl 10, New York, NY 10018
(212) 730-5003

Network Scenery Rentals
625 West 55th Street, New York, NY 10019
(212) 586-5243

Newth Lighting Company
363 Currybush Connection, Schenectady, NY 12306
(518) 372-3121

Novelty Scenic Studios Inc
40 Sea Cliff Avenue, Glen Cove, NY 11542
(516) 671-5940

One Dream Sound
431 Washington Street, New York, NY 10013
(212) 274-1115

Package Publicity Service Inc
158 West 27th Street 908, New York, NY 10001
(212) 255-2872

Packaged Lighting Systems Inc
29 Grant Street, Walden, NY 12586
(914) 778-3515

Paul Depass Inc
220 West 71st Street 1, New York, NY 10023
(212) 362-2648

Perfection Electricks
560 West 34th Street, New York, NY 10001
(212) 967-6676

Performance Inc
595 Targee Street, Staten Island, NY 10304
(718) 816-0885

Procomm Sound
8000 Cooper Avenue, Flushing, NY 11385
(718) 326-9112

Production Arts Lighting
630 9th Avenue Fl 14, New York, NY 10036
(212) 489-0312

Prop Company Kaplan & Associates
111 West 19th Street Fl 8, New York, NY 10011
(212) 691-7767

Propology Inc
1312 East 7th Street, Brooklyn, NY 11230
(718) 377-4874

Props For Today Inc
330 West 34th Street, New York, NY 10001
(212) 244-9600

R & B Sound Inc
55 Birch Street, Floral Park, NY 11001
(516) 327-9842

Ralph P Gibson Theater Consultant
308 Laburnam Crescent, Rochester, NY 14620
(716) 473-7655

Red Dot Scenic
203 West 90th Street 4H, New York, NY 10024
(212) 675-9041

Romeo Scenery Studio
115 Jackson Road, Hopewell Jct, NY 12533
(914) 454-1955

Rose Brand Wipers Inc
75 9th Avenue Fl 4, New York, NY 10011
(212) 594-7424

Royal Production Service
730 Fort Washington Avenue, New York, NY 10040
(212) 781-1440

SI Theatrical Rental Company
4 Hawthorne Avenue, Staten Island, NY 10314
(718) 698-3475

SK Light Shows
6203 Devoe Road, Camillus, NY 13031
(315) 487-0388

Scenic Specialties Inc
232 7th Street, Brooklyn, NY 11215
(718) 788-5379

Sensory Lighting & Sound Inc
651 Old Willets Path, Hauppauge, NY 11788
(516) 549-4724

Set Fabrications Inc
45 Crosby Street, New York, NY 10012
(212) 431-5696

ShowBiz Enterprises, Inc.
21-24 45th Road, Long Island City, NY 11101
(212) 989-5005

Showman Fabricators Inc
29 Imlay Street, Brooklyn, NY 11231
(718) 935-9899

Silent G Theatrical Lighting
2605 Colonial Street, Yorktown Heights, NY 10598
(914) 962-6242

SLD Lighting
318 West 47th Street, New York, NY 10036
(212) 541-5045

Spectrum Sound & Lighting
116 Killewald Avenue, Tonawanda, NY 14150
(716) 877-6438

Stage Dynamics
685 East Jericho Turnpike, Huntington Station, NY 11746
(516) 271-4981

State Supply Equipment & Props
210 11th Avenue Fl 2, New York, NY 10001
(212) 645-1430

Strand Lighting Inc
101 West 31st Street, New York, NY 10001
(212) 242-1042

Stroblite Company
430 West 14th Street 507, New York, NY 10014
(212) 929-3778

Syracuse Scenery & Stage Light
101 Monarch Drive, Liverpool, NY 13088
(315) 453-8096

Technical Supply Japan–USA
242 West 27th Street, New York, NY 10001
(212) 989-1272

Theatre Equipment Associates
244 West 49th Street 200, New York, NY 10019
(212) 246-6460

Theatrical Productions Service
100 Arden Street, New York, NY 10040
(212) 942-9382

Theatrical Props Inc
562 R 17M, Monroe, NY 10950
(212) 691-3359

Theatrical Services & Supply
1610 9th Avenue, Bohemia, NY 11716
(516) 588-9550

Theatrical Systems Service
265 New Hackensack Road 221, Wappingers Falls, NY 12590
(914) 462-4970

Times Square Lighting
2 Kay Fries Drive, Stony Point, NY 10980
(914) 947-3034

Tom Carroll Scenery Inc
98 Bayard Street, Brooklyn, NY 11222
(718) 963-6916

TPR Enterprises Limited
644 Fayette Avenue, Mamaroneck, NY 10543
(914) 698-1141

Unistage Inc
330 Genesee Street, Buffalo, NY 14204
(716) 853-6500

Unitech Productions Inc
165 West 46th Street 400, New York, NY 10036
(212) 997-2272

Variety Scenic Studio
2519 Borden Avenue, Long Island City, NY 11101
(718) 392-4747

Weller Fabrics Inc
24 West 57th Street Fl 1, New York, NY 10019
(212) 247-3790

North Carolina

ABRA Costumes Unlimited
1611 Central Avenue, Charlotte, NC 28205
(704) 334-2300

Audio & Light Inc
1604 Holbrook Street, Greensboro, NC 27403
(336) 294-1234

Bellows Drapery Inc
2705 Fairfax Road, Greensboro, NC 27407
(336) 852-6188

Capital City Supply
421 Greenway Drive, Eden, NC 27288
(336) 627-7551

Creative Stage Design Inc
1337 Central Avenue, Charlotte, NC 28205
(704) 375-1439

Custom Rigging Systems
830 Winston Street, Greensboro, NC 27405
(336) 370-4896

Dudley Theatrical Equipment
3401 Indiana Avenue, Winston Salem, NC 27105
(336) 722-3255

Lighting Supply Company
1026 Jay Street, Charlotte, NC 28208
(704) 372-7305

Morris Costumes
4300 Monroe Road, Charlotte, NC 28205
(704) 333-4653

National Mastercraft Stage
6 Deep Branch Road, South Brunswick, NC 28470
(910) 755-8080

Scenic Associates
115 North 2nd Street, Wilmington, NC 28401
(910) 254-4575

Stage Decoration & Supplies
3519 Associate Drive, Greensboro, NC 27405
(336) 621-5454

Stageworks Lighting & Production
123 Seaboard Avenue, Raleigh, NC 27604
(919) 839-2288

Total Production Service
6241 Westgate Road, Raleigh, NC 27613
(919) 787-7723

North Dakota

HB Sound & Light
3331 South University Drive 2, Fargo, ND 58104
(701) 775-1150

Northwestern Costume Theatre
3902 13th Avenue South, Fargo, ND 58103
(701) 282-7495

Sound Track Productions
4220 5th Avenue North, Grand Forks, ND 58203
(701) 772-1920

Ohio

Abyss Special FX
17577 Whitney Road Suite 311, Strongsville, OH 44136
(440) 779-5700
(330) 273-1221

Akron Theatrical Service
3217 Waterloo Road, Mogadore, OH 44260
(330) 628-5560

Alpha Audio Associates Inc
29491 Cedar Road, Cleveland, OH 44124
(440) 473-4290

American Theatre Equipment Company
4126 Anson Drive, Hilliard, OH 43026
(614) 876-6262

Back Stage Transfer
3136 West 70th Street, Cleveland, OH 44102
(216) 631-5931

Beck Studios Inc
1001 Tech Drive, Milford, OH 45150
(513) 831-6650

Best Devices Company
3190 West 32nd Street, Cleveland, OH 44109
(216) 651-8878

BGM Systems
PO Box 2401, Lancaster, OH 43130
(740) 653-8353

Bright Ideas
560 West Market Street, Lima, OH 45801
(419) 224-1777

Brite Lites Inc
4135 Westward Avenue, Columbus, OH 43228
(614) 272-1404

C & D Audio Productions & Design
3096 Colerain Avenue, Cincinnati, OH 45225
(513) 542-7038

Center of The World Stage Company
739 Bristol Champion Townline, Bristolville, OH 44402
(330) 889-3751

Cleveland Costume & Display Company
18489 Pearl Road, Cleveland, OH 44136
(216) 361-4200

Clown Alley Products Inc
5612 Carthage Avenue, Cincinnati, OH 45212
(513) 396-8080

Color Brite Fabrics & Display
212 East 8th Street, Cincinnati, OH 45202
(513) 721-4402

Dance Theatre Shop
3111 West Sylvania Avenue, Toledo, OH 43613
(419) 475-8829

Eighth Day Sound Systems Inc
1305 West 80th Street, Cleveland, OH 44102
(216) 961-2900

Electrastage Systems Inc
29315 Clayton Avenue, Wickliffe, OH 44092
(440) 585-0088

Erie Street Theatrical Service
3615 Superior Avenue East 44, Cleveland, OH 44114
(216) 426-0050

Fremont Theatre Supply
303 North Ohio Avenue, Fremont, OH 43420
(419) 334-2758

Mc Dougall Productions Inc
1420 East 30th Street, Cleveland, OH 44114
(216) 687-0017

Northcoast Theatrical
540 South Main Street, Akron, OH 44311
(330) 762-1768

Partech
8711 Reading Road, Cincinnati, OH 45215
(513) 821-8687

Perovsek Engineering
21850 Saint Clair Avenue, Cleveland, OH 44117
(216) 289-4748

Production Group
21515 Chagrin Boulevard, Cleveland, OH 44122
(216) 561-3600

River City Scenic Inc
3701 Red Bank Road, Cincinnati, OH 45227
(513) 272-2990

Schell Scenic Studio
841 South Front Street, Columbus, OH 43206
(614) 444-9550

Schenz Theatrical Supplies
2959 Colerain Avenue, Cincinnati, OH 45225
(513) 542-6100

Scott Costume Company
114 4th Street Northwest, Canton, OH 44702
(330) 452-6612

SFX Design
6099 Godown Road, Columbus, OH 43235
(614) 459-3222

Shoptalk Lingerie
5310 Warrensville Center Road, Cleveland, OH 44137
(216) 581-8888

Sideline Design
1588 East 40th Street, Cleveland, OH 44103
(216) 781-7880

Sketch-Lite Productions
4037 Tallmadge Road, Rootstown, OH 44272
(330) 325-9779

Stage Center Inc
908 North Main Street, Akron, OH 44310
(330) 535-7816

Stagecraft Theatrical
3950 Spring Grove Avenue, Cincinnati, OH 45223
(513) 541-6803

Syracuse Scenery & Stage
Medina, OH 44256
(330) 723-8677

Theatrics
2851 Noble Road, Cleveland, OH 44121
(216) 382-7169

Tiffin Scenic Studios Inc
146 Riverside Drive, Tiffin, OH 44883
(419) 447-1546

Toledo Theatre Supply
1016 North Summit Street, Toledo, OH 43604
(419) 241-7711

Oklahoma

Capitol Stage Equipment Company
3121 North Pennsylvania Avenue, Oklahoma City, OK 73112
(405) 524-9552

Cimarron Stage
5617 Northwest 82nd Street, Oklahoma City, OK 73132
(405) 722-1893

Jim French Design Shop
17 East Brady Street, Tulsa, OK 74103
(918) 583-2926

Journey Productions
3701 Southwest 11th Street, Lawton, OK 73501
(580) 355-1292

Show Biz Dance Wear
1214 West Gore Boulevard A, Lawton, OK 73501
(580) 248-6264

Showtek Inc
North of City, Chickasha, OK 73018
(405) 222-0632

Stage One Scenic
314 South Kenosha Avenue, Tulsa, OK 74120
(918) 592-1516

Tulsa Scenic
313 South Kenosha Avenue, Tulsa, OK 74120
(918) 582-8458

Oregon

4th Street Studio Inc
281 4th Street, Ashland, OR 97520
(541) 488-3228

Bud's Lites-Stage Lighting
32579 South Rachel Larkin Road, Molalla, OR 97038
(503) 829-8012

Cascade Sound Inc
1225 20th Street Southeast, Salem, OR 97302
(503) 581-5525

General American Theatre Supply
1506 Northeast Couch Street, Portland, OR 97232
(503) 231-5713

Hollywood Lights Inc
5251 Southeast McLoughlin Boulevard, Portland, OR 97202
(503) 232-9001

Northwest Theatrical
PO Box 3687, Sunriver, OR 97707
(541) 593-1270

Oregon Stage Lighting
3503 South Pacific Highway, Medford, OR 97501
(541) 535-7660

R A Reed Productions Inc
955 North Columbia Boulevard A, Portland, OR 97217
(503) 735-0003

Stage Right
2289 North Interstate Avenue, Portland, OR 97227
(503) 287-0361

Stagecraft Industries Inc
5051 North Lagoon Avenue, Portland, OR 97217
(503) 286-1600

West Coast Productions
1400 Northwest 15th Avenue, Portland, OR 97209
(503) 294-0412

Pennsylvania

AFM Productions Inc
28748 State Highway 77, Guys Mills, PA 16327
(814) 967-2336

Cenlyt Productions Ms Designs
111 Washington Avenue, Vandergrift, PA 15690
(724) 567-7474

Check Mate Productions Inc
689 Meadowbrook Lane, Media, PA 19063
(610) 565-9111

Dance Chateau
22 West Chestnut Street, Washington, PA 15301
(724) 228-2525

Declan Weir Productions
907 North Front Street, Philadelphia, PA 19123
(215) 829-1787

Designs Unlimited
4312 Butler Street, Pittsburgh, PA 15201
(412) 687-0437

Electrastage Systems Inc
101 Pfaff Road, Baden, PA 15005
(724) 869-2002

Flexitrol Lighting Company
311 East Main Street, Carnegie, PA 15106
(412) 276-3710

Ihtfp Theatricals
302 2nd Street, Charleroi, PA 15022
(724) 483-1824

Jeannie Costumes
Route 222, Maxatawny, PA 19538
(610) 683-0700

Jerry Habecker Lighting
5412 Legene Lane, Enola, PA 17025
(717) 728-0744

Keystone Concepts
1024 Saw Mill Run Boulevard, Pittsburgh, PA 15220
(412) 886-1025

M & M Lighting
572 Main Street, Stroudsburg, PA 18360
(570) 424-5200

Metropolis Studios
1410 South Darien Street, Philadelphia, PA 19147
(215) 463-3000

Midnight Productions Inc
4921 Upper Mountain Road, Buckingham, PA 18912
(215) 794-0782

Performance Lighting Rentals
5200 Harrison Street, Pittsburgh, PA 15201
(412) 781-5655

Phair Theatre & Stage Supply
110 Meadow Crest Drive, Nanticoke, PA 18634
(570) 735-5924

Pittsburgh Stage Inc
8325 Ohio River Boulevard, Pittsburgh, PA 15202
(412) 734-3902

Premier Production Service
5441 Jonestown Road, Harrisburg, PA 17112
(717) 541-4238

Prop Shop Inc
501 West Washington Street 4, Norristown, PA 19401
(610) 275-3130

Safeguard Lighting Systems Inc
114 West 5th Street, Chester, PA 19013
(610) 876-2800

Sapsis Rigging Inc
3883 Ridge Avenue, Philadelphia, PA 19132
(215) 228-0888

Scenery First Inc
34 North Whitehall Road, Norristown, PA 19403
(610) 539-0469 sceneryfst@aol.com

Scenery First Inc
207 Elmwood Avenue, Sharon Hill, PA 19079
(610) 583-2560

Skeletons In My Closets Production
112 East Washington Lane, Philadelphia, PA 19144
(215) 848-8223

Stage Works
510 Main Street, Pennsburg, PA 18073
(215) 541-9155

Stagestep Inc
2000 Hamilton Street, Philadelphia, PA 19130
(215) 636-9000

Tri State Theatrical Supply
622 California Avenue, Rochester, PA 15074
(724) 774-2133

Tri-Tech Stage Lighting Inc
1811 Edge Hill Road, Abington, PA 19001
(215) 659-4305

Vincent Lighting Systems
920 Vista Park Drive, Pittsburgh, PA 15205
(412) 788-5250

Rhode Island

Costume Chambers
880 East Main Road, Portsmouth, RI 02871
(401) 683-6660

High Output Inc
166 Valley Street, Providence, RI 02909
(401) 521-0676

Rosco Laboratories Inc
31 Walnut Street, Central Falls, RI 02863
(401) 725-6765

South Carolina

BMI Supply South
60 Airview Drive, Greenville, SC 29607
(864) 288-8983

Productions Unlimited Inc
208 Honey Horn Drive, Simpsonville, SC 29681
(864) 675-6146

Roberts Stage Curtains Inc
103 Shelton Road, Travelers Rest, SC 29690
(864) 834-1422

Southeast Stage Rigging & Curtains
2172 River Road A, Greer, SC 29650
(864) 848-9770

Theatrics Unlimited Inc
981 King Street, Charleston, SC 29403
(843) 722-2326

Tennessee

Bandit Lites
2233 Sycamore Drive, Knoxville, TN 37921
(423) 971-3071

Bandit Lites
1600 J P Hennessey Drive, La Vergne, TN 37086
(615) 641-9000

Booth Seating
650 Compress Drive A, Memphis, TN 38106
(901) 948-6515

Bradfield Stage Lighting
620 Davidson Street A, Nashville, TN 37213
(615) 256-0977

Cinema Products International
1015 5th Avenue North, Nashville, TN 37219
(615) 248-0771

Concert & Theatrical Service
4126 Mountain Creek Road 57, Chattanooga, TN 37415
(423) 875-9747

Interstate Lighting & Media
1921 Church Street, Nashville, TN 37203
(615) 329-2700

Joint Effort Productions
2224 Blount Avenue Southwest, Knoxville, TN 37920
(423) 573-2895

Knoxville Scenic
210 Sarvis Drive, Knoxville, TN 37920
(423) 577-5551

Marble Carbon Company
3102 Ambrose Avenue, Nashville, TN 37207
(615) 227-7772

Memphis Audio
749 North White Station Road, Memphis, TN 38122
(901) 761-3880

Memphis Scenic Inc
504 Cumberland Street, Memphis, TN 38112
(901) 458-8171

Mid America Entertainment Service
5700 Tennessee Avenue, Chattanooga, TN 37409
(423) 267-9060

Moonshine Lighting Inc
2635 Union Avenue Extension, Memphis, TN 38112
(901) 323-1111

Stage Lighting South
593 South Cooper Street, Memphis, TN 38104
(901) 274-4444

Television Production Service
3744 Old Hickory Boulevard B2, Nashville, TN 37209
(615) 352-8008

Thomas James Engineering
10603 Lexington Drive, Knoxville, TN 37932
(423) 671-2885

Tri State Theatre Supply Company
151 Vance Avenue, Memphis, TN 38103
(901) 525-8249

Texas

AV Professional Inc
2353 Santa Anna Avenue 23, Dallas, TX 75228
(214) 327-0453

Austin Theatrical Supply
4125 Todd Lane A, Austin, TX 78744
(512) 448-2001

Backstage Costumes
415 Schatzel Street 2, Corpus Christi, TX 78401
(361) 883-5224

Backstage Dancewear & Gifts
17170 Mill Forest Road, Webster, TX 77598
(281) 286-9894

Barhorst Theatrical Service
10214 Windriver Drive, Houston, TX 77070
(281) 955-9347

Billington Theater Supply
125 West McHarg Street, Stamford, TX 79553
(915) 773-2960

Bleisch Production Company
6330 Alder Drive, Houston, TX 77081
(713) 665-3558

Castleberry Cynthia Couture
3636 Executive Center Drive G50, Austin, TX 78731
(512) 231-8980

CINE Shoppe Inc
10217 Plano Road, Dallas, TX 75238
(214) 348-0025

Communilux Productions
4001 East Side Avenue, Dallas, TX 75226
(214) 821-8706

Costume World
13621 Inwood Road, Dallas, TX 75244
(972) 404-0584

Costumes Plus
2822 Nall Street, Port Neches, TX 77651
(409) 729-7015

DS Arts
1111 South Lamar Street, Dallas, TX 75215
(214) 565-7858

Dallas Costume Shoppe
3905 Main Street, Dallas, TX 75226
(214) 428-4613

Dallas Stage Lighting-Stalieco
1818 Chestnut Street, Dallas, TX 75226
(214) 428-1818

Dallas Stage Scenery Company
3917 Willow Street, Dallas, TX 75226
(214) 821-0002

Dance & Actionwear
3338 Broadway Boulevard 106, Garland, TX 75043
(972) 864-0565

Eagle Audio & Lighting Inc
3113 South University Drive 501, Fort Worth, TX 76109
(817) 926-4999

Gemini Stage Lighting & Equipment
10218 Miller Road, Dallas, TX 75238
(214) 341-4822

Hall's Cinema Products
2106 Villawood Lane, Garland, TX 75040
(972) 414-8229

High Energy Dance Lighting
2222 FM 1960 Road West C, Houston, TX 77090
(281) 880-9922

Independent Theatre Supply Inc
4038 North IH 35, San Antonio, TX 78219
(210) 226-3508

Inflated Egos
2512 Bisbee Street, Houston, TX 77017
(713) 645-8152

Kirchhoff's Kostume Kloset
120 East 5th Street, Plainview, TX 79072
(806) 296-7079

LD Systems Inc
483 West 38th Street, Houston, TX 77018
(713) 695-9400

LD Systems Inc
5913 Distribution, San Antonio, TX 78218
(210) 661-9700

Little Stage Lighting Company
10507 Harry Hines Boulevard, Dallas, TX 75220
(214) 358-3511

Lone Star Theatrical Service
4216 Murray Avenue C, Fort Worth, TX 76117
(817) 788-5544

Made In The Shade Fabrications
14501 Blanco Road, San Antonio, TX 78216
(210) 492-1832

National Stage Equipment Inc
801 North 15th Street, Waco, TX 76707
(254) 756-0651

Performing Arts Supply Company
11437 Todd Street, Houston, TX 77055
(713) 681-8688

Production & Rigging Resources
2551 Lombardy Lane 150, Dallas, TX 75220
(214) 350-6050

Props of Texas
8740 Diplomacy Row, Dallas, TX 75247
(214) 631-7767

R 'n 'r Service
1617 Harvard Street, Houston, TX 77008
(713) 862-3770

Safe Way Rental Equipment Inc
311 Bowie Street, Austin, TX 78703
(512) 476-7301

Samarco
1507 Sullivan Drive, Dallas, TX 75215
(214) 421-0757

SFX Design Inc
2500 East Interstate 20, Weatherford, TX 76087
(817) 599-0800

Showcrafters
1101 Quaker Street, Dallas, TX 75207
(214) 638-7469

Southern Importers & Exporters
4825 San Jacinto Street, Houston, TX 77004
(713) 524-8236

Stagelight Inc
2310 Richton Street, Houston, TX 77098
(713) 942-0555

Starline Costumes
1286 Bandera Road, San Antonio, TX 78228
(210) 435-3535

TW Design & Construction
1300 Crampton Street, Dallas, TX 75207
(214) 634-2965

Texas Costume-Norcostco
1231 Wycliff Avenue 300, Dallas, TX 75207
(214) 630-4048

Texas Scenic Company
5423 Jackwood Drive, San Antonio, TX 78238
(210) 684-0091

Texas Studio Rentals
10650 Rylie Road, Dallas, TX 75253
(972) 557-4226

Texas Theatre Supply
714 Finale Court, San Antonio, TX 78216
(210) 340-5766

Texas Theatrical Supply Inc
4102 Fannin Street, Houston, TX 77004
(713) 520-7076

Theatrical Supply
South of City, Pampa, TX 79065
(806) 665-0607

True West
Star, TX 76880
(915) 948-3768

Upstage Center
County Road 541, Alvin, TX 77511
(281) 331-6564

Winn Morton Designs
1921 Nokomis Road, Lancaster, TX 75146
(972) 227-0177

Wolf & Company Shop
5200 East Grand Avenue 6, Dallas, TX 75223
(214) 826-9490

Wrightworks Inc
2205 Cockrell Avenue, Dallas, TX 75215
(214) 426-2661

Utah

Claco Equipment & Service
1212 South State Street, Salt Lake City, UT 84111
(801) 355-1250

Delta AV Systems
309 South Main Street, Salt Lake City, UT 84111
(801) 466-7979

GTS General Theatrical Supply
2153 South 700 East, Salt Lake City, UT 84106
(801) 485-5012

Mountain West Stagecraft
2616 South 1030 West, Salt Lake City, UT 84119
(801) 974-9664

Nylander Rigging
855 3rd Avenue 5, Salt Lake City, UT 84103
(801) 532-3141

Oasis Stage Werks
249 Rio Grande Street, Salt Lake City, UT 84101
(801) 363-0364

Production Design
862 South Main Street, Brigham City, UT 84302
(435) 723-3642

Scenic Service Specialists
1240 East 800 North, Orem, UT 84097
(801) 224-4293

Signature Scenery
1565 West 200 South, Lindon, UT 84042
(801) 796-0400

Taylor Maid Beauty Supplies
562 South Main Street, Cedar City, UT 84720
(435) 628-5962

Voyager Productions Inc
690 West 200 North, Logan, UT 84321
(435) 753-7412

Vermont

Production Advantage
1 Main Street, Winooski, VT 05404
(802) 655-5100

Virginia

Act One Stage Lighting
PO Box 2204, Portsmouth, VA 23702
(757) 397-3406

Applied Electronics
716 Blue Crab Road, Newport News, VA 23606
(757) 591-9371

Associates Sound Service
7954 Angleton Court, Lorton, VA 22079
(703) 550-9550

Dr Bob's Theatricity
296 North Witchduck Road, Virginia Beach, VA 23462
(757) 499-0720

Event Technical Service
7619 Ansley Road, Richmond, VA 23231
(804) 222-0710

JeRM Productions
9113 Volunteer Drive, Alexandria, VA 22309
(703) 799-7899

Maryland Stage Lighting Inc
5160 Eisenhower Avenue, Alexandria, VA 22304
(703) 461-7872

Moonlight & Sound Inc
728 Etheridge Road, Chesapeake, VA 23322
(757) 482-8636

MTS Productions Inc
14508F Lee Road, Chantilly, VA 20151
(703) 631-2213

National Scenery Studios
7963 Conell Court, Lorton, VA 22079
(703) 550-9757

Scaena Studios
7963 Conell Court, Lorton, VA 22079
(703) 339-8308

Stage Right Lighting
296 North Witchduck Road 102, Virginia Beach, VA 23462
(757) 473-8548

Washington

Absolute Audio Inc/Northern
5503 232nd Street Southwest, Mountlake Ter, WA 98043
(425) 774-1905

Audio Service Company
215 North 4th Street, Yakima, WA 98901
(509) 248-7041

Avalanche Concert Lighting
2325 Tacoma Avenue South, Tacoma, WA 98402
(253) 627-2319

CITC Special Effects
2100 196th Street Southwest 138, Lynnwood, WA 98036
(425) 776-4950

Display & Costume Supply
11201 Roosevelt Way Northeast, Seattle, WA 98125
(206) 362-4810

Donovan Rigging Inc
2416 3rd Avenue West, Seattle, WA 98119
(206) 283-4419

Enterprise Professional Lghtng
3009 East Diamond Avenue, Spokane, WA 99207
(509) 533-1888

Gala Costume Shop
301 Northwest 82nd Street, Seattle, WA 98117
(206) 782-5332

Hollywood Lights Inc
433 8th Avenue North, Seattle, WA 98109
(206) 292-2353

Lackey Sound & Light Rentals
3425 Stone Way North, Seattle, WA 98103
(206) 632-7773

McRae Theater Equipment Inc
101 Nickerson Street 210, Seattle, WA 98109
(206) 285-8393

Pacific Northwest Theatre Association
333 Westlake Avenue North, Seattle, WA 98109
(206) 622-7850

Prop & Costume
5622 Corson Avenue South, Seattle, WA 98108
(206) 284-9002

Seattle Stage Lighting & Equipment
4442 27th Avenue West, Seattle, WA 98199
(206) 283-7464

Silhouette Lights & Staging
2432 South Inland Empire Way, Spokane, WA 99224
(509) 747-4804

Stagecraft Industries Inc
5503 6th Avenue South, Seattle, WA 98108
(206) 454-3089

Theatrical & Display Proudctio
PO Box 3442, Spokane, WA 99220
(509) 535-5582

West Virginia

Moore Theatre Equipment Company
213 Delaware Avenue, Charleston, WV 25302
(304) 344-4413

Wisconsin

Acme Corporation Production Service
6767 University Avenue, Suite 123, Madison, WI 53562
(608) 849-6429

Acme Corporation Production Service
529 West National Avenue, Milwaukee, WI 53204
(414) 645-7030

Clearwing Productions Inc
11101 West Mitchell Street, Milwaukee, WI 53214
(414) 258-6333

Custom Designed Lighting Equipment
2326 South Kinnickinnic Avenue, Milwaukee, WI 53207
(414) 744-0782

Festival Productions Inc
929 North Astor Street, Milwaukee, WI 53202
(414) 277-9606

John S Hyatt & Associates
122 State Street 304, Madison, WI 53703
(608) 280-0985

Madison Theatre Guild Inc
2410 Monroe Street, Madison, WI 53711
(608) 238-9322

Mainstage Theatrical Supply
129 West Pittsburgh Avenue, Milwaukee, WI 53204
(414) 278-0878

Mid-West Scenic & Stage Company Limited
224 West Bruce Street, Milwaukee, WI 53204
(414) 276-2707

Midwest Prototype & Design
4530 South Packard Avenue, Cudahy, WI 53110
(414) 481-4338

Stage One
106 Plummer Court, Neenah, WI 54956
(920) 729-6070

Sun Lighting Productions Inc
133 West Pittsburgh Avenue, Milwaukee, WI 53204
(414) 224-0443

Theatrical Construction Service
133 West Pittsburgh Avenue 205, Milwaukee, WI 53204
(414) 224-9037

National Theater Organizations

1-800 POSTCARDS

50 West 23rd Street 6th floor, New York, NY 10010
100 Wilshire Blvd. #1060, Santa Monica, CA 90401
Order Forms, Technical Details, Brochures by Fax : 212-271-5506 ext 3
New York Telephone : 212-271-5505
Customer Service : ext 600
Fax : 212-271-5506
Los Angeles Telephone : 310-319-0155
Customer Service : ext 6562
Fax: 310-319-0150
A very useful, economical, quick printer that delivers full color post-cards. A very popular service among the New York theater community.

Theatre Communications Group

355 Lexington Avenue, New York, NY 10017-0217
Telephone: 212-697-5230
Theatre Communications Group (TCG), the national organization for the American theater. They offer services to strengthen, nurture, and promote the not-for-profit American theater.

The League of American Theatres and Producers, Inc.,

226 West 47th Street, New York, NY 10036
Telephone: 212-764-1122
Fax: 212-719-4389
The League of American Theatres and Producers is the national trade association for the commercial theater industry.

ONStage!

http://www.onstage.org/
ONStage is also engaged in lobbying theatrical organizations on the Web to tailor their content specifically toward the needs of actors.

Theatrical Production Services (TPS)

100 Arden Street Suite F5, New York, N.Y. 10040
Telephone/Fax: (212) 942-9382
TPS serves the communities of professional opera, musical theater,

concert, and any performing arts organization in need of production staffing and guidance.

Stage Directors and Choreographers Foundation

1501 Broadway, Suite 1701, New York, NY 10036
Telephone: 212-302-6195, 212-391-1070
The Foundation is the only national organization dedicated exclusively to supporting and developing the professional director and choreographer.

American Association of Community Theatre

712 Enchanted Oaks, College Station, TX 77845
Telephone: 409-774-0611
Fax: 409-776-8718
E-mail: info@aact.org
The American Association of Community Theatre (AACT) exists to enable community theaters across the country to become the cornerstones of the creative life of their communities — to provide quality entertainment, intellectual stimulation, challenge and opportunity, to be worthy contributors to an improved quality of life for the communities which they serve.

Actors' Equity Association

The National Office, 165 West 46th Street, 15th Floor New York, NY 10036
Telephone: 212-869-8530
FAX:212-719-9815
AEA, founded in 1913, is the labor union representing actors and stage managers in the legitimate theater in the United States.

The American Society of Theatre Consultants

http://www.landb.com/ASTCIndex.htm
ASTC is a nonprofit corporation chartered to encourage and promote high standards of practice and procedure in many aspects of theater consulting work.

International Ticketing Association (INTIX)

The International Ticketing Association (INTIX), 250 West 57th Street, Suite 722, New York, NY 10107

Telephone: 212-581-0600
Fax: 212-581-0885
INTIX provides the premier forum for ticketing professionals world-wide.

Entertainment Services & Technology Association
875 Sixth Avenue, Suite 2302, New York, NY 10001 USA
Telephone: 212- 244-1505
Fax: 212-244-1502
ESTA is a nonprofit trade association representing the North American entertainment technology industry.

International Association of Assembly Managers
4425 W. Airport Freeway, Suite 590 Irving, TX 75062-5835 USA
Telephone: 972-255-8020
Fax: 972-255-9582
http://www.iaam.org/
IAAM's mission is to provide leadership, to educate, to inform, and to cultivate friendships among individuals involved in the management, operation, and support of public assembly facilities.

International Alliance of Theatrical Stage Employees
Suite 601, 1515 Broadway, New York, NY 10036
Telephone: 212-730-1770
The International Alliance of Theatrical Stage Employees, Moving Picture Technicians, Artists, and Allied Crafts of the United States and Canada is an association of people involved with many aspects of production.

The New England Theatre Conference, Inc.
c/o Department of Theatre, Northeastern University, 360 Huntington Ave., Boston, MA 02115
Telephone: 617 424 9275 · Fax: 617 424 1057
E-mail: NETC@world.std.com
The New England Theatre conference is a nonprofit educational corporation working to develop, expand and assist theater activity on the community, educational, and professional levels.

The United States Institute for Theatre Technology, Inc. (USITT)

6443 Ridings Road, Syracuse, NY 13206-1111
Telephone: 800-93USITT (800-938-7488) or 315-463-6463
Fax: 315-463-6525
usittno@pppmail.appliedtheory.com
The United States Institute for Theatre Technology, Inc. (USITT) is the association of design, production, and technology professionals in the performing arts and entertainment industry.

National Alliance of Musical Theatre

330 West 45th Street # B, New York, NY 10036
Telephone: 212-265-5376

American Arts Alliance

805 15th Street, N.W., Suite 500, Washington, D.C. 20005
Telephone: 202-289-1776
Fax: 202-371-6601
The mission of the American Arts Alliance is to be the principal advocate for America's professional nonprofit arts organizations in representing arts interests and advancing arts support before Congress and other branches of the federal government.

Americans for the Arts

1000 Vermont Avenue NW, 12th Floor , Washington DC 20005
Telephone: 202-371-2830
Fax: 202-371-0424
Americans for the Arts works with cultural organizations, arts, business and government leaders and patrons to provide leadership, research, visibility, professional development and advocacy to advance support and resources for the arts in communities across the country.

National Association of Artists' Organizations/NAAO

918 F Street N.W., Suite 611, Washington, DC 20004
NAAO has provided services to the primary creators of new, emerging, and often experimental work. They exist to strengthen the field from within, promote its many and varied accomplishments to the public, and to provide a national voice for artists' organizations in forums that debate issues of cultural policy.

Performing Arts Resources: PAR

88 East 3rd Street #19, New York, NY 10003

Telephone: 212-673-6343

PAR is a not-for-profit problem-solving resource for companies and individuals in the performing arts. PAR organizes seminars on a wide range of theater topics, including producing, acting, directing, and designing.

Up-To-Date Mailing Labels

449 W. 44th St. #3S, New York, NY 10036

Telephone: 212-265-0260

They provide mailing labels and a wide range of consulting services.

Volunteer Lawyers for the Arts

1 E. 53rd St., 6th Floor, New York, NY 10022

Telephone: 212-319-2787

VLA provides free legal services to nonprofit arts organizations, as well as to artists who can't afford legal services.

Bookstores

Act I Bookstore
2632 N. Lincoln Ave., Chicago, IL
Telephone: 773-348-6757
Act I is Chicago's first and only exclusively theater bookstore.

Appaluse
211 West 71st Street, New York, NY 10023
Telephone: 212-496-7511
A New York—based bookstore and publisher.

The Drama Book Shop, Inc.
723 7th Ave. (Corner of West 48th St., 2nd floor), New York, NY 10019
Telephone: 212-944-0595 or 800-322-0595
Fax: 212-921-2013
A New York bookstore located just off Times Square.

Rights and Royalties Agencies for Plays and Musicals

Anchorage Press
(Formerly the Children's Theatre Press)
P.O. Box 8067, New Orleans, LA 70182
Telephone: 504-283-8868
Fax: 504-866-0502

Aran Press
1036 S. Fifth St., Louisville, KY 40203
Telephone: 502-568-6622
Fax: 502-561-1124
E-mail: aranpres@aye.net

Bad Wolf Press
(Specializing in short musical plays)
5391 Spindrift Ct., Camarillo, CA 93012
Telephone: 888-827-8661
E-mail: ron@badwolfpress.com

Baker's Plays
100 Chauncy St., Boston, MA 02111-1783
Telephone: 617-482-1280
Fax: 617-482-7613
E-mail: info@bakersplays.com

Baymax Productions
(Children's story scripts)
2219 W. Olive Ave., Suite 130, Burbank, CA 91506
Telephone: 818-563-6105
Fax: 818-563-2968

Broadway Play Publishing, Inc.
56 East 81st St., New York, NY 10028
Telephone: 212-772-8334
Fax: 212-772-8358
E-mail: BroadwayPl@aol.com

Brown Bag Productions

(Children's plays and books)
2710 N Stemmons, Suite 60, Dallas, TX 75207
Telephone: 800-686-9484
Fax: 214-638-7747
E-mail: brownbag@pcico.com

Centerstage Press

P.O. Box 36688, Phoenix, AZ 85067
Telephone:602-242-1123
Fax: 602-861-2708
E-mail: info@cstage.com

Contemporary Drama Service

885 Elkton Dr., Colorado Springs, CO 80907
Telephone: 800-93-PLAYS
Fax: 719-594-9915
E-mail: MerPCDS@aol.com

Criminal Mischief

(Mystery Dinner Theater Plays—One Acts—Fundraisers)
65 Clear Creek Rd., Liberty Hill, TX 78642
Telephone: 512-515-5261
E-mail: bill.seward@usa.net

David Spicer Productions

(International musicals, pantomimes, plays, operettas)
274 Military Road, Dover Heights 2030 NSW, Australia
Telephone/Fax: 612-9371-8458
E-mail: dspice@ozemail.com.au

Dramatic Publishing Co.

311 Washington St., Woodstock, IL 60098
Telephone: 800-448-7469
Fax: 800-334-5302

Dramatists Play Service

440 Park Ave S., New York, NY 10016
Telephone: 212-683-8960
Fax: 212-213-1539

Eldridge Publishing Co.
P.O. Box 1595, Venice, FL 34284
Telephone: 800-HISTAGE
Fax: 800-453-5179
E-mail: info@histage.com

Empire Publishing Service
P.O. Box 1344, Studio City, CA 91614
Telephone: 818-784-8918

Encore Performance Publishing
P.O. Box 692, Orem Utah 84059
Telephone: 801-225-0605
E-mail: encoreplay@aol.com

Entertainment Marketing Management
(Musicals for all audiences)
367 Sausalito Blvd., Sausalito, CA 94965
Telephone: 415-331-6838
Fax: 415-331-6738
E-mail: Emktgmgmt@aol.com

FairAmount Entertainment, Inc.
P.O. Box 1245, Birmingham, MI 48012-1245
Telephone: 888-905-8188
E-mail: fairamount@mindspring.com

Fox Plays
(Plays, musicals, books, and music for all ages)
P.O. Box 2078 Richmond South 3121, Victoria Australia
Telephone: 03 9429 3004
Fax: 03 9428 9064
E-mail: cenfox@labyrinth.net.au

Generic Plays
(Works of women, gay men, lesbians, people of color, and other minorities)
P.O. Box 821, Bristol TN 37621-0081
E-mail: genericplays@hotmail.com

Hatful-Breindel Productions
78790 W. Harland Dr., La Quinta, CA 92253
Telephone: 619-345-2573

Herman & Apter
(Performable opera and operetta translations)
5748 W. Brooks Rd., Shepherd, MI 48883-9202
Telephone: 517-828-6987
E-mail: ronnie.apter@cmich.edu

Heuer Publishing Company
(Plays and musicals for schools and community theaters)
P.O. Box 248, Cedar Rapids, Iowa 52406
Telephone: 800-950-7529
Fax: 319-364-1771
E-mail: editor@hitplays.com

The Hollywood Legends
P.O. Box 8086, Calabasas, CA 91372
Telephone: 818-591-1963
Fax: 818-876-0069
E-mail: Druxy@ix.netcom.com

I. E. Clark Publications
P.O. Box 246, Schulenburg, TX 78956-0246
Telephone: 409-743-3232
Fax: 409-743-4765
E-mail: ieclark@cvtv.net

Jest for Funds
(Scripts for small theaters & dinner theater events)
RR2, Clinton, Ontario, Canada N0M 1L0
E-mail jestforfunds@odyssey.on.ca

KMR Scripts
(Deals primarily with children's musicals)
116 N 5th St., Medford, OK 73759-1002
Telephone/Fax: 580-395-2990
E-mail: kevin@kmrscripts.com

Lillenas Publishing
(Church, school, and dinner theater)
P.O. Box 419527, Kansas City MO 64141
Telephone: 800-877-0700

Musicline Publications
(Musical stage shows for schools)
18 Cadogan Road, Dosthill, Tamworth, Staffordshire,
United Kingdom B77 1PQ
Telephone: 01827 281431
Fax: 01827 284214

MusicLine USA
(Musicals and pantomimes for grade schools, high schools, and
youth groups)
771 Bailey Drive, Batavia, IL 60510
Telephone: 800-419-1028
Fax: 630-879-7023
E-mail 103512.3456@compuserve.com

Music Theatre International
421 W. 54th St., New York, NY 10019
Telephone: 212-541-4684
Fax: 212-397-4684
E-mail: Licensing@mtishows.com

Mysteries by Moushey
Kent, OH 44240
Telephone: 330-678-3893
Fax: 330-434-9376
E-mail: Mystmoush@aol.com

Pioneer Drama Service
P.O. Box 4267, Englewood, CO 80155
Telephone: 800-333-7262
Fax: 303-779-4315
E-mail: Piodrama@aol.com

Players Press
P.O. Box 1132, Studio City, CA 91614
Telephone: 818-780-4980

Playwrights Forum
E-mail: pforum@erols.com

Playwrights Union of Canada
54 Wolseley St., 2nd floor, Toronto, Ontario, Canada, M5T 1A5
Telephone: 416-703-0201
Fax: 416-703-0059
E-mail: cdplays@interlog.com

Popular Play Service
P.O. Box 1206, Woodbury, CT 06798
Telephone: 203-263-2546
Fax: 203-263-2632
E-mail: popplays@wtco.net

Return Engagement Plays
2720 Blaine Dr., Chevy Chase, MD 20815
Telephone: 301-585-9689
Fax: 301-585-9689

Rodgers & Hammerstein Theatre Library
229 W. 28th St., 11th floor, New York, NY 10001
Telephone: 212-564-4000
Fax: 212-268-1245

Samuel French
45 W. 25th St., New York, NY 10010
Telephone: 212-206-8990
Fax: 212-206-1429

7623 Sunset Blvd., Hollywood, CA 90046-2795
Telephone: 323-876-0570
Fax: 323-876-6822.
E-mail (for all offices): samuelfrench2earthlink.net

Select Entertainment Productions
23 Sugar Maple Ln., Tinton Falls, NJ 07724
Telephone: 908-741-8832
Fax: 908-741-1409

Smith and Kraus Publishers, Inc.
P.O. Box 127, Lyme NH 03768
Telephone: 800-895-4331
Fax: 603-795-1831
E-mail: SandK@sover.net

Stage Kids
(Children's Educational Theatre Productions)
The Edu-Tainment Company
1179A King Street West, Suite 111, Toronto,
Ontario, Canada M6K 3C5
Telephone: 888-537-8243 or 416-538-0299
Fax: 416-538-3609
E-mail: hello@stagekids.com

Tams-Witmark Music Library
560 Lexington Ave., New York, NY 10022
Telephone: 800-221-7196
Fax: 212-688-3232

Triad Productions
P.O. Box 578554, Chicago, IL 60657
Telephone: 877-TRIAD-77
Fax: 773-404-08016

The Way Off-Broadway Theatre Workshop
(Age-appropriate plays for children ages 7-17)
Telephone: 800-943-8628 (access code: 09)
E-mail: kidsplay@pacific.net

Regional Arts Organizations

Arts Midwest
Hennepin Center for the Arts, 528 Hennepin Avenue,
Suite 310, Minneapolis, MN 55403
Telephone: 612-341-0755
TT/Voice: 612-341-0901
E-mail: webcom@artsmidwest.org

Consortium for Pacific Arts & Cultures
2141C Atherton Road, Honolulu, HI 96822
Telephone: 808-946-7381

Mid-America Arts Alliance
912 Baltimore Avenue, Suite 700, Kansas City, MO 64105
Telephone: 816-421-1388

Mid Atlantic Arts Foundation
22 Light Street, #330, Baltimore, MD 21202
Telephone: 410-539-6656
TT: 410-539-4241
E-mail: maaf@midarts.usa.com

New England Foundation for the Arts
330 Congress Street, 6th Floor, Boston, MA 02210-1216
Telephone: 617-951-0010
E-mail: info@nefa.org

Southern Arts Federation
1401 Peachtree Street, Suite 460, Atlanta, GA 30309
Telephone: 404-874-7244
TT: 404-876-6240

Western States Arts Federation
1543 Champa St., Suite 220, Denver, CO 80202
Telephone: 303-629-1166
E-mail: staff@westaf.org

State Arts Agencies

Alabama State Council on the Arts
One Dexter Avenue, Montgomery, AL 36130
Telephone: 334-242-4076
TT/Relay: 800-548-2546

Alaska State Council on the Arts
411 West 4th Avenue, Suite 1E, Anchorage, AK 99501-2343
Telephone: 907-269-6610
E-mail: asca@alaska.net

American Samoa Council on Arts, Culture & Humanities
P.O. Box 1540 , Pago Pago, American Samoa 96799
Telephone: 011-684-633-4347

Arizona Commission on the Arts
417 West Roosevelt, Phoenix, AZ 85003
Telephone: 602-255-5882
E-mail: general@ArizonaArts.org

Arkansas Arts Council
1500 Tower Building, 323 Center Street, Little Rock, AR 72201
Telephone: 501-324-9766
E-mail: info@dah.state.ar.us

California Arts Council
1300 I Street, #930, Sacramento, CA 95814
Telephone: 916-322-6555
TT: 916-322-6569
E-mail: cac@cwo.com

Colorado Council on the Arts
750 Pennsylvania Street, Denver, CO 80203-3699
Telephone: 303-894-2617
TT: 303-894-2664
E-mail: coloarts@artswire.org

Connecticut Commission on the Arts
Gold Building 755 Main Street, Hartford, CT 06103
Telephone: 860-566-4770

Delaware Division of the Arts
State Office Building, 820 North French Street, Wilmington, DE 19801
Telephone: 302-577-3540
TT/Relay: 800-232-5460
E-mail: delarts@artswire.org

District of Columbia Commission on the Arts & Humanities
410 8th Street, NW, Washington, DC 20004
Telephone: 202-724-5613
TT: 202-727-3148
E-mail: carrien@tmn.com

Division of Cultural Affairs
Florida Department of State, The Capitol, Tallahassee, FL 32399-0250
Telephone: 904-487-2980
TT: 904-488-5779

Georgia Council for the Arts
530 Means Street, NW, Suite 115, Atlanta, GA 30318-5730
Telephone: 404-651-7920
E-mail: gca@gwins.campus.mci.net

Guam Council on the Arts & Humanities
Office of the Governor , P.O. Box 2950, Agana, GU 96910
Telephone: 011-671-647-2242
E-mail: arts@ns.gov.nu

State Foundation on Culture & the Arts
44 Merchant Street, Honolulu, HI 96813
Telephone: 808-586-0300
TTD: 808-586-0740
E-mail: sfca@sfca.state.hi.us

Idaho Commission on the Arts
P.O. Box 83720, Boise, ID 83720-0008
Telephone: 208-334-2119
E-mail: idarts@artswire.org

Illinois Arts Council
State of Illinois Center, 100 West Randolph,
Suite 10-500, Chicago, IL 60601
Telephone: 312-814-6750
TT: 312-814-4831
E-mail: ilarts@artswire.org

Indiana Arts Commission
402 West Washington Street, Room 072, Indianapolis, IN 46204-2741
Telephone: 317-232-1268
TT: 317-233-3001
E-mail: inarts@aol.com

Iowa Arts Council
600 East Locust, State Capitol Complex, Des Moines, IA 50319
Telephone: 515-281-4451
E-mail: jbailey@max.state.ia.us

Kansas Arts Commission
Jayhawk Tower, 700 Jackson, Suite 1004, Topeka, KS 66603
Telephone: 785-296-3335
TT/Relay: 800-766-3777

Kentucky Arts Council
31 Fountain Place, Frankfort, KY 40601
Telephone: 502-564-3757

Division of the Arts
Louisiana Department of Culture, Recreation, & Tourism
1051 North 3rd Street, P.O. Box 44247, Baton Rouge, LA 70804
Telephone: 504-342-8180
E-mail: arts@crt.state.la.us

Maine Arts Commission
55 Capitol Street, State House Station 25, Augusta, ME 04333
Telephone: 207-287-2724
TT: 207-287-5613

Maryland State Arts Council
601 North Howard Street, 1st Floor, Baltimore, MD 21201
Telephone: 410-767-6555
E-mail: msac@digex.net

Massachusetts Cultural Council
120 Boylston Street, 2nd Floor, Boston, MA 02116-4600
Telephone: 617-727-3668
TT: 617-338-9153

Michigan Council for Arts and Cultural Affairs
525 West Ottawa Street, P.O. Box 30705, Lansing, MI 48909-8205
Telephone: 517-241-4011

Minnesota State Arts Board
Park Square Court, 400 Sibley Street, Suite 200, St. Paul, MN 55101-1949
Telephone: 612-215-1600 or 800/8MN-ARTS
TT/Relay: 612-297-5353
E-mail: msab@tc.umn.edu

Mississippi Arts Commission
239 North Lamar Street, Second Floor, Jackson, MS 39201
Telephone: 601-359-6030

Missouri State Council on the Arts
Wainwright Office Complex, 111 North Seventh Street,
Suite 105, St. Louis, MO 63101
Telephone: 314-340-6845
E-mail: mac@state.mt.us

Montana Arts Council
316 North Park Avenue, Room 252, Helena, MT 59620
Telephone: 406-444-6430
TT/Relay: 00-833-8503
E-mail: mac@state.mt.us

Nebraska Arts Council
The Joslyn Castle Carriage House, 3838 Davenport Street, Omaha, NE 68131-2329
Telephone: 402-595-2122
TT/Voice: 402-595-2122
E-mail: nacart@synergy.net

Nevada Arts Council
Capitol Complex , 602 North Curry Street, Carson City, NV 89710
Telephone: 702-687-6680

New Hampshire State Council on the Arts
Phenix Hall, 40 North Main Street, Concord, NH 03301
Telephone: 603-271-2789
TT/Relay: 800-735-2964

New Jersey State Council on the Arts
20 West State Street, # 306, Trenton, NJ 08625-0306
Telephone: 609-292-6130
TT: 609-633-1186

New Mexico Arts Division
228 East Palace Avenue, Santa Fe, NM 87501
Telephone: 505-827-6490
TT: 505-827-6925
E-mail: artadmin@oca.state.nm.us

New York State Council on the Arts
915 Broadway, New York, NY 10010
Telephone: 212-387-7000
TT: 212-387-7049
E-mail: nysca@artswire.org

North Carolina Arts Council
Department of Cultural Resources, Raleigh, NC 27601-2807
Telephone: 919-733-2821

North Dakota Council on the Arts
418 East Broadway Ave., Suite 70, Bismarck, ND 58501-4086
Telephone: 701-328-3954
E-mail: thompson@pioneer.state.nd.us

Commonwealth Council for Arts & Culture
P.O. Box 553, CHRB, CNMI Convention Center, Commonwealth of the
Northern Mariana Islands, Saipan, MP 96950
Telephone: 9-011-670-322-9982

Ohio Arts Council
727 East Main Street, Columbus, OH 43205
Telephone: 614-466-2613
TT: 614-466-4541
E-mail: bfisher@mail.oac.ohio.gov or wlawson@mail.oac.ohio.gov

Oklahoma Arts Council
P.O. Box 52001-2001, Oklahoma City, OK 73152-2001
Telephone: 405-521-2931
E-mail: okarts@tmn.com

Oregon Arts Commission
775 Summer Street, NE, Salem, OR 97310
Telephone: 503-986-0082
TT: 503-378-3772
E-mail: oregon.artscomm@State.OR.US

Commonwealth of Pennsylvania Council on the Arts
Finance Building, Room 216A, Harrisburg, PA 17120
Telephone: 717-787-6883
TT/Relay: 800-654-5984

Institute of Puerto Rican Culture
Apartado Postal 4184, San Juan, PR 00902-4184
Telephone: 809-723-2115

Rhode Island State Council on the Arts
95 Cedar Street, Suite 103, Providence, RI 02903
Telephone: 401-277-3880
TT: 401-277-3880 info@risca.state.ri.us

South Carolina Arts Commission
1800 Gervais Street, Columbia, SC 29201
Telephone: 803-734-8696
E-mail: kenmay@scsn.net

South Dakota Arts Council
Office of Arts , 800 Governors Drive, Pierre, SD 57501-2294
Telephone: 605-773-3131
TT/Relay: 800-622-1770
E-mail: sdac@stlib.state.sd.us

Tennessee Arts Commission
Citizens Plaza, 401 Charlotte Avenue, Nashville, TN 37243-0780
Telephone: 615-741-1701
E-mail: btarleton@mail.state.tn.us

Texas Commission on the Arts
P.O. Box 13406, Austin, TX 78711-3406
Telephone: 512-463-5535
TTY: 512-475-3327
E-mail: front.desk@arts.state.tx.us

Utah Arts Council
617 East South Temple Street, Salt Lake City, UT 84102
Telephone: 801-533-5895
E-mail: dadamson@email.st.ut.us

Vermont Arts Council
136 State Street, Montpelier, VT 05633-6001
Telephone: 802-828-3291
TT/Relay: 800-253-0191
E-mail: info@arts.vca.state.vt.us

Virginia Commission for the Arts
223 Governor Street, Richmond, VA 23219
Telephone: 804-225-3132
TT: 804-225-3132
E-mail: vacomm@artswire.org

Virgin Islands Council on the Arts
41-42 Norre Gade, 2nd Floor, P.O. Box 103, St. Thomas, VI 00802
Telephone: 340-774-5984

Washington State Arts Commission
234 East 8th Avenue, P.O. Box 42675, Olympia, WA 98504-2675
Telephone: 360-753-3860
TT/Relay: 206-554-7400 or 800-833-6388
E-mail: wsac@artswire.org

Arts & Humanities Section
West Virginia Division of Culture & History, 1900 Kanawha Blvd.
East Capitol Complex, Charleston, WV 25305-0300
Telephone: 304-558-0220
TT: 304-348-0220

Wisconsin Arts Board
101 East Wilson Street, 1st Floor, Madison, WI 53702
Telephone: 608-266-0190
TT: 608-267-9629

Wyoming Arts Council
2320 Capitol Avenue, Cheyenne, WY 82002
Telephone: 307-777-7742
TT: 307-777-5964
E-mail: wyoarts@artswire.org

The Producer's Timetable: Suggested Parameters

Before Any Money Is Spent

14 Months before projected opening night

Begin budgeting process

- Estimate the cost of space
- Estimate the cost of personnel
- Estimate the cost of sets and costumes
- Estimate the cost of scripts/royalties
- Estimate the cost of marketing and public relations
- Estimate the cost of box office operations
- Estimate ticket revenue

Begin searching for space

- Network with other producers
- Consult resource books
- Check newspaper listings
- Contact technical equipment rental businesses
- Pitch the production to theater owners/managers

12 Months before projected opening night

Recruit a director

Recruit a stage manager

Recruit a set designer

Recruit a costume designer

Recruit a technical director

10 Months before projected opening night

Set fund-raising goals

Begin to negotiate and draft letters of agreement

If necessary, get appropriate IRS forms

Organize a reading of the play

8 Months before projected opening night

Create a media contact sheet (Names, addresses, e-mails)

Write a production "vision statement"

Plan specific fundraising strategies

Write thank-you notes to people who contributed to the effort

After this point, be prepared to spend money

6 Months before projected opening night
    Decide if the production effort will become a reality
    Begin marketing brainstorming sessions with the production
        team
    Interview press agents
    Write thank-you notes to people who contributed to the effort

5 Months before projected opening night
    Set actual production dates (Keep in mind conflicts and the
        seasonal nature of theater)
    Begin graphic design/photography for all aspects of print
        marketing and publicity
    Hire the press agent if necessary
    Organize fund-raising targets
    Write thank you notes to people who contributed to the effort

4 Months before projected opening night
    Secure the rights to the play
    Set ticket prices
    Decide on ticketing options
    Secure performance/rehearsal space
    Set payment schedules for personnel
    Prepare postcards/mailers
    Conduct fund-raising activities
    Organize the marketing team: Who is responsible for what
        activity?
    Brainstorm publicity angles with the production team
    Write press releases
    Write public service announcements
    Prepare the press kit
    Double check to be sure the aforementioned items were
        accomplished
    Circulate and sign letters of agreement
    Write thank-you notes to people who contributed to the effort

3 Months before projected opening night

Have the stage manager prepare rehearsal/tech/performance schedules

Begin to execute the marking plan

Submit magazine publicity articles

Distribute the press kits to magazines

Double check to be sure the aforementioned items were accomplished

Review the production "vision statement"

Write thank you notes to people who contributed to the effort

2 Months before projected opening night

Set up box office operations/reservations systems

Arrange preview articles in newspapers

Secure house/box office staff

Submit calendar listings to newspapers

Double check to be sure the aforementioned items were accomplished

Review the production "vision statement"

Write thank you notes to people who contributed to the effort

1 Month before projected opening night

Distribute press kits to newspapers

Send out invitations to opening night party

Approach radio and television stations for publicity

Distribute the press kit to TV and radio stations

Review all house procedures with house manager

Review the production "vision statement"

Review house/box office procedures with staff

Review technical/design needs with the production team

Review box office procedures

Review strike procedures

Have stage manager and director organize production run check-list

Invite agents and producers to opening night party

Inspect the performance space for any potential code violations

Double check to be sure the aforementioned items were accomplished

Write thank-you notes to people who contributed to the effort

Organize the opening night party

During Production Run

Inspect the performance space for any potential
code violations

Fax review to agents and producers

Deposit box office money

Monitor box office closely

Write thank-you notes to people who contributed to the effort

Acknowledgements

The book was researched by both the traditional means of examining the current publications on theatre production and by inter-
viewing dozens of theater producers in New York and the Midwest.
I am very grateful to the following people who gave their time and
wisdom.

Aaron Beall, Producer and Artistic Director of Todo Con Nada, New
York, N.Y. James Houghton, Producer and Artistic Director of the
Signature Theatre, New York, N.Y. Maggie Maes, Producer and Artis-
tic Director of The Actor's Loft, New York, N.Y. Kate Ryan, Producer
and Artistic Director of Five Bucks Unleaded, New York, N.Y. Richard
Foreman, Producer and Artistic Director of Ontologic Hysteric The-
atre, New York, N.Y. (Fringe-U, panel discussion). Paul Harris, Pro-
ducer and Artistic Director of Harris At Random, New York, N.Y. Ron
Lasko, Senior Press Representative, The Zeisler Group, New York,
N.Y. Annie Chadwick, President, Up-To-Date Mailing Labels, New
York, N.Y. Elizabeth Corley, Producer and Artistic Director of Har-
land Productions, New York, N.Y. Susannah and Timothy Nolan, Pro-
ducers and Artistic Directors of Present Tense Productions, New
York, N.Y. Donna E. Brady, President of Performing Arts Resources,
Inc., New York, N.Y. Donovan Johnson, Producer and Artistic Direc-
tor of The Oberon Theatre Ensemble, New York, N.Y. Micah Holling-
worth, Special Services Coordinator, The Dramatists Guild, Inc., New
York, N.Y. Ben Kolbert, President, The Producers Club Theatres, New
York, N.Y. Rita Spinosa, General Manager, The Producers Club The-
atres, New York, N.Y. Michele Rosenthal, Editor, *Showcase News*,
New York, N.Y. Dena Trakes, President, Select Entertainment, New
York. N.Y. Kristin Marting, Executive Director, HERE, New York, N.Y.
Donna DuCarme, Associate Producer, Westbeth Theatre Center, New
York, N.Y. Jerry Manning, Associate Producer, New York Theatre
Workshop, New York, N.Y. Patrick Kelsey, Director of Operations,
PACE Entertainment, New York, N.Y. Dee Dee Friedman, Producer,
Raw Space, New York, N.Y. Ellie Covan, Executive Director, Dixon

Place, New York, N.Y. Marsha Norman, Playwright, New York, N.Y., Phyllis Schuringa, Casting Director, Steppenwolf Theatre, Chicago, IL. Jean Adamak, Producer and Artistic Director, Footsteps Theatre, Chicago, IL. Brian Fonseca, Producer and Artistic Director, The Phoenix Theatre, Indianapolis, IN. Ron Spencer, Producer and Artistic Director, Theatre on the Square, Indianapolis, IN. Kathryn V. Lamkey, Central Regional Director of Actors' Equity Association, Chicago, IL, Volunteer Lawyer for the Arts. I also thank my colleagues at Ball State University for their support: Dr. Judy Yordon, Dr. Rodger Smith, Dr. Michael O'Hara, Dr. Don LaCasse, Prof. David C. Shawger, Prof. Kathleen Jaremski.

A special note of thanks goes to Dr. Don LaCasse, Chair of the Department of Theatre and Dance, and Dr. Margaret Merrion, Dean of the College of Fine Arts Ball State University for their support of my sabbatical.